T0178927

Advanced Techniques and Technology of
Computer-Aided Feedback Control

Series Editor
Jean-Paul Bourrières

Advanced Techniques and Technology of Computer-Aided Feedback Control

Jean Mbihi

WILEY

First published 2018 in Great Britain and the United States by ISTE Ltd and John Wiley & Sons, Inc.

ISTE Ltd
27-37 St George's Road
London SW19 4EU
UK

www.iste.co.uk

John Wiley & Sons, Inc.
111 River Street
Hoboken, NJ 07030
USA

www.wiley.com

Library of Congress Control Number: 2018937753

British Library Cataloguing-in-Publication Data
A CIP record for this book is available from the British Library
ISBN 978-1-78630-249-6

Contents

Preface

This book presents an in-depth study of advanced design techniques and modern technology for the implementation of computer-aided feedback control systems for deterministic and stochastic dynamic processes.

It is addressed to stakeholders (students, teachers and researchers) in engineering schools, teacher training schools for technical education, PhD schools and applied science research centers.

This book will provide readers with:

– techniques for building canonical discrete state models of dynamic processes, as well as methods for the design of discrete state feedback digital controllers;

– a detailed case study of the creation and effective implementation of a new computer-aided multimedia test bench for servomechanisms, based on virtual toolboxes of PIDF (proportional, integral and derivative with filter) controllers, state feedback controllers (with or without observer) and virtual instruments;

– detailed algorithmic schemes of deterministic or stochastic optimal control, with finite or infinite optimization time;

– secrets of the creation and prototyping of a new remote virtual Matlab®/GUI platform, the rapid design of systems for deterministic and stochastic optimal control;

– infrastructural topologies of real-time remote feedback control systems;

– a detailed case study of the creation and effective implementation of a new remotely operated automation laboratory (REOPAULAB) via the Internet;

– Matlab programs for teaching purposes, allowing the replication, if needed, of the numerical and graphic results presented in this book;

– corrected exercises at the end of each chapter, aimed at consolidating the acquired technical knowledge.

The content of this book is the outcome of the experiences gathered by the author throughout the last 15 years with ENSET (École Normale Supérieure d'Enseignement Technique) and UFD (Unité de Formation Doctorale) in Engineering Sciences at the University of Douala, which involved multiple activities:

– lectures on "deterministic and stochastic optimal control" and "Matlab-aided advanced programming";

– scientific research of new flexible teaching platforms;

– support for the development of computer-aided control technology in modern automated process engineering.

The author wishes to commend the state of Cameroon for the scientific research grant awarded via the Ministry of Higher Education, which allowed him to cover a part of the costs involved for preparing and editing this book.

The author wishes to sincerely thank:

– Prof. Womonou Robert, director and promoter of ESSET at the University of Douala and Nkongsamba, for his motivational support in completing this book.

– Prof. Nneme Nneme Léandre, director of ENSET at the University of Douala, who participated in the study of the remotely operated automation laboratory, which is presented in Chapter 8.

– Pauné Félix, PhD lecturer in the Computer Science Engineering department of ENSET at the University of Douala, who is the main author and the system administrator of the above-mentioned remotely operated automation laboratory, a subject that he has studied and implemented in his PhD thesis, conducted under the author's supervision.

– Lonlac Konlac Karvin Jerry PhD lecturer and head of the department of Computer Science Engineering of ENSET at the University of Douala. While abroad, during his post-doctoral studies at Lens, in France, he was the first remote test operator without online assistance of the above-mentioned remote automation laboratory.

– The ISTE editorial team, for their excellent collaboration throughout all the editing phases of this book.

– His wife, Mrs. Mbihi, born Tsafack Pélagie Marthe, who offered her close assistance, and all those who have substantially contributed to the production of this book.

Jean Mᴮɪʜɪ

March 2018

Introduction

I.1. Architecture of computer-aided control systems

The general architecture of a complete computer-aided control system is represented in Figure I.1, where the main constitutive subsystems are designated as follows:

– real dynamic process to be controlled;

– multifunction data acquisition (MDAQ) interface;

  multimedia PC for closed digital control;

– stations for the remote control of the real process via the Internet.

The next sections of this book offer a detailed study of these constituent subsystems.

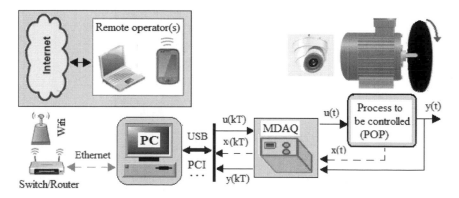

Figure I.1. *Architecture of a complete system for computer-aided control*

I.2. Dynamic processes to be controlled

The real dynamic process to be controlled corresponds to the power and operative part (POP) of an open-loop regulation system. In the POP, u, x and y notations designate direct control, state and output physical quantities, respectively. These quantities are obviously continuous time variables.

I.3. Multifunction data acquisition (MDAQ) interface

An MDAQ interface is in reality a macrocontroller (unified microcontroller system). It acts as a communication protocol interpreter between the dynamic analog process and a digital computer.

The detailed study of modern MDAQ interfaces is a broad, topical subject in industrial computing [MBI 12]. Here, the focus will be on reviewing the elements of strategic knowledge, allowing the mastery of selection criteria and real-time programming operational scheme of an MDAQ interface in industrial automation and computing.

I.3.1. *Input/output buses*

An MDAQ interface used in computer aided feedback control technology has an input/output bus-specific system. Table I.1 summarizes the types of buses used in computer-aided instrumentation.

Class	Type	Year	Packet (*) D, C	Maximum data rate	Range
Ports	RS232	1962	8, 3	7 Ko/s	30 m
	LPT	1992	8, 0	2 Mo/s	3 m
	USB	1995	1024, 1027	1.5 Go/s	1.8 m
	Ethernet	1980	–	40 Gb/s	100 m
Slots	PCI	1992	32, 0	132 Mo/s	Narrow
	PCI-X	1999	32, 0	160 Mo/s	Narrow
			64, 0	320 Mo/s	Narrow
	PCI-E	2004	128, 130	8 Go/s	Narrow
Other	WiFi	1997	–	11 Mbits/s	400 m

(*) D (bits): data per packet; C (bit): control per packet

Table I.1. *Buses used in computer-aided instrumentation*

In practice, RS232 and LPT buses are no longer relevant. On the contrary, multimedia PC motherboards support PCI, PCI-X, PCI-E and WiFi buses.

I.3.2. *Unified software structure*

In micro-computer science, the software structure of a microsystem designates a simplified descriptive scheme of internal programmable components that are accessible in real time through an application program. Figure I.2 presents the software structure of an MDAQ interface viewed from the computer side and from the POP (power and operative part) side of the dynamic process.

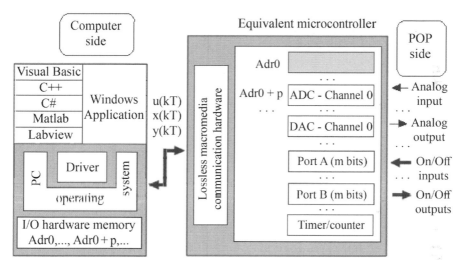

POP: power and operative part; ADC: analog-to-digital converter; DAC: digital-to-analog converter

Figure I.2. *Software structure unified by an MDAQ interface*

In other words, the physical chain comprises the computer motherboard, the connector and the MDAQ interface bus controller can be modeled by a lossless communication macromedia between the computer software environment and the programmable instrumentation resources of the MDAQ interface.

The main types of programmable instrumentation resources that are present in the software structure of modern MDAQ interfaces are the following:

– analog-to-digital converter (ADC);

– digital-to-analog converter (DAC);

– specialized input module (for thermocouple, optical encoders, etc.);

– specialized PWM (pulse width modulation) output module;

– timer for the management of periodic tasks;

– on/off input/output ports, Bluetooth, WiFi, etc.

Each programmable resource of an MDAQ interface is accessible in real time on the software side of a Windows application by relative addressing via a computer memory area allocated to hardware input/output targets. This area starts at a base installation address "Ard0" that is automatically assigned after the detection of an MDAQ interface by the operating system.

Thus, the control, state and output quantities of a dynamic process, designated by $u(t)$, $x(t)$ and $y(t)$ are expressed on the computer side as discrete quantities $u(kT)$, $x(kT)$ and $y(kT)$, respectively, where T is the sampling period.

I.3.3. *Real-time programming operational diagram*

The historical operational diagram of real-time programming of an MDAQ interface is presented in Figure I.3, which illustrates the compatibility between generations of software development tools and computer operating systems.

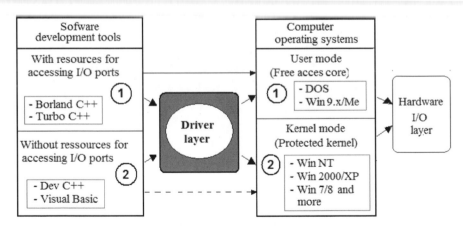

Figure I.3. *Operational diagram of real-time programming of an MDAQ interface*

Indeed, the history of real-time programming of an MDAQ interface reveals:

– two generations of software development tools, which are distinguishable by the resources for accessing hardware input/output ports. Thus, Turbo C++ and Borland C++ are examples of historical development tools equipped with functions for addressing hardware input/output ports, which is not the case for Dev C++ and Visual Basic;

– two generations of operating systems, which are distinguishable by the security conditions for effective access to hardware input/output ports addressing the kernel. Thus, DOS and Windows 9.x/Me are examples of historical operating systems equipped with a kernel whose access conditions are not secure, which is not the case for Windows NT, Windows 2000, Windows XP, etc.

Based on this historical information, the following four cases of association between development tools and operating systems can be considered:

– Case 1 → 1: technically interesting, but no longer topical;

– Case 1 → 2: problematic in terms of the direct addressing of ports;

– Case 2 → 1: more problematic than the previous one;

– Case 2 → 2: unrealistic.

In practice, problems related to real-time addressing of hardware ports can be solved by using a software driver provided by the producer of the MDAQ interface to be used.

I.3.4. *MDAQ interface driver*

In Windows programming, an MDAQ interface driver is a category of dynamic link library (*.DLL) that provides ranges of specialized functions for the management of available instrumentation resources.

The instrumentation functions of an MDAQ interface are executable in real time in "Kernel" mode under import/export call from an application program properly developed with any programming tool recommended in the product user manual.

Table I.2 summarizes the examples of instrumentation functions integrated in the K8055.dll driver of a Velleman USB/VM110 card. This K8055.dll driver is intended for popular Windows programming tools in Delphi, Visual Basic, C++ and C# languages.

Description		Declaration syntax in a Visual Basic program	Example of use in a Visual Basic program
Role	Names in K8055.dll		
Open	OpenDevice	Private Declare Function OpenDevice Lib "k8055d.dll" (ByVal CardAddress As Long) As Long	If card 0 installed: OpenDevice (0)
Close	CloseDevice	Private Declare Sub CloseDevice Lib "k8055d.dll" ( )	CloseDevice ( )
A/D Conversion	ReadAnalogChannel	Private Declare Function ReadAnalogChannel Lib "k8055d.dll" (ByVal Channel As Long) As Long	Ncan = ReadAnalogChannel(1)
D/A Conversion	OutputAnalogChannel	Private Declare Sub OutputAnalogChannel Lib "k8055d.dll" (ByVal Channel As Long, ByVal Data As Long)	'Ncna = 254 : 'No. of channel = 1 OutputAnalogChannel (1, Ncna)

A/D: analog/digital; D/A: digital/analog

Table I.2. *Examples of basic functions of an MDAQ interface driver: case of K8055.dll driver of USB/VM110 card*

I.3.5. *A/D and D/A conversions in an instrumentation program*

As shown in Table I.2, it is worth noting that, in general, the A/D (analog/digital) conversion function of the considered MDAQ interface driver returns in reality to the calling instrumentation program of the integer code value *Ncan* of a voltage y to be measured. Therefore, the effective measurement should be digitally reconstructed in the instrumentation program based on the input/output characteristic of the real ADC (A/D converter) operating in the MDAQ interface.

Thus, in the case of an ADC operating within a voltage range $[U_m \ U_M]$ by binary coding shifted by n bits, the effective measurement y represented by an integer code *Ncan* can be reconstructed in the calling instrumentation program using the formula:

$$y = \left(\frac{U_M - U_m}{2^n} \right) \text{Ncan} + U_m \qquad\qquad [\text{I.1}]$$

Moreover, if the measurement of y, given by [I.1], corresponds in reality to the output voltage of a sensor of arbitrary physical quantity v, it would then suffice to reconstruct the effective value of v using the reverse characteristic $v(y)$ of the said sensor.

In a similar way, the argument of the DAC function of a driver corresponds in general to the integer value $Ncna$ of a digital code of n bits to be applied as input of the DAC operating in the MDAQ interface. Under operating conditions that are theoretically reciprocal to [I.1], this coded value $Ncna$ should therefore be reconstructed from the real voltage u of digital control using the following formula:

$$N_{cna} = E\left(\frac{u - U_m}{q}\right) \tag{I.2}$$

where $q = \dfrac{U_M - U_m}{2^n}$ and E(.) designate the operator that extracts the integer part on the left of its argument. Quantity q defined in [I.2] designates the quantum of the converter and corresponds to the smallest value that can be accurately converted.

In general, for unipolar converters $U_m = 0$ and $U_M > 0$ in [I.1] and [I.2]. On the contrary, the most popular bipolar converters offer a symmetrical operating range, which involves $U_M = -U_m = U > 0$ in [I.1] and [I.2].

Detailed descriptions of implementation technologies for A/D and D/C conversions can be found in Mbihi [MBI 12] and Moffo and Mbihi [MBI 15].

I.3.6. *Further practical information on the MDAQ interface*

A summary of complementary practical information on MDAQ interface drivers includes:

– an MDAQ interface driver can be developed by various types of programming tools such as Visual C++, Visual C#, Builder C++, Matlab®, Labview, etc. However, this development requires advanced skills of Windows programming;

– in practice, each MDAQ interface is delivered with its driver, which can be freely downloaded from the producer's website. Moreover, the instrumentation functions of a driver can be operated by any external program developed with a programming tool recommended in the user manual of the said driver;

– in general, an MDAQ interface producer also provides examples of programs and tests for the driver instrumentation functions. Given their educational focus, these programs are the basis for the development of advanced applications for computer-aided feedback control of dynamic processes;

– the basic C++ driver of an MDAQ interface can be used as a software component for building a new extended driver, intended for a higher level programming tool. Chapter 3 will present the secrets of the creation of an MEX-C++ driver for Matlab applications using the basic C++ driver of a Velleman USB/VM110 card.

I.4. Multimedia PC

A multimedia PC is a computerized device whose hardware and software resources support the real-time production and operation of multimedia applications.

In the context of computer-aided digital feedback control, a multimedia PC has the following main tasks:

– collect and reconstruct input quantities issued by the man–machine interface (MMI) and by the MDAQ interface;

– calculate and format the digital control values to be applied to hardware output ports;

– update the output constituents of MMI (spreadsheet programs, message boxes, graphic components, audio/video components, state indicators, etc.);

– manage databases and production log book;

– manage web services, if needed.

I.5. Remote access stations

The stations observed in Figure I.1 are wired or wireless computer equipment, allowing authorized remote operators to remotely control a real dynamic process via the local computer network or the Internet.

As described in Chapters 7 and 8, in virtual instrumentation, the minimum software of a remote control station for dynamic processes via the Internet is a web browser (Internet Explorer, Mozilla, etc.). However, depending on the technology and on the tool used for server implementation in the local computer, compatible runtime software could also be installed on the station side.

I.6. Organization of the book

This book is organized in three parts, each of which is structured into coherent chapters.

The first part presents advanced elements as well as a multimedia test bench for computer-aided feedback control of servomechanisms. Thus, the canonical discrete state models of dynamic processes are studied in Chapter 1, while the design of digital state feedback control systems is presented in detail in Chapter 2. Moreover, the secrets of building a multimedia test bench for computer-aided feedback control of servomechanisms are revealed in Chapter 3.

The second part deals with deterministic and stochastic optimal digital feedback control. Chapter 4 of this part will allow the readers to acquire the fundamental elements, as well as the main results of the theory of optimal feedback control of deterministic dynamic processes. In Chapter 5, readers will find a clear summary of the theory of optimal feedback control of stochastic dynamic processes. In Chapter 6, the reader will discover a methodology for the study of a project of creation and implementation of a newly deployed Matlab/GUI platform for the design and computer-aided virtual simulation for stochastic optimal control systems, over a finite or infinite time horizon.

The third part covers the computer-aided feedback control systems remotely operated via the Internet. In Chapter 7 of this last part, the reader will get acquainted with infrastructural topologies of remote control systems. Chapter 8 will reveal the secrets involving the design and effective creation of a new remotely operated automation laboratory (REOPAULAB) via the Internet.

Finally, it is also worth remembering that each chapter of the book ends with corrected exercises. Moreover, Appendix 1 provides the readers with a table of z-transforms, and Appendix 2, a table that summarizes the Matlab elements used in the teaching programs presented in this book. Finally, Appendix 3 offers a summary of the results of methods for the discretization of transfer functions of dynamic processes and analog PIDF (proportional, integral, derivative with filter) controllers.

Part 1

Advanced Elements and Test Bench of Computer-aided Feedback Control

1

Canonical Discrete State
Models of Dynamic Processes

1.1. Interest and construction of canonical state models

Even though a dynamic process can be described in the state space by an infinity of discrete state models, the types of discrete state models of greatest interest in practice are structurally canonical.

Indeed, the morphology of the parametric space of a canonical state model offers:

– maximum number of null terms, which substantially reduces the cost of numerical analysis, if needed;

– several apparent elements indicative for the fundamental dynamic properties of the model, such as: stability (imposed by the nature of eigenvalues), controllability, observability, etc.

A canonical discrete state model can be obtained from:

– canonical realization of the z-transfer function of the same process;

– canonical transformation of an existing discrete state model.

Canonical realizations and transformations presented in this chapter can be extended to the multivariable case [FOU 87].

1.2. Canonical realizations of a transfer function G(z)

Canonical realizations result from the transformation of a z-transfer function defined by [1.1]:

$$G(z) = \frac{y(z)}{u(z)} = \frac{b_1 z^{n-1} + b_2 z^{n-2} + \ldots + b_{n-1} z + b_n}{z^n + a_1 z^{n-1} + a_2 z^{n-2} + \ldots + a_{n-1} z + a_n} \qquad [1.1]$$

Three main types of canonical realizations can be distinguished as follows:

– Jordan canonical realization;

– controllable canonical realization;

– observable canonical realization.

1.2.1. *Jordan canonical realization*

The construction of the Jordan discrete state model requires the decomposition of $G(z)$ into simple elements (see [1.2]).

1.2.1.1. *G(z) admits distinct real poles*

If all the poles of the transfer function $G(z)$ defined by [1.1] are simple, the latter could be decomposed into [1.2], where a_i designates the pole i of [1.1] with $i = 1$, $2,\ldots, n$, and k_i is the static gain associated with pole a_i:

$$G(z) = \sum_{i=1}^{n} \frac{k_i}{(z - a_i)} = \sum_{i=1}^{n} \left(\frac{\left(\dfrac{1}{z} \right)}{\left(1 - \dfrac{a_i}{z} \right)} \right) k_i \qquad [1.2]$$

The block diagram associated with this decomposition into simple elements corresponds to Figure 1.1, in which the fixed state vector corresponds to $x = [x_1 \ x_2 \ \ldots \ x_n]^T$.

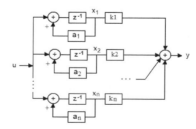

Figure 1.1. *Block diagram of a Jordan realization of G(z): case of distinct simple poles*

The specific choice of the elements of vector x in Figure 1.1 leads to the following Jordan discrete canonical state model:

$$
\begin{cases}
x(k+1) = \begin{bmatrix} a_1 & 0 & 0 & . & . & 0 & 0 \\ 0 & a_2 & 0 & . & . & 0 & 0 \\ . & 0 & . & . & . & 0 & . \\ 0 & 0 & 0 & . & . & a_i & 0 \\ 0 & 0 & 0 & . & . & 0 & a_n \end{bmatrix} x(k) + \begin{bmatrix} 1 \\ 1 \\ . \\ 1 \\ 1 \end{bmatrix} u(k) \\
y(k) = \begin{bmatrix} k_1 & k_2 & . & . & & k_n \end{bmatrix} x(k)
\end{cases}
\qquad [1.3]
$$

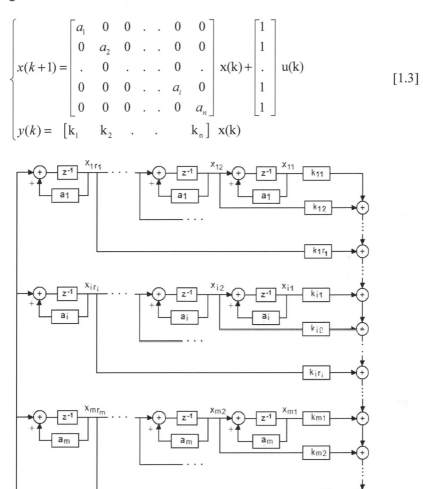

Figure 1.2. *Block diagram of a Jordan realization of G(z): case of multiple poles*

1.2.1.2. *G(z) admits multiple real poles*

Let us consider the specific case of a discrete transfer function $G(z)$ that admits m poles with multiplicity orders $r_1, r_2,..., r_m$, respectively, with $r_1 + r_2 + ... + r_m = n$, then $G(z)$ can be decomposed into the following form:

$$G(z) = \sum_{i=1}^{m} \left(\sum_{j=1}^{r_i} \left(\frac{k_{ij}}{(z-a_i)^{r_i-j+1}} \right) \right)$$ [1.4]

This decomposition leads to the block diagram in Figure 1.2.

The specific choice of given state variables leads to the following Jordan canonical model:

$$\begin{cases} x(k) = \begin{pmatrix} A_1 & 0 & 0 & . & . & 0 & 0 \\ 0 & A_2 & 0 & . & . & 0 & 0 \\ . & 0 & & . & . & . & 0 \\ 0 & 0 & 0 & . & . & A_{r-1} & 0 \\ 0 & 0 & 0 & . & . & 0 & A_r \end{pmatrix} x(k) + \begin{bmatrix} B_1 \\ B_2 \\ . \\ B_{m-1} \\ B_m \end{bmatrix} u(k) \\ y(k) = \begin{bmatrix} C_1 & C_2 & . & . & C_{m-1} & C_m \end{bmatrix} x(k) \end{cases}$$ [1.5]

with:

$$A_i = \begin{bmatrix} a_i & 1 & 0 & . & . & 0 & 0 \\ 0 & a_i & 1 & . & . & 0 & 0 \\ . & 0 & & . & . & . & 1 & . \\ 0 & 0 & 0 & . & . & a_i & 1 \\ 0 & 0 & 0 & . & . & 0 & a_i \end{bmatrix}_{(r_i \times r_i)} \quad ; \quad B_i = \left. \begin{bmatrix} 0 \\ 0 \\ . \\ 0 \\ 1 \end{bmatrix} \right\} r_i \; lines$$ [1.6]

$$C_i = \begin{bmatrix} \underbrace{k_{i1} \quad k_{i2} \quad ... \quad k_{iri}}_{r_i \; columns} \end{bmatrix}$$

1.2.1.3. *Problems raised by Jordan realization*

Jordan canonical realization raises two practical problems. The first problem is posed by the difficulty in factorizing the denominator of the transfer function for a degree above 3. The second problem stems from the difficulty in implementing subsystems admitting complex poles.

In the first case, the solution involves factorization by means of an advanced numerical analysis tool, such as Matlab®, using, for example, the "roots" command. The solution to the second problem results from the properties of block diagrams. Indeed, given that complex poles of a dynamic model are necessarily present in conjugated pairs, then each pair of conjugated poles appears in the decomposed form of the transfer function in the following form:

$$G(z) = \frac{k}{(z-a)^2 + b^2} = \frac{\dfrac{1}{(z-a)^2}}{1 + \dfrac{b^2}{(z-a)^2}} k \qquad [1.7]$$

Relation [1.7] corresponds to two first-order systems in cascade, forming a closed-loop system with a negative feedback of b^2 and an output gain k. The resulting block diagram is presented in Figure 1.3.

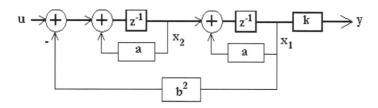

Figure 1.3. *Block diagram of a Jordan realization of G(z): case of complex poles*

1.2.2. *Controllable canonical realization*

The concept of controllability of dynamic systems will be clarified further. For the time being, let us consider a discrete transfer function $G(z)$ given by [1.1]. It is easy to prove that it can be written as a z^{-1} function that has the form [1.8]:

$$G(z) = \frac{y(z)}{u(z)} = \frac{b_1 z^{-1} + b_2 z^{-2} + \dots + b_{n-1} z^{-(n-1)} + b_n z^{-n}}{1 + a_1 z^{-1} + a_2 z^{-2} + \dots + a_{n-1} z^{-(n-1)} + a_n z^{-n}} \qquad (a)$$

$$= \frac{\left(b_1 z^{-1} + b_2 z^{-2} + \dots + b_{n-1} z^{-(n-1)} + b_n z^{-n} \right)}{\left(1 + a_1 z^{-1} + a_2 z^{-2} + \dots + a_{n-1} z^{-(n-1)} + a_n z^{-n} \right)} \left(\frac{w(z)}{w(z)} \right) \qquad (b) \qquad [1.8]$$

where $w(z)$ is a fictitious function.

Relation [1.8] leads to the following equalities:

$$u(z) = (1 + a_1 z^{-1} + \ldots + a_{n-1} z^{-(n-1)} + a_n z^{-n}) w(z) \tag{1.9}$$

$$y(z) = (b_n z^{-n} + b_{n-1} z^{-(n-1)} + \ldots + b_1 z^{-1}) w(z) \tag{1.10}$$

Therefore:

$$w(z) = u(z) - (a_1 z^{-1} w(z) - \ldots - a_{n-1} z^{-(n-1)} w(z) - a_n z^{-n} w(z)) \tag{1.11}$$

and:

$$y(z) = b_n z^{-n} w(z) + b_{n-1} z^{-(n-1)} w(z) + \ldots + b_1 z^{-1} w(z) \tag{1.12}$$

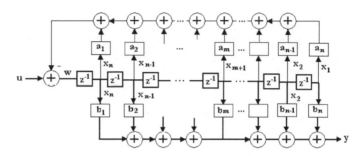

Figure 1.4. *Block diagram of the controllable realization of G(z)*

Expressions [1.9] to [1.12] lead to the block diagram of controllable realization of G(z), which is represented in Figure 1.4. The choice of the system of state variables:

$$x_n(z) = z^{-1} w(z)$$

$$x_{n-1}(z) = z^{-1} x_n(z) \tag{1.13}$$

$$\ldots$$

$$x_1(z) = z^{-1} x_2(z)$$

leads to the controllable discrete state model given by [1.14]:

$$\begin{cases} x(k+1) = \begin{bmatrix} 0 & 1 & 0 & . & . & . & 0 \\ 0 & 0 & 1 & 0 & . & . & 0 \\ . & & . & . & . & 1 & . \\ 0 & 0 & . & . & . & 0 & 1 \\ -a_n & -a_{n-1} & . & . & . & -a_2 & -a_1 \end{bmatrix} x(k) + \begin{bmatrix} 0 \\ 0 \\ . \\ 0 \\ 1 \end{bmatrix} u(k) \\ y(k) = \begin{bmatrix} b_n & b_{n-1} & . & . & b_m & \ldots & b_1 \end{bmatrix} x(k) \end{cases} \tag{1.14}$$

EXAMPLE.– Let us consider:

$$G(z) = \frac{y(z)}{u(z)} = \frac{0.5z^2 + 2.5z + 1}{z^3 + 6z^2 + 10z + 8} \qquad [1.15]$$

In this case, the following relations are obtained:

$$x(k+1) = \begin{bmatrix} 0 & 1 & 0 \\ 0 & 0 & 1 \\ -8 & -10 & -6 \end{bmatrix} x(k) + \begin{bmatrix} 0 \\ 0 \\ 1 \end{bmatrix} u(k)$$

$$y(k) = \begin{bmatrix} 1 & 2.5 & 0.5 \end{bmatrix} x(k) \qquad [1.16]$$

1.2.3. *Observable canonical realization*

The concept of observability of dynamic systems will be clarified further. Given a transfer function G(z), the following can be written as:

$$G(z) = \frac{y(z)}{u(z)} \frac{z^{-n}}{z^{-n}} = \frac{\left(b_1 z^{-1} + b_2 z^{-2} + \dots + b_{n-1} z^{-(n-1)} + b_n z^{-n} \right)}{\left(1 + a_1 z^{-1} + a_{n-2} z^{-2} + \dots + a_{n-1} z^{-(n-1)} + a_n z^{-n} \right)} \qquad [1.17]$$

therefore:

$$y(z)(1 + a_1 z^{-1} + a_2 z^{-2} + \dots + a_n z^{-n}) = u(z)(b_1 z^{-1} + \dots b_{n-1} z^{-(n-1)} + b_n z^{-n}) \qquad [1.18]$$

hence, the following relation:

$$y(z) = (-a_n y(z) + b_n u(z))z^{-n}$$

$$= (-a_{n-1} y(z) + b_{n-1} u(z))z^{-(n-1)} + \dots + (-a_1 y(z) + b_1 u(z))z^{-1} \qquad [1.19]$$

This relation leads to the block diagram of the observable realization of G(z), which is represented in Figure 1.5.

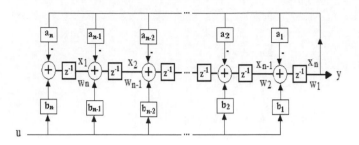

Figure 1.5. *Block diagram of the observable realization of G(z)*

The choice of the system of state variables $\{x_1, x_2, \ldots, x_n\}$ leads to equations [1.20]:

$$zx_1(z) = -a_n x_n(z) + b_n u(z)$$

$$zx_2(z) = x_1(z) - a_{n-1} xn(z) + bn_{-2} u(z) \qquad [1.20]$$

$\ldots$

$$zx_n(z) = x_{n-1} - a_1 xn(z) + b_1 u(z)$$

that facilitate the writing in discrete time of the full observable state model in the following form:

$$\begin{cases} x(k) = \begin{bmatrix} 0 & 0 & 0 & . & . & 0 & -a_n \\ 1 & 0 & 0 & . & . & 0 & -a_{n-1} \\ . & 1 & 0. & . & . & 0 & . \\ 0 & 0 & 1 & . & . & 0 & -a_2 \\ 0 & 0 & 0 & . & . & 1 & -a_1 \end{bmatrix} x(k) + \begin{bmatrix} b_n \\ b_{n-1} \\ . \\ . \\ b_1 \end{bmatrix} u(k) \\ y(k) = \begin{bmatrix} 0 & 0 & . & . & 0 & 1 \end{bmatrix} x(k) \end{cases} \qquad [1.21]$$

On the contrary, the choice of the system of state variables $\{w_1 = xn, w_2 = xn - 1, \ldots, w_n = x_1\}$ leads to the following new relations:

$$zw_1(z) = -a_1 w_1(z) + w_2(z) + b_1 u(z))$$

$$zw_2(z) = -a_2 w_1(z) + w_3(z) + b_2 u(z)) \qquad [1.22]$$

$\ldots$

$$zw_n(z) = -a_n w_1(z) + b_n u(z))$$

and in this case, the observable state model that results in discrete time is written as follows:

$$\begin{cases} w(k) = \begin{bmatrix} -a_1 & 1 & 0 & . & . & 0 & 0 \\ -a_2 & 0 & 1 & . & . & 0 & 0 \\ ... & ... & 0. & . & . & 1 & . \\ -a_{n-1} & 0 & 0 & . & . & 0 & 1 \\ -a_n & 0 & 0 & . & . & 0 & 0 \end{bmatrix} w(k) + \begin{bmatrix} b_1 \\ b_2 \\ . \\ b_{n-1} \\ b_n \end{bmatrix} u(k) \\ y(k) = \begin{bmatrix} 1 & 0 & .... & & 0 & 0 \end{bmatrix} w(k) \end{cases}$$ [1.23]

EXAMPLE.– Let us consider:

$$G(z) = \frac{y(z)}{u(z)} = \frac{0.5z^2 + 2.5z + 1}{z^3 + 6z^2 + 10z + 8}$$ [1.24]

The state model can thus be written in the following form:

$$\begin{cases} w(k+1) = \begin{bmatrix} -8 & 1 & 0 \\ -10 & 0 & 1 \\ -6 & 0 & 0 \end{bmatrix} w(k) + \begin{bmatrix} 1 \\ 2.5 \\ 0.5 \end{bmatrix} u(k) \\ y(k) = \begin{bmatrix} 1 & 0 & 0 \end{bmatrix} w(k) \end{cases}$$ [1.25]

1.3. Canonical transformations of discrete state models

Canonical transformations allow for the construction of discrete canonical state models (controllable, observable and Jordan realizations) based on arbitrary discrete state models.

Each type of transformation is based on an appropriate choice of reversible transformation matrix $P = Q^{-1}$, allowing the description of the same dynamic process by means of a new state vector $\overline{x}$, in such a way that:

$$\overline{x}(k) = P\,x(k) = Q^{-1}x(k)$$ [1.26]

The new representation obtained after expansion of [1.26] can be written as:

$$\begin{cases} \overline{x}(k+1) = \underbrace{\left(P \; A \; P^{-1} \right)}_{\overline{A}} \overline{x}(k) + \underbrace{P \; B}_{\overline{B}} \, x(k) \\ y(k) = \underbrace{C \; P^{-1}}_{\overline{C}} x(k) + \underbrace{D}_{\overline{D}} u(k) \end{cases} \equiv \left\{ \overline{A}, \overline{B}, \overline{C}, \overline{D} \right\} \qquad [1.27]$$

It is worth noting here that:

– if the choice of P in [1.26] is not appropriate, then the resulting state model [1.27] would be just similar to the original state model, without offering any canonical structure;

– the fundamental properties of discrete state models are conserved during canonical transformations.

In practice, the most commonly used transformations are those of Luenberger (Jordan, controllable and observable) and those of Kalman. The difference between them resides in the structure of the transformation matrix P.

These properties are:

– stability;

– controllability;

– observability.

1.3.1. *Jordan canonical transformation*

In a Jordan canonical transformation, Q represents the matrix of eigen vectors and can be calculated with Matlab command:

$$[Q, D] = \text{eig}(A,B); \qquad [1.28]$$

Thus, considering $P = Q^{-1}$, then:

$$\begin{cases} \overline{x}(k+1) = \underbrace{\left(P \; A \; P^{-1} \right)}_{\overline{A}} \overline{x}(k) + \underbrace{P \; B}_{\overline{B}} \, x(k) \\ y(k) = \underbrace{C \; P^{-1}}_{\overline{C}} x(k) + \underbrace{D}_{\overline{D}} u(k) \end{cases} \equiv \left\{ \overline{A}, \overline{B}, \overline{C}, \overline{D} \right\} \qquad [1.29]$$

EXAMPLE OF JORDAN TRANSFORMATION.– Let us consider:

$$x(k+1) = \begin{bmatrix} 2 & 1 & 1 \\ 0 & 1 & 0 \\ 1 & 0 & 1 \end{bmatrix} x(k) + \begin{bmatrix} 0 \\ 1 \\ 0 \end{bmatrix} u(k)$$

$$y(k) = \begin{bmatrix} 0 & 0 & 1 \end{bmatrix} x(k)$$

[1.30]

In this case, it can be verified that:

$$Q = \begin{bmatrix} 0.8507 & -0.5257 & 0 \\ 0 & 0 & 0.7071 \\ 0.5257 & 0.8507 & -0.7071 \end{bmatrix}$$

[1.31]

therefore:

$$P = Q^{-1} = \begin{bmatrix} 0.8507 & 0.5257 & 0.5257 \\ -0.5257 & 0.8507 & 0.8507 \\ 0 & 1.4142 & 0 \end{bmatrix}$$

[1.32]

Thus, the controllable form can be written as follows:

$$\bar{A} = PAQ = \begin{bmatrix} 2.6180 & 0 & 0 \\ 0 & 0.3820 & 0 \\ 0 & 0 & 1 \end{bmatrix}, \; \bar{B} = PB = P\begin{bmatrix} 0 \\ 1 \\ 0 \end{bmatrix} = \begin{bmatrix} 1.3764 \\ 0.3249 \\ 0 \end{bmatrix}$$

[1.33]

$$\bar{C} = CQ = \begin{bmatrix} 0 & 0 & 1 \end{bmatrix} Q = \begin{bmatrix} 0.5257 & 0.8507 & -0.707 \end{bmatrix}$$

1.3.2. Controllable canonical transformation

In a controllable canonical transformation, Q can be built using the controllability matrix U_c defined by:

$$U_c = \begin{bmatrix} B & AB & AB^2 & \dots & A^r B & \dots & A^{n-1}B \end{bmatrix}$$

[1.34]

If the rank of U_c is equal to n, then:

$$Q = U_c = \left[B \ AB \ AB^2 ... \ AB^r ... \ A^{n-1}B \right] \qquad [1.35]$$

Otherwise, if the rank of U_c is equal to $r < n$, then:

$$Q = \left[\underbrace{B \ AB ... A^{r-1}B}_{r \ columns} \ \underbrace{R_1 ... \ R_{n-r}}_{(n-r)} \right] \qquad [1.36]$$

which is composed of r linearly independent columns of U_c, selected from left to right, and of an arbitrary choice of $n - r$ remaining columns R_1, R_2, ..., R_{n-r}, so that Q is regular (rank n). In this case, the resulting controllable canonical system $\{\bar{A}, \bar{B}, \bar{C}, \bar{D}\}$ takes the following form:

$$\begin{cases} \bar{x}(k+1) = \begin{bmatrix} \bar{A}_c & \bar{A}_{12} \\ 0 & \bar{A}_{\bar{c}} \end{bmatrix} \bar{x}(k) + \begin{bmatrix} \bar{B}_c \\ 0 \end{bmatrix} u(k) \\ y(k) = \begin{bmatrix} \bar{C}_c & \bar{C}_{\bar{c}} \end{bmatrix} \bar{x}(k) + \underset{\bar{D}}{\underline{D}} u(k) \end{cases} \qquad [1.37]$$

EXAMPLE OF TRANSFORMATION OF A CONTROLLABLE MODEL.– Let us consider.

$$\begin{aligned} x(k+1) &= \begin{bmatrix} 2 & 1 & 1 \\ 0 & 1 & 0 \\ 1 & 0 & 1 \end{bmatrix} x(k) + \begin{bmatrix} 0 \\ 1 \\ 0 \end{bmatrix} u(k) \\ y(k) &= \begin{bmatrix} 0 & 0 & 1 \end{bmatrix} x(k) \end{aligned} \qquad [1.38]$$

In this case, it can be verified that the rank of $U_c = \begin{bmatrix} 0 & 1 & 3 \\ 1 & 1 & 1 \\ 0 & 0 & 1 \end{bmatrix}$ is 3, and it can be considered that:

$$Q = U_c = \begin{bmatrix} 0 & 1 & 3 \\ 1 & 1 & 1 \\ 0 & 0 & 1 \end{bmatrix}$$

Therefore:

$$P = Q^{-1} = \begin{bmatrix} -1 & 1 & 2 \\ 1 & 0 & -3 \\ 0 & 0 & 1 \end{bmatrix} \qquad [1.39]$$

Thus, the controllable form can be written as follows:

$$\bar{A} = PAQ = \begin{bmatrix} 0 & 0 & 1 \\ 1 & 0 & -4 \\ 0 & 1 & 4 \end{bmatrix}, \; \bar{B} = PB = \begin{bmatrix} -1 & 1 & 2 \\ 1 & 0 & -3 \\ 0 & 0 & 1 \end{bmatrix} \begin{bmatrix} 0 \\ 1 \\ 0 \end{bmatrix} = \begin{bmatrix} 1 \\ 0 \\ 0 \end{bmatrix} \qquad [1.40]$$

$$\bar{C} = CQ = \begin{bmatrix} 0 & 0 & 1 \end{bmatrix} \begin{bmatrix} 0 & 1 & 3 \\ 1 & 1 & 1 \\ 0 & 0 & 1 \end{bmatrix} = \begin{bmatrix} 0 & 0 & 1 \end{bmatrix} \qquad [1.41]$$

EXAMPLE OF TRANSFORMATION OF AN UNCONTROLLABLE MODEL.– Let us consider:

$$x(k+1) = \begin{bmatrix} 2 & 1 & 1 \\ 0 & 1 & 0 \\ 1 & 0 & 1 \end{bmatrix} x(k) + \begin{bmatrix} 1 \\ 0 \\ 1 \end{bmatrix} u(k)$$

$$y(k) = \begin{bmatrix} 1 & 0 & 0 \end{bmatrix} x(k)$$

$$[1.42]$$

In this case, it can be verified that the rank of $U_c = \begin{bmatrix} 1 & 3 & 8 \\ 0 & 0 & 0 \\ 1 & 2 & 5 \end{bmatrix}$ is 2. The first two

columns are chosen (they are linearly independent), together with an arbitrary vector $[1 \; 1 \; 0]^T$ in order to form:

$$Q = \begin{bmatrix} 0 & 3 & 1 \\ 1 & 0 & 1 \\ 0 & 2 & 0 \end{bmatrix}$$

or:

$$P = Q^{-1} = \begin{bmatrix} -2 & 2 & 3 \\ 1 & -1 & -1 \\ 0 & 1 & 0 \end{bmatrix}$$

[1.43]

which yields:

$$\overline{A} = PAQ = \begin{bmatrix} 0 & -1 & 5 \\ 1 & 3 & 3 \\ 0 & 0 & -1 \end{bmatrix}, \ \overline{B} = PB = \begin{bmatrix} -2 & 2 & 3 \\ 1 & -1 & -1 \\ 0 & 1 & 0 \end{bmatrix} \begin{bmatrix} 0 \\ 1 \\ 1 \end{bmatrix} = \begin{bmatrix} 1 \\ 0 \\ 0 \end{bmatrix}$$

[1.44]

$$\overline{C} = CQ = \begin{bmatrix} 0 & 0 & 1 \end{bmatrix} \begin{bmatrix} 0 & 3 & 1 \\ 1 & 0 & 1 \\ 0 & 2 & 0 \end{bmatrix} = \begin{bmatrix} 1 & 3 & 1 \end{bmatrix}$$

[1.45]

and it can be verified that the subsystem defined by:

$$\overline{A}_c = \begin{bmatrix} 0 & -1 \\ 1 & 3 \end{bmatrix}, \ \overline{B}_c = \begin{bmatrix} 1 \\ 0 \end{bmatrix}$$

[1.46]

is controllable.

1.3.3. *Observable canonical transformation*

In an observable canonical transformation, Q can be built using the observability matrix U_0 defined by:

$$U_o = \begin{bmatrix} C \\ CA \\ \dots \\ CA^r \\ \dots \\ CA^{n-1} \end{bmatrix}$$

[1.47]

If the rank of U_0 is equal to n, it can be considered that $P = U_0$, or $Q = (U_0)^{-1}$, and otherwise, if the rank of U_0 is equal to $r < n$, matrix [1.48] is considered:

$$
P = \begin{bmatrix}
\left.\begin{matrix} C \\ C\,A \\ ... \\ C\,A^{r-1} \end{matrix}\right\} r\ lines \\
\left.\begin{matrix} R_1 \\ ... \\ R_{n-r} \end{matrix}\right\} (n-r)\ lines
\end{bmatrix}
\qquad [1.48]
$$

It is composed of r linearly independent lines of U_0 selected from up to down and the remaining $n - r$ lines are arbitrarily chosen, so that the rank of P is n. In this case, the resulting observable canonical system $\{\bar{A}, \bar{B}, \bar{C}, \bar{D}\}$ can be written in the following form:

$$
\begin{cases}
\bar{x}(k+1) = \begin{bmatrix} \bar{A}_o & 0 \\ \bar{A}_{21} & \bar{A}_{\bar{o}} \end{bmatrix} \bar{x}(k) + \begin{bmatrix} \bar{B}_o \\ \bar{B}_{\bar{o}} \end{bmatrix} u(k) \\
y(k) = \begin{bmatrix} \bar{C}_o & 0 \end{bmatrix} x(k) + \underset{\bar{D}}{D}\, u(k)
\end{cases}
\qquad [1.49]
$$

For example, let us consider:

$$
\begin{aligned}
x(k+1) &= \begin{bmatrix} 2 & 1 & 1 \\ 0 & 1 & 0 \\ 1 & 0 & 1 \end{bmatrix} x(k) + \begin{bmatrix} 1 \\ 0 \\ 1 \end{bmatrix} u(k) \\
y(k) &= \begin{bmatrix} 0 & 0 & 1 \end{bmatrix} x(k)
\end{aligned}
\qquad [1.50]
$$

In this case, it can be verified that the rank of $U_o = \begin{bmatrix} 0 & 0 & 1 \\ 1 & 0 & 1 \\ 3 & 1 & 2 \end{bmatrix}$ is 3, and it can be

considered that $P = U_o = \begin{bmatrix} 0 & 0 & 1 \\ 1 & 0 & 1 \\ 3 & 1 & 2 \end{bmatrix}$ and therefore $Q = P^{-1} = \begin{bmatrix} -1 & 1 & 0 \\ 1 & -3 & 1 \\ 1 & 0 & 0 \end{bmatrix}$.

Thus, the observable canonical form can be written as:

$$\bar{A} = PAQ = \begin{bmatrix} 0 & 1 & 0 \\ 0 & 0 & 1 \\ 1 & -4 & 4 \end{bmatrix}, \ \bar{B} = PB = \begin{bmatrix} 1 \\ 2 \\ 5 \end{bmatrix} \qquad [1.51]$$

$$\bar{C} = CP^{-1} = \begin{bmatrix} 1 & 0 & 0 \end{bmatrix}$$

Let us also consider the following discrete observable model:

$$x(k+1) = \begin{bmatrix} 2 & 1 & 1 \\ 0 & 1 & 0 \\ 1 & 0 & 1 \end{bmatrix} x(k) + \begin{bmatrix} 1 \\ 0 \\ 1 \end{bmatrix} u(k)$$

$$y(k) = \begin{bmatrix} 1 & 0 & 0 \end{bmatrix} x(k) \qquad [1.52]$$

Once again, it can be verified that the rank of $U_o = \begin{bmatrix} 1 & 0 & 0 \\ 2 & 1 & 1 \\ 5 & 3 & 3 \end{bmatrix}$ is 2, and matrix P

can be chosen, so that $P = \begin{bmatrix} 1 & 0 & 0 \\ 2 & 1 & 1 \\ 1 & 0 & 1 \end{bmatrix}$ composed of the first two lines of U_0 and of a

third arbitrary line [1 0 1]. In this case, it can be readily verified that P is regular.

Therefore, $Q = P^{-1} = \begin{bmatrix} 1 & 0 & 0 \\ -1 & 1 & -1 \\ -1 & 0 & 1 \end{bmatrix}$. Thus, the observable canonical form sought for

can be written as:

$$\bar{A} = PAQ = \begin{bmatrix} 0 & 1 & 0 \\ -1 & 3 & 0 \\ 0 & 1 & 1 \end{bmatrix}, \ \bar{B} = PB = \begin{bmatrix} 1 \\ 3 \\ 2 \end{bmatrix} \qquad [1.53]$$

$$\bar{C} = CP^{-1} = \begin{bmatrix} 1 & 0 & 0 \end{bmatrix}$$

1.3.4. *Kalman canonical transformation*

Kalman canonical transformation relies on an orthogonal matrix H (in the sense of Householder) of sequential decomposition of A, which means:

$$A = HR \qquad [1.54]$$

with $H^{-1} = H^T$ (orthogonality condition), R being an upper triangular matrix. In this case, the required orthogonal transformation matrix is $Q = P^{-1} = H^T$. The calculation of $H = Q^T$ can be done with Matlab command:

$$\gg [Q, R] = qr(A) \qquad [1.55]$$

For example, let us consider:

$$x(k+1) = \begin{bmatrix} 2 & 1 & 1 \\ 0 & 1 & 0 \\ 1 & 0 & 1 \end{bmatrix} x(k) + \begin{bmatrix} 0 \\ 1 \\ 0 \end{bmatrix} u(k)$$

$$y(k) = \begin{bmatrix} 0 & 0 & 1 \end{bmatrix} x(k) \qquad [1.56]$$

Under these conditions, using Matlab to calculate $H = Q$ and R yields:

$$Q = \begin{bmatrix} -0.8944 & 0.1826 & -0.4082 \\ 0 & -0.9129 & 0.4082 \\ -4472 & 0.3651 & 0.8165 \end{bmatrix}, R = \begin{bmatrix} -2.2361 & -0.8944 & -1.3416 \\ 0 & -1.0954 & 0.1826 \\ 0 & 0 & 0.4082 \end{bmatrix} \qquad [1.57]$$

Therefore:

$$\bar{A} = PAQ = \begin{bmatrix} 2.6000 & 0.7348 & -0.5477 \\ -0.0816 & 1.0667 & -0.2981 \\ -0.1826 & 0.1491 & 0.3333 \end{bmatrix}, \bar{B} = PB = \begin{bmatrix} 0 \\ -0.9129 \\ 0.4082 \end{bmatrix} \qquad [1.58]$$

$$\bar{C} = CP^{-1} = \begin{bmatrix} -0.4472 & 0.3651 & 0.8165 \end{bmatrix}$$

1.4. Canonical decomposition diagram

The previous review of canonical structures of discrete state models of dynamic processes leads to the diagram in Figure 1.6 which represents the canonical decomposition of the state model of a discrete process.

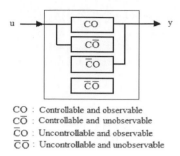

CO : Controllable and observable
CŌ : Controllable and unobservable
C̄O : Uncontrollable and observable
C̄Ō : Uncontrollable and unobservable

Figure 1.6. *Diagram of canonical decomposition*

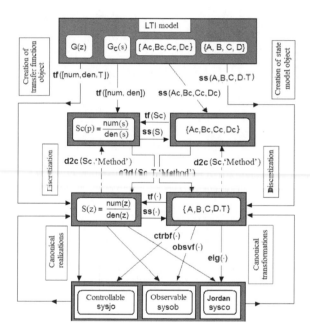

Figure 1.7. *Discretization and canonical transformations of dynamic models using Matlab*

1.5. Discretization and canonical transformations using Matlab

The diagram in Figure 1.7 presents the examples of Matlab commands for discretization and canonical transformation of models of linear and time invariant dynamic processes. Each arrow indicates the direction of creation of a new structure of dynamic model based on the corresponding initial model.

It is worth remembering that "Sc" and "S" denote "continuous object model" and "discrete object model", respectively. On the contrary, the models created with "ss" are "structures of state model objects".

1.6. Exercises and solutions

Exercise 1.1.

A dynamic process is described by the following transfer function in z:

$$G(z) = \frac{Y(z)}{U(z)} = \frac{z^2 + 2z + 2}{10\,z^3 + z^2 + 3z + 1}$$

Find:

a) a controllable state representation;

b) an observable state representation.

Solution – Exercise 1.1.

The first step is to set $G(z)$ in the form [1.1], then in the form [1.8a] and deduce a controllable structure corresponding to [1.14].

a) A controllable state representation is given by:

$$\begin{cases} x(k) = \begin{bmatrix} 0 & 1 & 0 \\ 0 & 0 & 1 \\ -0.1 & -0.3 & -0.1 \end{bmatrix} x(k) + \begin{bmatrix} 0 \\ 0 \\ 1 \end{bmatrix} u(k) \\ y(k) = \begin{bmatrix} 0.2 & 0.2 & 0.1 \end{bmatrix} \text{x(k)} \end{cases}$$

b) An observable state representation is given by:

$$\begin{cases} x(k+1) = \begin{bmatrix} 0 & 0 & -0.1 \\ 1 & 0 & -0.3 \\ 0 & 1 & -0.1 \end{bmatrix} x(k) + \begin{bmatrix} 0.2 \\ 0.2 \\ 0.1 \end{bmatrix} u(k) \\ y(k) = \begin{bmatrix} 0 & 0 & 1 \end{bmatrix} \text{x(k)} \end{cases}$$

Exercise 1.2.

A process is described by the z-transfer function:

$$G(z) = \frac{Y(z)}{U(z)} = \frac{1}{(z+1)(z+2)}$$

Find a Jordan canonical state realization.

Solution – Exercise 1.2

$$G(z) = \frac{1}{(z+1)(z+2)} = G(z) = \frac{1}{z+1} - \frac{1}{z+2} = \frac{\frac{1}{z}}{1+\frac{1}{z}} - \frac{\frac{1}{z}}{1+\frac{2}{z}}$$

Therefore, a Jordan state representation is:

$$\begin{cases} x(k+1) = \begin{bmatrix} -1 & 0 \\ 0 & -2 \end{bmatrix} x(k) + \begin{bmatrix} 1 \\ 1 \end{bmatrix} u(k) \\ y(k) = \begin{bmatrix} 1 & 1 \end{bmatrix} x(k) \end{cases}$$

Exercise 1.3.

A process is described by the z-transfer function:

$$G(z) = \frac{Y(z)}{U(z)} = \frac{1}{(z+1)^2(z+2)}$$

Find a Jordan canonical state realization.

Solution – Exercise 1.3.

$$G(z) = \frac{Y(z)}{U(z)} = \frac{1}{(z+1)^2(z+2)} = \frac{1}{(z+1)^2} - \frac{1}{z+1} + \frac{1}{z+2}$$

A Jordan canonical state realization leads to:

$$\begin{cases} x(k+1) = \begin{bmatrix} -1 & 1 & 0 \\ 0 & -1 & 0 \\ 0 & 0 & -2 \end{bmatrix} x(k) + \begin{bmatrix} 0 \\ 1 \\ 1 \end{bmatrix} u(k) \\ y(k) = \begin{bmatrix} 1 & 1 & 1 \end{bmatrix} x(k) \end{cases}$$

Exercise 1.4.

The block diagram of a servomechanism that is digitally controlled by a discrete PI controller corresponds to Figure 1.8, where K_p and b designate the parameters of the transfer function $D(z)$ of the controller, K_m and a being the parameters of the z-transfer function of the dynamic process (with $0 < a < 1$).

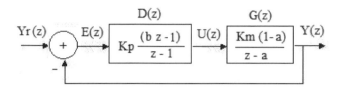

Figure 1.8. *Block diagram of a servomechanism controlled by a discrete PI controller*

a) Find and represent an equivalent block diagram of this servomechanism in the discrete state space based on the respective (Jordan) canonical realizations of $G(z)$ and $D(z)$.

b) Find the discrete state feedback control law, as well as the discrete state equation of this control system.

c) Knowing that $\{K_m = 1.1;\ a = 0.8065;\ K_p = 0.7;\ T = 0.2\ \text{s}\}$, use Matlab to generate the simulation results of the unit step response of the complete discrete state feedback control system. Then, proceed to the interpretation of the graphical results obtained.

Solution – Exercise 1.4.

a) A simple expansion leads to new expressions $G(z) = K_m\,(1-a)\,\dfrac{1/z}{1-1/z}$ and

$D(z) = b\,K_p\,(1 + \dfrac{(1-1/b)\,(1/z)}{1-1/z})$. Jordan block diagrams of $G(z)$ and $D(z)$ are presented in Figure 1.9.

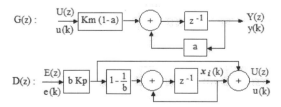

Figure 1.9. *Jordan block diagrams of $G(z)$ and $D(z)$*

The combined control block diagram that results in the discrete state space is presented in Figure 1.10.

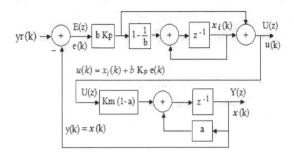

Figure 1.10. *Block diagram of discrete state space control*

b) Given the state variables x and x_i chosen in Figure 1.10, the discrete state feedback control law can be written as:

$$u(k) = \begin{bmatrix} -b \ K_p & 1 \end{bmatrix} \begin{bmatrix} x(k) \\ x_i(k) \end{bmatrix} + b \ K_p \ y_r(k)$$

Then, the discrete state equation of the control system is given by:

$$\begin{bmatrix} x(k+1) \\ x_i(k+1) \end{bmatrix} = \begin{bmatrix} a - Km \ (1-a) \ b \ K_p & Km \ (1-a) \\ -(1-(1/b)) \ K_p & 1 \end{bmatrix} \begin{bmatrix} x(k) \\ x_i(k) \end{bmatrix} + \begin{bmatrix} Km \ (1\text{-}a) \ b \ K_p \\ (1-(1/b)) \ b \ K_p \end{bmatrix} y_r(k)$$

$$y(k) = \begin{bmatrix} 1 & 0 \end{bmatrix} \begin{bmatrix} x(k) \\ x_i(k) \end{bmatrix}$$

c) Figure 1.11 presents the obtained simulation results. The Matlab program in Figure 1.12 can then be used to replicate these results. From a numerical point of view, the closed-loop results are:

$$\begin{cases} \begin{bmatrix} x(k+1) \\ x_i(k+1) \end{bmatrix} = \begin{bmatrix} 0.6157 & 0.2129 \\ -0.1965 & 1.0000 \end{bmatrix} \begin{bmatrix} x(k) \\ x_i(k) \end{bmatrix} + \begin{bmatrix} 0.1908 \\ 0.1965 \end{bmatrix} yr(k) \\ y(k) = \begin{bmatrix} 1 & 0 \end{bmatrix} \begin{bmatrix} x(k) \\ x_i(k) \end{bmatrix} \end{cases}$$

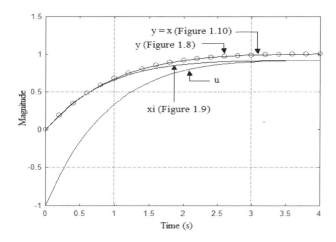

Figure 1.11. *Result of the Matlab-based simulation*

It can be noted that the block diagrams described in the frequency domain (Figure 1.8) and in the discrete state space (Figure 1.10) are equivalent from the input/output point of view, but they are not similar at the internal level, where the control of state x_i is explicit in the state space. Moreover, knowing that

$$u(\infty) = \begin{bmatrix} -b \ K_P & 1 \end{bmatrix} \begin{bmatrix} x(\infty) \\ x_i(\infty) \end{bmatrix} + b \ K_P \ y_r(\infty), \text{ if } y(\infty) = x(\infty) - y_r(\infty), \text{ then } u(\infty) = x_i(\infty)$$

(see Figure 1.11).

```
               % EXERCISE_I4.m
    Km = 1.1    a = 0.8065;  b = 1.2807;   Kp = 0.7;   T= 0.2;
                t = 0:T:4;  N = length(t);   z = tf('z');
                Dz = Kp*(b*z-1)/(z-1);       Gz = Km*(1-a)/(z-a);
           [numF, denF] = tfdata(feedback(series(Dz, Gz),1));

        Ytf = dstep(numF,denF, N);         % Simulation Figure 1.8
        A = [a - Km*(1-a)*b*Kp   Km*(1-a);   -(1-(1/b))*b*Kp   1];
        B = [Km*(1-a)*Kp*b ;    b*Kp*(1-(1/b))];
        C = [1   0];   D = 0;
        [Yss, X] = dstep(A,B,C,D,1,N);        % Simulation Figure 1.10
            Yr = ones(N,1);  Er = Yr-Yss;  U = X(:,2) - Er;  % {u(k}
        plot(t, Ytf,'o', t,X(:,1),'k',t,X(:,2),'k',t,U,'b');  grid
```

Figure 1.12. *Example of Matlab program for the simulation of the control system in the discrete state space*

Design and Simulation of Digital State Feedback Control Systems

2.1. Principle of digital state feedback control

The methods for the discretization of dynamic models studied in basic automation [MBI 17b], whose results are summarized in Appendix 3, allow for the construction of block diagrams of digital control systems in the discrete state space. An example of a basic block diagram is presented in Figure 2.1.

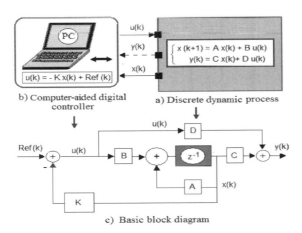

b) Computer-aided digital
controller

a) Discrete dynamic process

c) Basic block diagram

Figure 2.1. *Block diagram of a digital control system in the discrete state space*

Without loss of generality, it could be considered, where necessary, that Ref(*k*) = 0.

The structure of the complete discrete state model is given by [2.1]:

$$\begin{cases} x(k+1) = A\,x(k) + B\;u(k) \\ u(k) = -K\,x(k) + \operatorname{Re} f(k) \end{cases} \rightarrow \begin{cases} x(k+1) = (A - B\,K)\,x(k) + B\operatorname{Re} f(k) \\ y(k) = (C - D\,K)\,x(k) + D\operatorname{Re} f \end{cases} \quad [2.1]$$

Thus, for an appropriate choice of the gain K, the stability of [2.1] can be guaranteed.

Among the classical and modern methods for calculating the gain K, the simplest one, whose algorithm is available in most of the tools for simulating automated control systems, is based on the pole placement principle.

2.2. Calculation of the gain K using pole placement

The principle of the pole placement method involves finding the gain K for which the poles of the closed-loop system coincide with the poles that are fixed according to the desired specifications. This means that the characteristic polynomial of matrix $(A - BK)$ must coincide with the one whose roots represent the desired eigenvalues.

Let us consider:

$$- K = [K_1, K_2, \ldots, K_n] \,; \tag{[2.2]}$$

    $d(z)$: the desired closed loop characteristic polynomial,

– $b(z, K)$: characteristic polynomial of the closed-loop system of the gain K.

Then, $d(z)$ and $b(z, K)$ can be written as follows:

$$d(z) = z^n + d_{n-1}z^{n-1} + d_{n-2}z^{n-2} + \ldots + d_1 z + d_0 \tag{[2.3]}$$

$$b(z, K) = |zI_n - A + BK| = z^n + b_{n-1}(K)z^{n-1} + b_{n-2}(K)z^{n-2} + \ldots + b_1(K)z + b_0(K) \tag{[2.4]}$$

Under these conditions, the gain K can be calculated in several ways:

– through identification of the coefficients of characteristic polynomials $d(z)$ and $b(z, K)$. This involves solving the following system of n equations with n unknowns $K_1, K_2, \ldots, K_n$:

$$\begin{cases} b_{n-1}(K_1, K_2, \ldots, K_n) = d_{n-1} \\ b_{n-2}(K_1, K_2, \ldots, K_n) = d_{n-2} \\ \ldots \\ b_0(K_1, K_2, \ldots, K_n) = d_0 \end{cases} \tag{[2.5]}$$

– Ackermann's formula:

$$K = \begin{bmatrix} 0 & 0 & \dots & 0 & 1 \end{bmatrix} \begin{bmatrix} B & AB & A^2B \dots A^{n-1}B \end{bmatrix}^{-1} \left(A^n + d_{n-1}A^{n-1} + \dots + d_1A + d_0I_n \right) \qquad [2.6]$$

It is clear that relation [2.6] is applicable if the controllability matrix $\begin{bmatrix} B & AB & A^2B \dots A^{n-1}B \end{bmatrix}$ is regular. The Matlab® command "acker" allows for the numerical calculation of the gain K if the data {A, B, desired poles} are specified.

2.3. State feedback with complete order observer

2.3.1. *Problem statement*

Real-time implementation of the discrete state feedback control law defined by [2.1] is not possible in practice unless all measured values of the state vector $x(k)$ are available for calculating control sequences $u(k)$. There are however practical applications for which:

– the components of vector x are difficult or even impossible to measure directly (rotor flux of a cage induction motor);

– components of state x make no physical sense (case of fictitious variables that result from canonical or homogeneous transformations);

– reduction of the number of physical sensors to be deployed is intended, for reasons related to costs and operating constraints.

Provided that the dynamic model of the process is observable, all these critical cases can use an observer for real-time reconstruction of the missing state components from the sequences of the dynamic process control quantities $u(k)$ and output quantities $y(k)$. Depending on whether the observation process concerns all or part of the state vector, this state observer is qualified as "complete" or "partial", respectively.

2.3.2. *Structure of the complete or full state observer*

Let us consider, for example, a linear dynamic process, which is time-invariant and supposed observable, described by the discrete state model [2.7]:

$$\begin{cases} x(k+1) = A\,x(k) + B\,u(k) \\ y(k) = C\,x(k) \end{cases} \qquad [2.7]$$

with:

- matrix A of order $n \times n$;

- matrix B of order $n \times p$;

- C being a line vector to be determined according to observation needs.

Under these conditions, the structure of the observer model can logically be deduced from the process structure, taking into account possible errors to be corrected between the observed state $\hat{x}(k)$ and the theoretical state $x(k)$.

Thus, the state observer schematically presented in Figure 2.2 is described by the linear state model [2.8]:

$$\begin{cases} \hat{x}(k+1) = A\,\hat{x}(k) + B\,u(k) + L\,(y(k) - \hat{y}(k)) \\ \hat{y}(k) = C\,\hat{x}(k) \end{cases}$$

[2.8]

where L designates the observation gain to be determined.

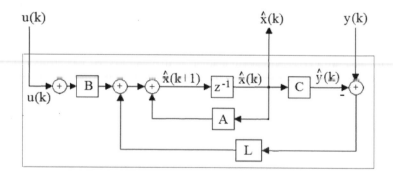

Figure 2.2. *Structure of a complete state observer*

Combining equations [2.7] and [2.8], then considering $\varepsilon(k) = (x(k) - \hat{x}(k))^{\mathrm{T}}$, the following is obtained:

$$\varepsilon^{\mathrm{T}}(k+1) = \varepsilon^{\mathrm{T}}(k)\left(A - LC\right)^{\mathrm{T}} = \varepsilon^{\mathrm{T}}(k)\left(A^{\mathrm{T}} - C^{\mathrm{T}}L^{\mathrm{T}}\right)$$

[2.9]

The dynamic behavior of the observer is therefore imposed by the eigenvalues of matrix $A - LC = (A^{\mathrm{T}} - C^{\mathrm{T}}L^{\mathrm{T}})^{\mathrm{T}}$ or by those of $A^{\mathrm{T}} - C^{\mathrm{T}}L^{\mathrm{T}}$. Thus, by analogy to the characteristic matrix $A - BK$ of a state feedback law of gain K, the calculation of L^{T} or that of L can be made using the pole placement technique considering the pair

(A^T, C^T). In this case, Ackermann's formula to be used is written in one of the following equivalent forms:

$$L^T = [0 \; 0 \; ... \; 0 \; 0 \; 1][C^T \; A^T C^T \; ... \; (A^{n-1})^T C^T]^{-1} \Phi(A^T)$$

$$L = \Phi(A) \begin{bmatrix} C \\ CA \\ ... \\ CA^{n-2} \\ CA^{n-1} \end{bmatrix}^{-1} \begin{bmatrix} 0 \\ 0 \\ ... \\ 0 \\ 1 \end{bmatrix} \quad\quad [2.10]$$

where $\Phi(A)$ is the image of A given by the desired closed-loop characteristic polynomial.

2.3.3. Synthesis diagram of the state feedback with complete observer

2.3.3.1. *Separation principle*

Let us consider the process and complete observer models, given respectively by:

$$\begin{cases} x(k+1) = A\,x(k) + B\,u(k) \\ y(k) = C\,x(k) \end{cases}$$

and:

$$\begin{cases} \hat{x}(k+1) = A\,\hat{x}(k) + B\,u(k) + L\,(y(k) - \hat{y}(k)) \\ \hat{y}(k) = C\,\hat{x}(k) \end{cases} \quad\quad [2.11]$$

Given an observer state feedback control law defined by:

$$u(k) = -K\,\hat{x}(k) \quad\quad [2.12]$$

relations [2.11] and [2.12] lead to the synthesis block diagram of a state feedback control system with complete order observer, which is represented in Figure 2.3.

If, instead of using states $x(k)$ and $\hat{x}(k)$, new states $x(k)$ and $\varepsilon(k) = x(k) - \hat{x}(k)$ are considered, the previous equations can be written as follows:

$$\begin{bmatrix} x(k+1) \\ \varepsilon(k+1) \end{bmatrix} = \begin{bmatrix} A - BK & BK \\ 0 & A - LC \end{bmatrix} \begin{bmatrix} x(k) \\ \varepsilon(k) \end{bmatrix} \quad\quad [2.13]$$

$$y(k) = Cx(k)$$

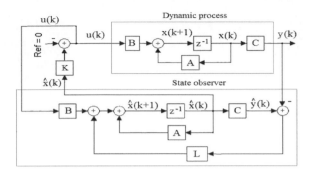

Figure 2.3. *Block diagram of a state feedback control system with complete order observer*

It can then be noted that the eigenvalues of the resulting dynamic joint system of order $2n$ are constituted of those of state feedback matrices $(A - BK)$ and observer matrices $(A - LC)$. This leads to the separation principle.

The separation principle stipulates that for a state feedback control system with complete observer, the respective gains K and L of the state feedback and of the observer can be calculated separately, and then applied to the joint system whose control law is given by [2.12].

Since the observer state $\hat{x}(k)$ serves as input data for the controller, the observer response time should be shorter (for example, 5 times shorter) than that of the state feedback controller.

2.3.3.2. *Implementation algorithm*

When the system's parameters (A, B, C) as well as the respective gains K and L of the controller and of the observer have defined numerical values, the algorithm shown in Figure 2.4 allows for the implementation of the digital state feedback control system with complete order observer. A real-time implementation (in contrast to simulation) requires at each discrete instant $t_k = kT$:

– a *timer* of sampling period T;

– writing the digital code of the numerically calculated command $u(k)$ to the D/A conversion port;

– measurement of response $y(k)$ at instant $t_k = kT$, by reading the corresponding digital code at the A/D conversion port, followed by decimal conversion of this code;

– waiting for the next discrete instant $(n + 1)T$.

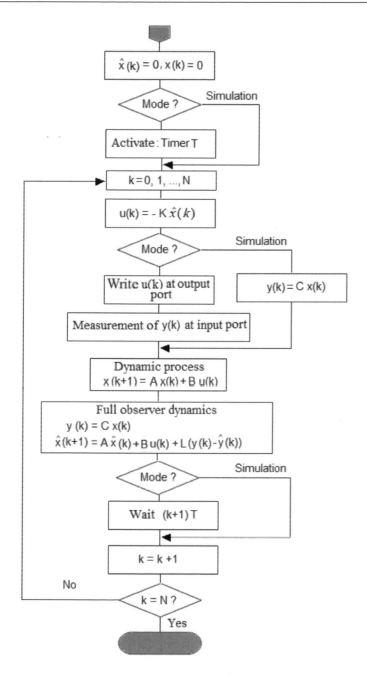

Figure 2.4. *Algorithm of state feedback with complete observer*

2.4. Discrete state feedback with partial observer

2.4.1. *Problem statement*

Let us once again consider the discrete process described by the following state model, which is supposed observable:

$$\begin{cases} x(k+1) = A\, x(k) + B\, u(k) \\ y(k) = C\, x(k) \end{cases}$$
[2.14]

with:

– matrix A of order $n \times n$;

– matrix B of order $n \times p$;

– C being a matrix that should be determined depending on observation needs.

If m components of the state are accessible to measurement, an estimate of the remaining $n - m$ states should be made by means of a partial state observer.

2.4.2. *Structure of the partial state observer*

Given that m components of the state are available, it is always possible to reorder the components of $x(k)$, so that the new adequately ordered vector $\chi(k) = \begin{bmatrix} \chi_m(k) \\ \chi_o(k) \end{bmatrix}$, which is obtained by the similarity transformation $\chi(k) = \begin{bmatrix} \chi_m(k) \\ \chi_o(k) \end{bmatrix} = Px(k)$, leads to a new dynamic equation of the form:

$$\begin{cases} \chi(k+1) = \begin{bmatrix} \chi_m(k+1) \\ \chi_o(k+1) \end{bmatrix} = \begin{bmatrix} A_{mm} & A_{mo} \\ A_{om} & A_{oo} \end{bmatrix} \begin{bmatrix} \chi_m(k) \\ \chi_o(k) \end{bmatrix} + \begin{bmatrix} B_m \\ B_o \end{bmatrix} u(k) \\ y(k) = \chi_m(k) = \begin{bmatrix} I & 0 \end{bmatrix} \begin{bmatrix} \chi_m(k) \\ \chi_o(k) \end{bmatrix} \end{cases}$$
[2.15]

with:

– $\chi_m(k)$: vector of m measurable states of $x(k)$;

– $\chi_o(k)$: the remaining part of $x(k)$ to be observed.

Moreover, for a particular choice of $\chi_m(k)$ and $\chi_o(k)$, vectors $x(k)$ and $\chi(k)$ are necessarily equivalent, in which case there is a regular transformation matrix P, so that $\chi(k) = Px(k)$. Thus, state $x(k)$ can be calculated as follows:

$$x(k) = \mathrm{P}^{-1}\chi(k) = Qx(k) = [Q_m \mid Q_o]\chi(k) \qquad [2.16]$$

with $Q = \mathrm{P}^{-1}$.

Therefore, [2.15] can be written in the form [2.17]:

$$\begin{cases} \chi_o(k+1) = A_{om}\chi_m(k) + A_{oo}\chi_o(k) + B_o\,u(k) & \text{(a)} \\ \chi_m(k+1) = A_{mm}\chi_m(k) + A_{mo}\chi_o(k) + B_m\,u(k) & \text{(b)} \end{cases} \qquad [2.17]$$

or in the equivalent form:

$$\begin{cases} \chi_o(k+1) = A_{oo}\chi_o(k) + \underbrace{A_{om}\chi_m(k) + B_o u(k)}_{u_O(k)} \\ \underbrace{\chi_m(k+1) - A_{mm}\chi_m(k) - B_m\,u(k)}_{y_O(k)} = A_{mo}\chi_o(k) \end{cases} \qquad [2.18]$$

Given [2.18], and considering:

$$\begin{cases} u_o(k) = A_{om}\chi_m(k) + B_o\,u(k) \\ y_0(k) = A_{mo}\chi_o(k) = \chi_m(k+1) - A_{mm}\chi_m(k) - B_m\,u(k) \end{cases} \qquad [2.19]$$

the above leads to:

$$\begin{cases} \chi_o(k+1) = A_{oo}\chi_o(k) + u_o(k) = \underbrace{A_{oo}\chi_o(k) + A_{om}\chi_m(k) + B_o\,u(k)}_{\text{Term known at step } k+1} & \text{(a)} \\ y_o(k) = A_{mo}\chi_o(k) = \overbrace{x_m(k+1) - A_{mm}\chi_m(k) - B_m(k)u(k)}^{\text{Term known at step } k+1} & \text{(b)} \end{cases} \qquad [2.20]$$

The problem of partial state observation has a solution, which is given by:

$$\begin{cases} \hat{\chi}_o(k+1) = A_{oo}\hat{\chi}_o(k) + A_{om}\chi_m(k) + B_o\,u(k) + L_o(y_o - \hat{y}_0) \\ L_o y_o(k) = L_o\left(x_m(k+1) - A_{mm}\chi_m(k) - B_m u(k)\right) \\ L_o \hat{y}_o(k) = L_o A_{mo}\hat{\chi}_o(k) \end{cases} \qquad [2.21]$$

Now combining the first equation and the last two equalities in [2.21], a single equation results, which is given by:

$$\hat{\chi}_o(k+1) = A_{oo}\hat{\chi}_o(k) + A_{om}\chi_m(k) + B_o\,u(k)$$
$$+L_o(x_m(k+1) - A_{mm}\chi_m(k) - B_m u(k)) - L_o A_{mo}\hat{\chi}_0(k))$$

[2.22]

After regrouping of similar terms in [2.22], relation [2.23] is obtained:

$$\hat{\chi}_o(k+1) = (A_{oo} - L_o A_{mo})\,\hat{\chi}_o(k) + (A_{om} - L_o A_{mm})\chi_m(k)$$
$$+ (B_o - L_o B_m)\,u(k)\ +\ L_o\chi_m(k+1)$$

[2.23]

In order to study the behavior of the observation error defined by [2.24]:

$$\varepsilon_o(k) = \chi_o(k) - \hat{\chi}_o(k)$$

[2.24]

regrouping of [2.20a] and [2.23] leads to [2.25]:

$$\begin{cases} \chi_o(k+1) = A_{oo}\chi_o(k) + A_{om}\chi_m(k) + B_o u(k) \\ \hat{\chi}_o(k+1) = (A_{oo} - L_o A_{mo})\,\hat{\chi}_o(k) + (A_{om} - L_o A_{mm})\chi_m(k) + (B_o - L_o B_m)\,u(k) \\ \quad +\ L_o\chi_m(k+1) \end{cases}$$

[2.25]

At this stage, if the expression of $\chi_m(k+1)$ given by [2.17b] is used in [2.25], then subtraction of the two terms of [2.25] yields the dynamic model of the observation error $\varepsilon(k)$, which is described by [2.26]:

$$\varepsilon_o(k+1) = \chi_o(k+1) - \hat{\chi}(k+1) = (A_{oo} - L_o A_{mo})\varepsilon_o(k)$$

[2.26]

Therefore, the gain L_o of the partial observer can still be found, so that it guarantees observation stability if and only if the pair (A_{oo}, A_{mo}) is observable.

Moreover, if the term $\chi_m(k+1)$ in [2.23] is replaced by its expression [2.17b], then [2.23] becomes after simplification:

$$\hat{\chi}_o(k+1) = (A_{oo} - L_o A_{mo})\,\hat{\chi}_o(k) + (A_{om} - L_o A_{mm})\chi_m(k)$$
$$+ (B_o - L_o B_m)\,u(k)$$
$$+\ L_o\ (A_{mm}\chi_m(k) + A_{mo}\chi_o(k) + B_m\,u(k))$$
$$= (A_{oo} - L_o A_{mo})\,\hat{\chi}_o(k) + A_{om}\,\chi_m(k) + L_o\,A_{mo}\chi_o(k)$$
$$+ B_o\,u(k)$$

[2.27]

Moreover, if in [2.17b], the first term of [2.25] and [2.27] are regrouped, the following dynamic equations of the joint system (dynamic process and partial state observer) are obtained after simplification:

$$\begin{cases} \chi_m(k+1) = A_{mm}\,\chi_m(k) + A_{mo}\chi_o(k) + B_m u(k) \\ \chi_o(k+1) = A_{oo}\chi_o(k) + A_{om}\chi_m(k) + B_o u(k) \\ \hat{\chi}_o(k+1) = (A_{oo} - L_o A_{mo})\,\hat{\chi}_o(k) + (A_{om})\chi_m(k) \;+\; L_o A_{mo}\chi_o(k) + B_o u(k) \end{cases} \qquad [2.28]$$

In conclusion, relation [2.28] describes a digital state feedback control system with partial observer, as shown in Figure 2.5.

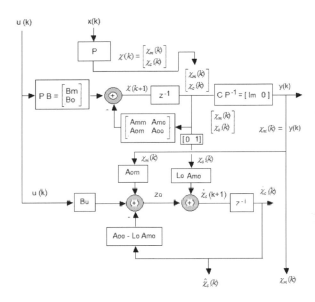

Figure 2.5. *Detailed block diagram of the partial state observer*

2.4.3. *Diagram of discrete state feedback with partial observer*

2.4.3.1. *Separation principle*

Knowing that the state model of the system formed of process and partial observer is given by:

$$\begin{cases} \chi_m(k+1) = A_{mm}\chi_m(k) + A_{mo}\chi_o(k) + B_m u(k) \\ \chi_o(k+1) = A_{oo}\chi_o(k) + A_{om}\chi_m(k) + B_o u(k) \\ \hat{\chi}_o(k+1) = (A_{oo} - L_o A_{mo})\,\hat{\chi}_o(k) + (A_{om})\chi_m(k) \;+\; L_o A_{mo}\chi_o(k) + B_o u(k) \end{cases} \qquad [2.29]$$

and considering the state feedback law defined by:

$$u(k) = -K_m \chi_m(k) - K_o \hat{\chi}_o(k) \tag{2.30}$$

after the introduction of [2.30] into [2.29], simplification and regrouping of the resulting expressions, the following final structure is obtained:

$$
\begin{bmatrix} \chi_m(k+1) \\ \chi_o(k+1) \\ \hat{\chi}_o(k+1) \end{bmatrix} = \begin{bmatrix} A_{mm} - B_m K_m & A_{mo} - B_m K_o & 0 \\ A_{om} - B_o K_m & A_{oo} - B_o K_o & 0 \\ A_{om} - B_o K_m & -B_o K_o + L_o A_{mo} & A_{oo} - L_o A_{mo} \end{bmatrix} \begin{bmatrix} \chi_m(k) \\ \chi_o(k) \\ \hat{\chi}_o(1) \end{bmatrix}
$$
$$
+ \begin{bmatrix} B_m K_m & B_m K_o \\ B_o K_m & B_o K_o \\ B_o K_m & B_o K_o \end{bmatrix} \begin{bmatrix} \chi_{rm} \\ \chi_{ro} \end{bmatrix} \tag{2.31}
$$

Thus, relation [2.31] describes the final structure of a state feedback control system with partial observer and corresponds to the block diagram in Figure 2.6.

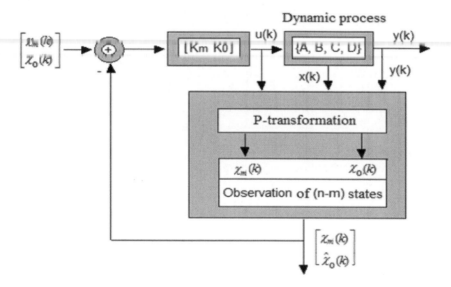

Figure 2.6. *Diagram of state feedback control with partial observer*

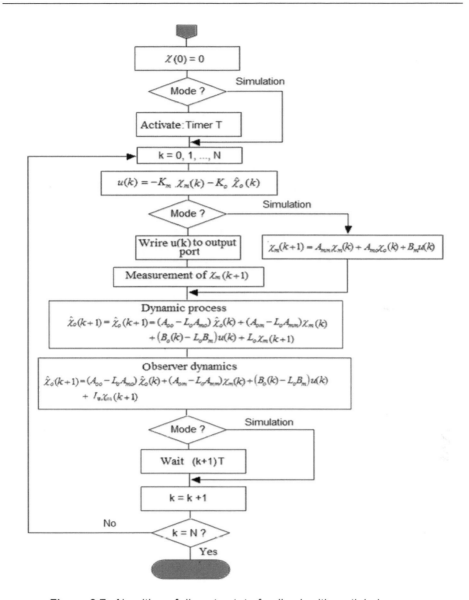

Figure 2.7. *Algorithm of discrete state feedback with partial observer*

The structure of [2.31] shows that the eigenvalues of the joint system are constituted of those of the system and of the partial observer. The separation principle is also applicable to the design of a state feedback control system with partial estimator.

2.4.3.2. *Implementation algorithm*

When the numerical values of the system's parameters A_{mm}, B_{mo}, A_{om}, A_{oo}, B_m, B_o, C, K_m, K_o and L_o are known, the algorithm allows the implementation of the state feedback control system with partial observer corresponding to Figure 2.7.

2.5. Discrete state feedback with set point tracking

This type of controller is of great interest if, besides the stability of the state feedback loop, a closed loop with high static performance has to be obtained. In this case, the block diagram of the state feedback control system with set point tracking device corresponds to Figure 2.8.

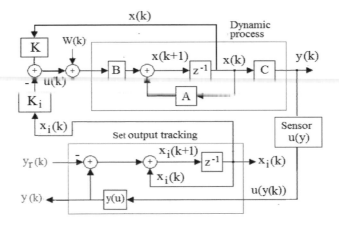

Figure 2.8. *Diagram of discrete state feedback with set point tracking*

2.6. Block diagram of a digital control system

The complete diagram in Figure 2.9 shows a synthesis of the developments of various configurations of digital state feedback control.

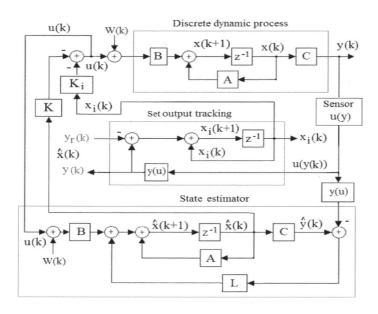

Figure 2.9. *Block diagram of digital discrete state feedback controller with estimator*

2.7. Computer-aided simulation of a servomechanism

2.7.1. *Simulation of a speed servomechanism*

2.7.1.1. *Canonical discrete state model with input delay*

It is worth remembering that the open-loop transfer functions $G_c(s)$ and $G(z)$ of a servomechanism with input delay τ_0 are written in the following form:

$$G_c(s) = \frac{Y(s)}{U(s)} = G_0(s)\, e^{-\tau_0\, s} \qquad\qquad [2.32]$$

$$G(z) = z^{-m}\, \frac{(z-1)}{z}\, Z\!\left(\frac{G_0(s)}{s}\right) \qquad\qquad [2.33]$$

where $G_0(s)$ is a rational transfer function, and m is an adequately fixed integer in order to rationalize the dynamic model of the effect of pure delay τ_0.

The discrete state model of the open-loop servomechanism will be elaborated by the canonical realization of [2.33].

For a speed servomechanism, relations [2.32] and [2.33] become:

$$G_c(s) = \frac{Y(s)}{U(s)} = \frac{K_s}{(1+\tau s)} e^{-\tau_0 s}$$ [2.34]

$$G(z) = \frac{K_s (1-e^{-\frac{1}{\tau}T})}{z^{m+1} - e^{-\frac{1}{\tau}T} z^m}$$ [2.35]

Thus, for $m = 8$, the observable realization of [2.35] leads to the following canonical state model of dimension $(m + 1) = 9$:

$$\begin{cases} x(k+1) = A\,x(k) + B\,u(k) \\ y(k) = C\,x(k) \end{cases}$$ [2.36]

with:

$$A = \begin{bmatrix} e^{-\frac{1}{\tau}T} & 1 & 0 & \cdots & 0 & 0 \\ 0 & 0 & 1 & 0 & 0 & 0 \\ \cdots & 0 & 0 & \cdots & 0 & \cdots \\ 0 & 0 & 0 & \cdots & 1 & 0 \\ 0 & 0 & 0 & 0 & 0 & 1 \\ 0 & 0 & 0 & . & 0 & 0 \end{bmatrix}_{(m+1)\,\mathrm{x}\,(m+1)} \quad B = \begin{bmatrix} 0 \\ 0 \\ \cdots \\ 0 \\ 0 \\ K_s\left(1-e^{-\frac{1}{\tau}T}\right) \end{bmatrix}_{(m+1)\,\mathrm{x}\,1}$$ [2.37]

$$C = \begin{bmatrix} 1 & 0 & 0 & \cdots & 0 & 0 \end{bmatrix}_{1\,\mathrm{x}\,(m+1)}$$

2.7.1.2. Diagram of state feedback control with observer

Relations [2.35]–[2.37] involve $m = 8$ fictitious state variables, which result from the rationalization of the input delay, out of a total of $(n + m)$ state variables. This constraint requires the use of a complete state observer for the state feedback. Moreover, a speed set output tracking sub-loop is also required for good static performance.

The full diagram of digital state feedback control with complete observer is represented in Figure 2.10. This diagram corresponds to the graphic interpretation of the joint dynamic equations of the dynamic subsystems in the digital control loop:

$$
\begin{cases}
\begin{cases} x(k+1) = A\,x(k) + B\,u(k) + B\,w(k) & \text{(a)} \\ y(k) = C\,x(k) \end{cases} \\[4pt]
u(k) = \begin{cases} -K\,x(k) \; -K_i\,x_i(k)\,, \\ \qquad\quad \text{or} \\ -K\,\hat{x}(k) \; -K_i\,x_i(k) \end{cases} & \text{(b)} \qquad\qquad [2.38] \\[4pt]
x_i(k+1) = x_i(k) + y\,(k) - y_r\,(k) & \text{(c)} \\[4pt]
\begin{cases} \hat{x}(k+1) = A\,\hat{x}(k) + B\,u(k) + B\,w(k) \\ \qquad\quad + L\,(y(k) - C\,\hat{x}(k)) \\ \hat{y}(k) = C\,\hat{x}(k) \end{cases} & \text{(d)}
\end{cases}
$$

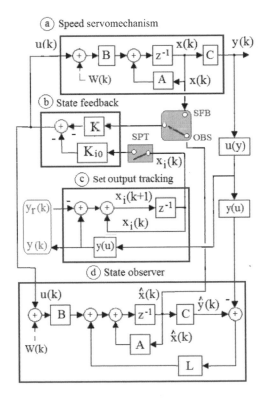

Figure 2.10. *Block diagram of digital state feedback control with complete observer of a speed servomechanism*

2.7.1.3. *Digital simulations and results*

The following data have been used for the calculation of gain matrices of the controller and observer:

– process parameters: $K_s = 0.5$; $\tau = 0.5$ s; $\tau_0 = 0.25$ s;

– set output value: $y_r = 3$ units;

– sampling period: $T = 40$ ms;

– required closed-loop characteristic polynomial $p(\lambda)$:

$$p(\lambda) = \lambda^{10} - 1.9210\ \lambda^9 + 0.9205\ \lambda^8 + 0.0006\ \lambda^7$$
$$- 0.0001\ \lambda^4 + 0.0001\ \lambda^3 + 0.0046\ \lambda^2 \qquad [2.39]$$
$$+ 0.0198\ \lambda - 0.0216$$

Calculation of the roots of [2.39] using the Matlab "roots" command yields:

$$r = \begin{bmatrix} -0.5828 \\ -0.434\ + j0.3982 \\ -0.434\ - j0.3982 \\ -0.0485 + j0.6090 \\ -0.0485 - j0.6090 \\ 0.4144 - j0.5042 \\ 0.4144 + j0.5042 \\ 0.9489 - j0.0299 \\ 0.9489 + j0.0299 \\ r_i = -0.7437 \end{bmatrix} \qquad [2.40]$$

where r_i is the pole associated with the dynamic behavior of the set output tracking state. It is worth noting that in the complex z-plane, all the roots of [2.39] have modules below one. Thus, the studied digital control system is stable. Moreover, the numerical resolution of the pole placement problem using the Matlab "place" command yields the following gain matrix of discrete state feedback:

$$K = [0.31\ \ 0.05\ \ 0.001\ \ 0.002\ \ 0.004\ \ 0.006\ \ 0.008\ \ 0.01\ \ 0.02],$$
$$K_i = 0.03 \qquad [2.41]$$

where K_i is the gain of the set output tracking state feedback. Moreover, the gain L of the observer is fixed in a manner that allows for sufficiently rapid comparison of its dynamic behavior to that of the process. The chosen gain is given by the following relation:

$$L = 4K \qquad\qquad [2.42]$$

Figure 2.11 shows the simulation results of the response at the step $y_r = 3$ units of the state feedback control system for the speed servomechanism.

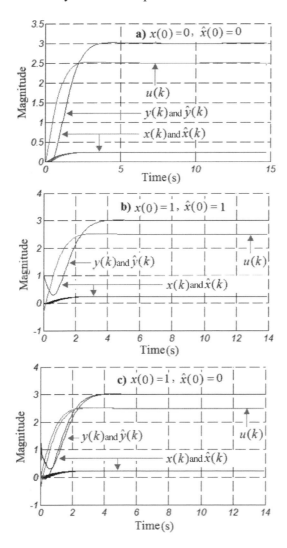

Figure 2.11. *Graphic results of the step response of time delay servomechanism*

As shown in Figures 2.11(a) and 2.11(b), when the initial conditions of the process states and of the estimated states are identical, the trajectories of the dynamic process signals coincide at each moment with those of the estimator. Otherwise, the trajectories of the estimated signals rapidly converge towards those of the process within 0.5 seconds, as can be noted in Figure 2.11(c).

2.7.2. Computer-aided simulation of a position servomechanism

In this case, the analytical relations required for digital simulation are similar to those developed for a speed servomechanism. These relations are summarized as follows:

$$G_C(s) = \frac{Y(s)}{U(s)} = \frac{K_s}{s\,(1+\tau\,s)}\,e^{-\tau_0\,s} \qquad\qquad [2.43]$$

$$G(z) = K_s\left(\frac{\left[T-\tau(1-e^{-\frac{1}{\tau}T})\right]z - Te^{-\frac{1}{\tau}T} + \tau(1-e^{-\frac{1}{\tau}T})}{z^{m+2} - (1+e^{-\frac{1}{\tau}T})\,z^{m+1} + e^{-\frac{1}{\tau}T}\,z^{m}}\right) \qquad\qquad [2.44]$$

$$\begin{cases} x(k+1) = A\,x(k) + B\,u(k) \\ y(k) = C\,x(k) \end{cases} \qquad\qquad [2.45]$$

with:

$$\begin{cases} A = \begin{bmatrix} a_1 & 1 & 0 & \dots & 0 & 0 \\ a_2 & 0 & 1 & 0 & 0 & 0 \\ 0 & 0 & 0 & \dots & 0 & \dots \\ \dots & 0 & 0 & \dots & 1 & 0 \\ 0 & 0 & 0 & 0 & 0 & 1 \\ 0 & 0 & 0 & . & 0 & 0 \end{bmatrix}_{(m+2)x(m+2)}, B = \begin{bmatrix} 0 \\ 0 \\ \dots \\ 0 \\ 0 \\ b_9 \\ b_{10} \end{bmatrix}_{(m+2)x1} \\ C = \begin{bmatrix} 1 & 0 & 0 & . & 0 & 0 \end{bmatrix} \end{cases} \qquad [2.46]$$

with:

$$\begin{cases} a_1 = 1 + e^{-\frac{1}{\tau}T}, \ a_2 = e^{-\frac{1}{\tau}T}; \ b_9 = K_s\left(T - \tau(1 - e^{-\frac{1}{\tau}T})\right) \\ b_{10} = K_s\left(-Te^{-\frac{1}{\tau}T} + \tau(1 - e^{-\frac{1}{\tau}T})\right) \end{cases}$$

[2.47]

The following data have been used for the calculation of gain matrices of the controller and estimator:

– process parameters: $K_s = 0.5$; $\tau = 0.5$ s; $\tau_0 = 0.25$ s;

– set output value: $y_r = 12$ units;

– sampling period: $T = 40$ ms;

– required closed-loop characteristic polynomial $p(\lambda)$:

$$p(\lambda) = \lambda^{11} - 2.9229\,\lambda^{10} + 2.8458\,\lambda^9 - 0.9228\,\lambda^8$$
$$+ \ 0.0009\,\lambda^2 - 0.0008$$

[2.48]

The calculation of the roots of [2.48] using the Matlab "roots" command yields:

$$r = \begin{bmatrix} 0.9868 + j0.0204 \\ 0.9868 - j0.0204 \\ 0.4285 + j0.2469 \\ 0.4285 - j0.2469 \\ 0.0991 + j0.4147 \\ 0.0991 - j0.4147 \\ -0.3446 + j0.1238 \\ -0.3446 - j0.1238 \\ -0.1911 + j0.3376 \\ -0.1911 - j0.3376 \\ r_i = 0.9655 \end{bmatrix}$$

[2.49]

where r_i designates the pole associated with the dynamic behavior of set output tracking state. It can readily be verified that all the roots contained in [2.49] have modules below one; therefore, the stability conditions of the digital control system are met.

Moreover, the numerical resolution of the pole placement problem using the Matlab "place" command makes it possible to determine the following gain matrix of discrete state feedback:

$$K = 10^{-2} \begin{bmatrix} 48 & 0.6 & 0.1 & 0.01 & 0.01 & 0.01 & 0.01 & 0.01 & 0.01 & 0.002 \end{bmatrix},$$
$$K_i = 0.00585$$

[2.50]

Moreover, the observer gain is fixed by the following relation:

$$L = 4K$$

[2.51]

Figure 2.12 presents the simulation results of a set output response at a step $y_r = 12$ units of the digital state feedback control system of the position servomechanism being studied.

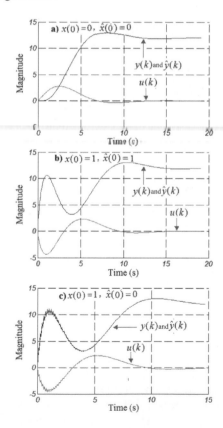

Figure 2.12. *Results of simulation of the step response of the digital state feedback control system of the servomechanism*

As shown in Figures 2.12(a) and 2.12(b), the dynamic behavior of the observer is perfect when the initial conditions of the estimated state vector coincide with that of the process. Moreover, as shown in Figure 2.12(c), when these initial conditions are different, the observer behavior rapidly converges towards that of the dynamic process.

2.8. Exercises and solutions

Exercise 2.1.

Let us consider a system described in the discrete state space by the following data: $A = \begin{bmatrix} 1 & \alpha \\ 0 & 1 \end{bmatrix}$ and $B = \begin{bmatrix} \alpha^2/2 \\ \alpha \end{bmatrix}$, for which the following closed-loop characteristic equation should be obtained:

$$z^2 - 1.6z + 0.7 = 0$$

Find the required state feedback gain K using:

a) the technique involving identification of the terms of characteristic polynomials;

b) Ackermann's formula.

Solution – Exercise 2.1.

a) The closed-loop characteristic polynomial for a state feedback gain $K = [K_1 \ K_2]$ is written as:

$$b(z, K) = |zI_2 - A + BK| = 0$$

$$\rightarrow \left| z \begin{bmatrix} 1 & 0 \\ 0 & 1 \end{bmatrix} - \begin{bmatrix} 1 & \alpha \\ 0 & 1 \end{bmatrix} + \begin{bmatrix} \alpha^2/2 \\ \alpha \end{bmatrix} [K_1 \ K_2] \right|$$

$$\rightarrow b(z, K) = \left| z \begin{bmatrix} z\text{-}1 & -\alpha \\ 0 & z\text{-}1 \end{bmatrix} + \begin{bmatrix} (\alpha^2/2)K_1 & (\alpha^2/2)K_2 \\ \alpha K_1 & \alpha K_2 \end{bmatrix} \right|$$

$$\rightarrow b(z, K) = z^2 + \alpha K_2 + \left((\alpha^2/2) K_1 - 2 \right) z + (\alpha^2/2) K_1 - \alpha K_2 + 1$$

Now the gain K can be determined through identification of the coefficients of characteristic polynomials:

$$b(z,K) = z^2 + \alpha K_2 + \left(\left(\alpha^2 / 2 \right) K_1 - 2 \right) z + \left(\alpha^2 / 2 \right) K_1 - \alpha K_2 + 1$$

and:

$$d(z) = z^2 - 1.6\ z + 0.7$$

which involves solving the following system of linear equations:

$$\begin{cases} \alpha K_2 + \left(\alpha^2 / 2 \right) K_1 \ -2 = -1.6 \\ \left(\alpha^2 / 2 \right) K_1 - \alpha K_2 + 1 = 0,7 \end{cases}$$

which yields the sought-for solution:

$$K = \begin{bmatrix} \dfrac{0.1}{\alpha^2} & \dfrac{0.35}{\alpha} \end{bmatrix}$$

b) The system's controllability matrix is:

$$[B\ AB] = \begin{vmatrix} \alpha^2 / 2 \\ \alpha \end{vmatrix} \begin{bmatrix} 1 & \alpha \\ 0 & 1 \end{bmatrix} \left(\begin{matrix} \alpha^2 / 2 \\ T \end{matrix} \right) = \begin{vmatrix} \alpha^2 / 2 & \alpha^2 + \alpha^2 / 2 \\ \alpha & \alpha \end{vmatrix}$$

Moreover:

$$[B\ AB]^{-1} = -\frac{1}{\alpha^3} \begin{bmatrix} \alpha & -\alpha^2 - \alpha^2 / 2 \\ -\alpha & \alpha^2 / 2 \end{bmatrix} = -\frac{1}{\alpha^2} \begin{bmatrix} 1 & -\dfrac{3}{2}\alpha \\ -1 & \alpha / 2 \end{bmatrix}$$

or:

$$A^2 = \begin{bmatrix} 1 & \alpha \\ 0 & 1 \end{bmatrix} \begin{bmatrix} 1 & \alpha \\ 0 & 1 \end{bmatrix} = \begin{bmatrix} 1 & 2\alpha \\ 0 & 1 \end{bmatrix};\ -1.6\ A = \begin{bmatrix} -1.6 & -1.6\ \alpha \\ 0 & -1.6 \end{bmatrix}$$

$$0,7 I_2 = \begin{bmatrix} 0.7 & 0 \\ 0 & 0.7 \end{bmatrix}$$

$$A^2 - 1.6A + 0.7I_2 = \begin{bmatrix} 1 & 2\alpha \\ 0 & 1 \end{bmatrix} + \begin{bmatrix} -1.6 & -1.6\ \alpha \\ 0 & -1.6 \end{bmatrix} + \begin{bmatrix} 0.7 & 0 \\ 0 & 0.7 \end{bmatrix}$$

$$= \begin{bmatrix} 0.1 & 0.4\ \alpha \\ 0 & 0.1 \end{bmatrix}$$

Therefore:

$$K = \begin{bmatrix} 0 & 1 \end{bmatrix} \left(-\frac{1}{\alpha^2} \begin{bmatrix} 1 & -\dfrac{3}{2}\alpha \\ -1 & \dfrac{\alpha}{2} \end{bmatrix} \right) \begin{bmatrix} 0.1 & 0.4\alpha \\ 0 & 0.1 \end{bmatrix} = \begin{bmatrix} 0.1 & 0.35 \\ \dfrac{0.1}{\alpha^2} & \alpha \end{bmatrix}$$

Exercise 2.2.

Let us consider the problem of control of the process described by the following transfer function:

$$G_c(s) = \frac{K_m}{s\ (1 + \tau\ s)}$$

where:

- $K_m = 11$;

- $\tau = 0.14$ s.

Let us also consider the corresponding state model:

$$\begin{cases} \dfrac{dx}{dt} = \begin{bmatrix} 0 & \dfrac{Km}{\tau} \\ 0 & -\dfrac{1}{\tau} \end{bmatrix} x + \begin{bmatrix} 0 \\ 1 \end{bmatrix} u \\ y = \begin{bmatrix} 1 & 0 \end{bmatrix} x \end{cases}$$

as well as a discrete state feedback law of gain $K = [K_1\ \ K_2]$ that can provide the closed-loop poles:

- $p_1 = -46.05 + 36.98j$;

- $p_2 = -46.05 - 36.98j$.

a) Considering a sampling period $T = 1$ ms, use a Matlab program to calculate the equivalent discrete model of the process and the required gain of the discrete state feedback. Then simulate and graphically represent the states of digital control corresponding to a set state $x_r = [1 \ 0]^T$.

b) Generate the obtained simulation results.

Solution – Exercise 2.2.

The problem of pole placement can be solved under these conditions using the Matlab "gain.m" source code (see Figure 2.13).

In this program, the process state model is discretized using the Matlab "c2d (sysproc, T)" command. This discretization yields the parameters A, B, C and D of the equivalent discrete state model, as follows:

$$A = \begin{bmatrix} 0 & 0.15603 \\ 0 & 0.98588 \end{bmatrix}; \ B = \begin{bmatrix} 0.0001564 \\ 0.0019858 \end{bmatrix}; C = [1 \ 0]; D = 0$$

It is worth noting that, in the discrete domain, the rank of the controllability matrix:

$$[B \ AB \ A^2B] = \begin{bmatrix} 0.0002 & 0.0005 & 0.0008 \\ 0.0020 & 0.0020 & 0.0019 \end{bmatrix}$$

is 2; therefore, the controllability property has been preserved during discretization.

Furthermore, the gain K is calculated in the previous program using one of the following Matlab primitives:

$- K\_place = place(A,B,[z1 \ z2])$;

$- K\_acker = acker(A,B,[z1 \ z2])$.

with:

$$z_1 = e^{p_1T} = e^{(-46.05 + 36.9j)(0.002)} = 0.9095 + j0.0674$$

$$z_2 = e^{p_2T} = e^{(-46.05 - 36.9j)(0.002)} = 0.9095 - j0.0674$$

which yields the required closed-loop characteristic polynomial:

$$\Phi(\lambda) = (\lambda - z_1)(\lambda - z_2) = \lambda^2 - (z_1 + z_2)\lambda + z_1 z_2 = \lambda^2 - 1.819\lambda + 0.8318$$

The value of the gain obtained as result of running the previous Matlab program is:

$$K = [40.7870\ \ 80.7733]$$

Matlab "gain.m" program
| ```
% Matlab-aided calculation of the gain K by pole placement
T = 0.002 ;  t=0:T:0.14;

% Continuous Process Model
km =11; tau = 0.14;
Ac = [0 km/tau; 0 -1/tau]; Bc = [0; 1]; Cc = [1 0]; Dc=0;
Sysproc = ss(Ac,Bc,Cc,0);

% Closed-loop required poles
p1= - 46.05 + 36.98j;   p2 = - 46.05 - 36.98j; % Continuous poles
z1=exp(T*p1),  z2 = exp(T*p2)   % Discrete poles

% Discretization of continuous process
sysdproc = c2d(sysproc,T)  % Display of the following numerical values
                % of parameters
A=sysdproc.a
B= sysdproc.b
% Calculation of feedback gain with place and Acker
K_place = place(A,B,[z1  z2]) % Pole placement
K_acker = acker(A,B,[z1  z2]) % Ackermann's formula

% Reference states refx1=step  and refx2=0;
refx1 = ones(length(t)); refx1=refx1(:,1);
refx2 = zeros(length(t)); refx2=refx2(:,1);
refx = [refx1 refx2];

% Simulations of closed-loop state evolution
[y,x] = dlsim(A-B*K_place,B*K_place,[1 0],0,refx)
 plot(t,x(:,1),'.',t,x(:,2),'+'); grid
``` |

Figure 2.13. Matlab "gain.m" program
```

Figure 2.14 presents the obtained simulation results when running the previously described Matlab "gain.m" program.

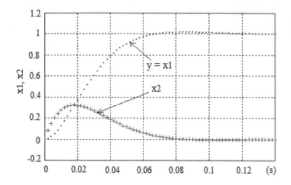

Figure 2.14. *Results of running the Matlab "gain.m" program*

Exercise 2.3.

Let us consider a process described by the following discrete state model:

$$\begin{cases} x(k+1) = \begin{bmatrix} 0 & 0.15603 \\ 0 & 0.98588 \end{bmatrix} x(k) + \begin{bmatrix} 0.0001564 \\ 0.0019858 \end{bmatrix} u(k) \\ y(k) = \begin{bmatrix} 1 & 0 \end{bmatrix} x(k) \end{cases}$$

The sampling period used is $T = 1$ ms.

a) Is this model observable?

b) Use Matlab to calculate the gain L of the complete order observer required when process states are not available in real time. To answer this question, let us suppose that the observation process should be five times faster than the one of state feedback and the state feedback poles in the discrete domain are:

- $z_1 = 0.9095 + j0.0674$;

- $z_2 = 0.9095 - j0.0674$.

c) Find the discrete state model of the state feedback and observer system.

d) Propose a complete Matlab program, allowing the simulation and graphic representation of the estimated and real states of digital control for a set state $x_r = [1\ 0]^T$.

e) Generate the obtained simulation results.

Solution – Exercise 2.3.

a) The system is observable, as the rank of the observability matrix defined by:

$$\begin{bmatrix} C \\ CA \\ CA^2 \end{bmatrix} = \begin{bmatrix} 1 & 0 \\ 1 & 0.156 \\ 1 & 0.3098 \end{bmatrix}$$

is equal to 2.

b) For a sampling period $T = 1$ ms, the state feedback poles in the continuous domain are:

- $p_1 = -46.05 + 36.98j$;

- $p_2 = -46.05 - 36.98j$.

If the aim is to have an observation process that is five times faster than the state feedback, the observer poles should be chosen as follows:

- $z_{1o} = e^{\frac{s_1 T}{5}} = 0.9816 + j0.0145$;

- $z_{2o} = e^{\frac{s_1 T}{5}} = 0.9816 - j0.0145$;

in which case, the observer gain L can be calculated using the Matlab command $L = place(A', C', [z1o\ z2o])$, which yields:

$$L = [0.0226\ \ 0.0015]^T$$

c) For the joint closed-loop system, the following can be written as:

$$\begin{cases} \begin{bmatrix} x(k+1) \\ x(k+1) - \hat{x}(k+1) \end{bmatrix} = \begin{bmatrix} A - BK & BK \\ 0 & A - LC \end{bmatrix} \begin{bmatrix} x(k) \\ x(k) - \hat{x}(k) \end{bmatrix} \\[2em] \qquad = \begin{bmatrix} 0.9936 & 0.1434 & 0.0064 & 0.0126 \\ -0.0810 & 0.8254 & 0.0810 & 0.1604 \\ 0 & 0 & 0.9774 & 0.1560 \\ 0 & 0 & -0.0015 & 0.9858 \end{bmatrix} \begin{bmatrix} x(k) \\ x(k) - \hat{x}(k) \end{bmatrix} \\[2em] z(k) = \begin{bmatrix} 1 & 0 \\ 0 & 1 \end{bmatrix} \begin{bmatrix} x(k) \\ x(k) - \hat{x}(k) \end{bmatrix} = \begin{bmatrix} x(k) \\ x(k) - \hat{x}(k) \end{bmatrix} \end{cases}$$

```
% "RetEtaObsCom.m" Program
% STATE FEEDBACK WITH COMPLETE ORDER OBSERVER
    clear
    Tech = 0.0001; Tfin=0.005; t=0:Tech:Tfin;
    Nech = length(t);  u = ones(1,Nech);


        z1 = 6.52e-001 +9.6e-002i
        z2 = 6.52e-001 -9.6e-002i
    A = [0.95577        22.324  ;  -0.00043348     0.0043314];
     B = [0.034428  ;   0.00043693]; C = [1   0];   D = 0;
Polyz = conv([1 -z1],[1 -z2]) % Charact. polynomial
    K= place(A,B,[z1 ; z2])
   Af = A-B*K; Bf = B*K;
   r1=1* ones(1,length(t))';   r2 = 0.0*ones(1,length(t))'
```

```
            X0 = [0.0 ; 0]
            syszf  = ss(Af,Bf,[1 0], 0,Tech);
             [Y,X] = dlsim(Af,Bf,[1 0], 0,[r1 r2], X0);
                % Observer
            L = [0.175 -0.003];
            x1e(1) = 0; x2e(1) = 0; x1(1) = 0; x2(1) = 0
            y(1) = 0
Nech1= Nech-1;
        for n=1:Nech1
            uc(n) =  -K(1)*(x1e(n))-K(2)*x2e(n)+K*[r1(1) r2(1)]';
            y(n) = C(1)* x1(n) + C(2)*x2(n);
           x1(n + 1) = A(1,1) * x1(n) + A(1,2) * x2(n) + B(1) * uc(n) ;
           x2(n + 1) = A(2,1) * x1(n) + A(2,2) * x2(n) + B(2) * uc(n);
           x1e(n + 1) = A(1,1) * x1e(n) + A(1,2) * x2e(n) + B(1) * uc(n) ...
                   + L(1) * (y(n) - C(1) * x1e(n)-C(2)*x2e(n));
           x2e(n + 1) = A(2,1) * x1e(n) + A(2,2) * x2e(n) + B(2) * uc(n) ...
                   + L(2) * (y(n) - C(1) * x1e(n)-C(2)*x2e(n));
        end
uc(n+1) = uc(n);
plot(t,x1, t,x1e,'*', t,1000*x2,t,1000*x2e,'+',t,uc ); grid
axis([0 max(t) -2.5  2.5]);
```

Figure 2.15. *Matlab "RetEtaObsCom.m" program*

Using the Matlab *eig*([A-B*K   B*K; *zeros*(2)   A-L'*C]) command, it can be verified that the eigenvalues of the joint closed-loop system are:

- controller poles:

$$0.9095 + 0.0674i$$

$$0.9095 - 0.0674i$$

- observer poles:

$$0.9816 + 0.0145i$$

$$0.9816 - 0.0145i$$

d) The Matlab "RetEtaObsCom.m" program in Figure 2.15 can be used to rapidly make all the previous numerical calculations and automatically generate the results presented.

e) The obtained simulation results are shown in Figure 2.16.

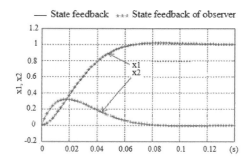

Figure 2.16. *Simulation results of a state feedback control system with and without complete order observer*

Exercise 2.4.

Case study of a state feedback with reduced observer. Let us consider a discrete system defined by:

$$\begin{cases} x(k+1) = \begin{bmatrix} 0.95577 & 22.324 \\ -0.00043348 & 0.0043314 \end{bmatrix} x(k) + \begin{bmatrix} 0.034428 \\ 0.00043693 \end{bmatrix} u(k) \\ y(k) = \begin{bmatrix} 1 & 0 \end{bmatrix} x(k) \end{cases}$$

with a sampling period $T = 0.1$ ms. Let us suppose that a previous study has yielded a state feedback gain $K = [1.834 - 931.784]$ and an estimation in practice of the second component $x(k)$ is required, by a partial state observer of gain $L_o = -0.01$.

"RetEtaObsRed.m" Program

```
% STATE FEEDBACK WITH REDUCED OBSERVER
clear
Tech = 0.0001; Tfin = 0.005; t = 0:Tech:Tfin;
Nech = length(t);
A= [0.95577    22.324;   -0.00043348    0.0043314];
B= [0.034428  ;  0.00043693];
C = [1  0];   D = 0;
% ----------------
            Amm = 0.95577;    Amo = 22.324;
            Aom = -0.00043348 ; Aoo = 0.0043314;
            Bm = 0.034428;  Bo = 0.00043693;
    u(1) = ;  Xm(1) = 0; Xo(1)=0;
zo(1) = 0; u(1) = 0;
    Xrm = 1* ones(1,length(t))';
    Xro =  0.0*ones(1,length(t))'
    Lo = -0.01;
K = [1.834 -931.784];  Km = K(1);  Ko = K(2);
% Observer
% --------------
Af=A-B*K; Bf=B*K;
r1 = 1* ones(1,length(t))';  r2 = 0.0*ones(1,length(t))'
X0 = [0.0 ; 0]
Syszf = ss(Af,Bf,[1 0], 0,Tech);
 [Y,X] = dlsim(Af,Bf,[1 0], 0,[r1 r2], X0);
Nech1 = Nech-1;
for n = 1:Nech1
  u(n) = -Km*(Xm(n)-Xrm(n))-Ko*(Xo(n)-Xro(n));
Xm(n + 1) = Amm*Xm(n) + Amo*Xo(n)+Bm*u(n);
zo(n+1) = (Aoo-Lo*Amo)*Xo(n) ...
  +(Aom-Lo*Amm)*Xm(n)+(Bo-Lo*Bm)*u(n);
Xo(n+1) = zo(n+1)+Lo*Xm(n+1);
end
u(n+1) = u(n);
plot(t,Xm,t,X(:,1),'+', t,1000*Xo, t,1000*X(:,2),'+',t,u ); grid
title('State feedback and partial observer: x1 (V) and x2(mA)')
```

Figure 2.17. *Matlab "RetEtaObsRed.m" program*

a) Propose a Matlab program for the simulation of the closed loop control system without and with reduced order observer.

b) Present the obtained simulation results.

Solution – Exercise 2.4.

– In this specific case, the following can be written as:

- $[\chi_m(k)\ \chi_o(k)] = x(k) = [x_1(k)\ x_2(k)]$;

- $[K_m\ K_o] = K = [K_1\ K_2]$.

Under these conditions, the Matlab "RetEtaObsRed.m" program (see Figure 2.17) allows for the simulation of the closed-loop control system without and with reduced observer.

– The obtained simulation results are presented in Figure 2.18.

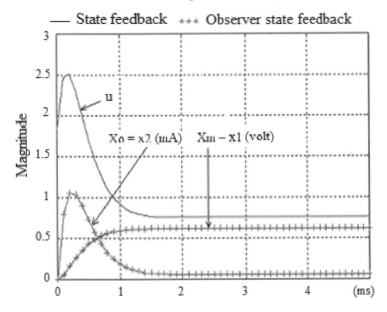

Figure 2.18. *Results of the simulation of a state feedback control system with or without partial observer*

Multimedia Test Bench for Computer-aided Feedback Control

3.1. Context and interest

3.1.1. *Context*

ServoSys multimedia test bench, presented in this chapter, is a flexible work station for computer-aided feedback control of servomechanisms. It is the result of major overhauls and upgrades, followed by the combination and expansion of previous research efforts of Mbihi [MBI 15a, MBI 15b].

The design of automatic operating modes of this platform relies on modeling approaches using main SFC (Sequential Function Chart), macro-step expansion SFC and subprogram SFC [MBI 05], while the implementation uses MMMI (multimedia man–machine interface) technology.

Moreover, the virtual range of control strategies offered features P, PI, PID and PIDF controllers, as well as state feedback control laws with or without observer. This virtual range also offers advanced tools for open-loop testing and real-time experimental modeling of target dynamic processes.

The dynamic process considered is a modular servomechanism. It is a driver of mechanical load with adjustable speed/position. This type of device can be applied to:

– hard disks;

– machine tools;

– powered conveyers;

– textile cutter machines;

– steering devices for vehicles (car, boat, aircraft and spacecraft);

– robots (industrial, surgical and remotely operated);

– arm or leg prostheses, etc.

In practice, operational performances of a servomechanism are validated before effective use by means of an appropriate, precise, user-friendly and flexible test bench.

3.1.2. *Scientific/teaching interest*

The ServoSys multimedia platform differs from most of the test benches in practical automation due to the following advantages:

– multiple dynamic targets, with optional output variable;

– a source of virtual set output with adjustable parameters;

– open-loop control with an option for prior automatic identification of the parameters of the dynamic process to be controlled;

– multiple control laws;

– multiple operating modes: simulation, tests, shutdown, configuration, etc.;

– virtual multimedia control panel (text, image and video).

3.1.3. *Platform presentation methodology*

In this chapter, section 3.2 reviews the hardware and software components that allow the creation of a test bench for teaching purposes. Moreover, section 3.3 presents the normalized descriptive SFC of functional and operational specifications, while sections 3.4 and 3.5 cover the software implementation and the simulation and experimental test results obtained, respectively.

3.2. Hardware constituents of the platform

Figure 3.1 presents the hardware architecture of the ServoSys multimedia test bench. This platform comprises the following subsystems:

– PC (Figure 3.1(a));

– MDAQ (multifunction data acquisition) interface (Figure 3.1(b));

– modular servomechanism (Figure 3.1(c));

– USB webcam (Figure 3.1(d)).

Moreover, the specific constituents of a modular servomechanism (Figure 3.1(c)) are:

– power interface, featuring a ± 15 volts symmetrical power source and a controllable amplifier with direct voltage u provided by an analog output channel of MDAQ interface;

– servomotor;

– magnetic load (perturbation) with adjustable position.

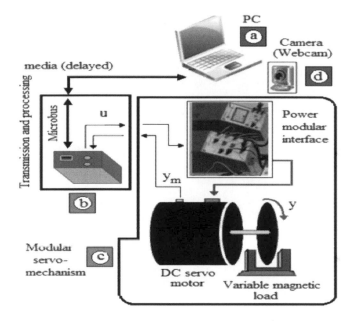

Figure 3.1. *ServoSys hardware architecture*

3.3. Design elements of the ServoSys software application

3.3.1. *Fundamental elements*

3.3.1.1. *Diagram of feedback control systems under consideration*

Figure 3.2 presents the digital control diagrams of the ServoSys multimedia platform. The names of given *.png files are numerical images of feedback control diagrams viewable in real time according to the operating mode selected by the operator.

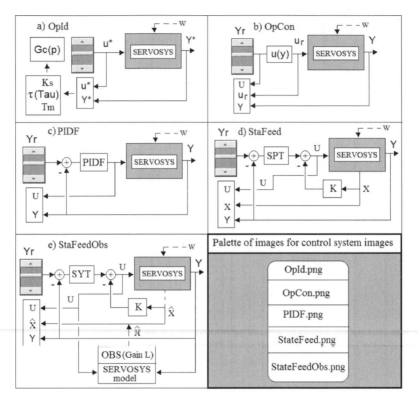

Figure 3.2. *Range of ServoSys feedback control diagrams*

There are five categories of control diagrams, as follows:

– OpId (open-loop identification of parameters), see Figure 3.2(a);

– OpCon (open-loop control), see Figure 3.2(b);

– PIDF (PIDF controller), see Figure 3.2(c);

– StaFeed (state feedback without observer), see Figure 3.2(d);

– StaFeedObs (state feedback with observer), see Figure 3.2(e).

3.3.1.2. *Parametric identification and open-loop control*

For parametric identification systems (OpId) and open-loop control systems (OpCon), the target dynamic processes of the ServoSys platform are described by a transfer function of the following general form:

$$G_c(s) = \frac{Y(s)}{U(s)} = G_0(s)\, e^{-\tau_0 s} \qquad\qquad [3.1]$$

with:

– U: command quantity;

– Y: output quantity;

– $G_0(s)$: rational transfer function, of order n and strictly proper.

The specific structures of [3.1], retained here for the modular servomechanism, are defined by:

$$G_c(s) = \frac{Y(s)}{U(s)} = \begin{cases} \dfrac{K_s}{1+\tau s}\, e^{-\tau_0 s} & \text{if } Y \text{ is the speed} \quad\text{(a)} \\[2mm] \dfrac{K_s}{s(1+\tau s)}\, e^{-\tau_0 s} & \text{if } Y \text{ is the position} \quad\text{(b)} \end{cases} \qquad [3.2]$$

with:

– K_s: static gain;

– τ: time constant;

– τ_0: input delay time.

Parameters K_s, τ and τ_0 of [3.2] can be identified in a Matlab® script from the open-loop experimental response of the servomechanism to be controlled using the "tfest" command. Moreover, for digital simulation needs of the closed-loop control system, the process transfer function G(z) is obtained by discretizing [3.2] using the technique of index invariance defined by $G(z) = z^{-m}\left(\dfrac{z-1}{z}\right) Z\left(\dfrac{G_{cr}(s)}{s}\right)$, where

$G_{cr}(s)$ designates the rational part of [3.2], while parameter m is the order of delay encapsulation of pure delay τ_0. On the contrary, the transfer function D(z) of the PIDF controller results from the discretization of [3.3] using the Tustin technique:

$$D_c(s) = \frac{Y(s)}{E(s)} = K_p \left(1 + \frac{1}{T_i s} + \frac{T_d s}{1+T_f s} \right) \tag{3.3}$$

Other techniques for the discretization of transfer functions of the PIDF controllers, according to Mbihi [MBI 18], are summarized in Appendix 3.

Thus, the resulting transfer function G(z) is given by:

$$G(z) = \begin{cases} \dfrac{K_s\,(1-e^{-\frac{1}{\tau}T})}{z^{m+1} - e^{-\frac{1}{\tau}T} z^m} & \text{if } y = \text{speed (a)} \\[4mm] K_s \dfrac{\left(T - \tau\,(1-e^{-\frac{T}{\tau}})\right) z - Te^{-\frac{T}{\tau}} + \tau\,(1-e^{-\frac{T}{\tau}})}{z^{m+2} - (1+e^{-\frac{T}{\tau}}) z^{m+1} + e^{-\frac{T}{\tau}} z^m} & \text{if } y = \text{position (b)} \end{cases} \tag{3.4}$$

where m denotes the order of delay encapsulation τ_0 by the modified z-transform. Furthermore, the transfer function D(z) of the PIDF controller, obtained through the Tustin method, followed by simple expansion and restructuring of the parameters of numerator and denominator, can be written as:

$$D(z) = K_p \frac{(b_0 z^2 + b_1 z + b_0)}{z^2 + a_1 z + a_2} \tag{3.5}$$

with:

$$\begin{cases} b_0 = K_p \dfrac{\left((1+\frac{T}{2T_i})\,(T+2T_f) + 2\,T_d\right)}{T+2T_f}, \quad b_1 = K_p \dfrac{\left(\frac{T^2}{T_i} - 4\,(T_f + T_d)\right)}{T+2T_f} \\[6mm] b_2 = K_p \dfrac{\left((\frac{T}{2T_i} - 1)\,(T-2T_f) + 2\,T_d\right)}{T+2T_f}, \quad a_1 = \dfrac{-4\,T_f}{T+2T_f}, \quad a_2 = \dfrac{2\,T_f - T}{T+2T_f} \end{cases} \tag{3.6}$$

3.3.1.3. State feedback without or with observer

As regards state feedback control systems without observer (StaFeed) or with observer (StaFeedObs) for a speed servomechanism, the parameters {A, B, C, D} of the state model of the process deduced from [3.4a] using observable canonical realization have the following form:

$$A = \begin{bmatrix} e^{-\frac{1}{\tau}T} & 1 & 0 & \dots & 0 & 0 \\ 0 & 0 & 1 & 0 & 0 & 0 \\ \dots & 0 & 0 & \dots & 0 & \dots \\ 0 & 0 & 0 & \dots & 1 & 0 \\ 0 & 0 & 0 & 0 & 0 & 1 \\ 0 & 0 & 0 & . & 0 & 0 \end{bmatrix}_{(m+1)\,\text{x}\,(m+1)} \qquad B = \begin{bmatrix} 0 \\ 0 \\ \dots \\ 0 \\ 0 \\ K_s\left(1-e^{-\frac{1}{\tau}T}\right) \end{bmatrix}_{(m+1)\,\text{x}\,1} \qquad [3.7]$$

$$C = \begin{bmatrix} 1 & 0 & 0 & \dots & 0 & 0 \end{bmatrix}_{1\,\text{x}\,(m+1)}$$

For the position servomechanism, canonical realization of [3.4b] yields the following parameters {A, B, C, D}:

$$\left\{ \begin{aligned} A &= \begin{bmatrix} a_1 & 1 & 0 & \dots & 0 & 0 \\ a_2 & 0 & 1 & 0 & 0 & 0 \\ 0 & 0 & 0 & \dots & 0 & \dots \\ \dots & 0 & 0 & \dots & 1 & 0 \\ 0 & 0 & 0 & 0 & 0 & 1 \\ 0 & 0 & 0 & . & 0 & 0 \end{bmatrix}_{(m+2)\text{x}(m+2)}, \quad B = \begin{bmatrix} 0 \\ 0 \\ \dots \\ 0 \\ 0 \\ b_9 \\ b_{10} \end{bmatrix}_{(m+2)\text{x}1} \\ C &= \begin{bmatrix} 1 & 0 & 0 & . & 0 & 0 \end{bmatrix} \end{aligned} \right. \qquad [3.8]$$

with:

$$\left\{ \begin{aligned} a_1 &= 1 + e^{-\frac{1}{\tau}T}, \quad a_2 = e^{-\frac{1}{\tau}T}; \quad b_9 = K_s\left(T - \tau(1 - e^{-\frac{1}{\tau}T})\right) \\ b_{10} &= K_s\left(-Te^{-\frac{1}{\tau}T} + \tau(1 - e^{-\frac{1}{\tau}T})\right) \end{aligned} \right. \qquad [3.9]$$

In both cases, the law of digital state feedback control is given by:

$$u(k) = \begin{cases} -K\,x(k) - K_i\,x_i(k)\,, & \text{(a) if without observer} \\ \qquad\qquad \text{ou} \\ -K\,\hat{x}(k) - K_i\,x_i(k) & \text{(b) if with observer} \end{cases} \qquad [3.10]$$

where x_i is the integral state of the set output tracking error.

3.3.2. Elements of software programming

3.3.2.1. *Elements of MEX-C++ programming technology*

3.3.2.1.1. Concept of MEX-C++

MEX-C++ is a programming technology which allows the development of C++ programs that are specifically compilable and executable in real time in the Matlab environment. This MEX-C++ technology proves its usefulness for creating software interfaces between Matlab and C++ *drivers* and data acquisition boards that are not supported by Matlab. Thus, a MEX-C++ function is a compiled MEX-C++ program, whose call syntax is identical to that of a Matlab function.

It is worth mentioning here that, compared to a classical C++ program, a MEX-C++ program has the following specificities.

– its compilation requires specialized "windows.h" and "mex.h" libraries to be declared in the header of the MEX-C++ program;

– the following input function is identified by the key word "mexFunction":

void mexFunction (Arguments)

{ // Definition of variables

   // Import/export data recovery and testing

   // Call of standard C++ functions and of global functions

   // of C++ program for data processing

}

– the "mexFunction" input function supports "mxArray" arguments, which refer to structures of pointer tables;

– a MEX-C++ program compiled for a 32 bits execution target admits *.mexh32 as extension;

– before compiling a MEX-C++ source program, the C++ compiler to be used should be specified by first typing the following Matlab command line:

>> mex –setup

A choice should then be made from the list of compilers available in the computer. At this stage, "Lcc" compiler of C language embedded in Matlab can be chosen from this list, if needed:

– the syntax for compiling the MEX-C++ file is the following:

>> mex Nomfchier.c   % if C/C++ compiler

>> mcx Nomfchicr.cpp % if C++ compiler

On the contrary, a MEX-C++ library is a set of MEX-C++ functions placed in one system file. Figure 3.3 presents the relational model of a MEX-C++ library with other software entities of a Matlab environment for the time control of dynamic process.

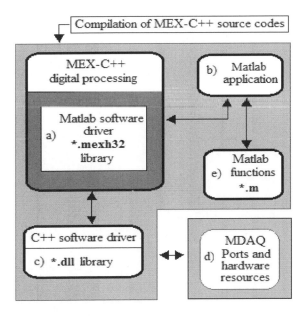

Figure 3.3. *Relational model of a MEX-C++ library with other Matlab environment software entities*

Structure of a MEX-C++ program

```
// Source program Mex-C++ - MyMexCpp.Cpp
// Section S1 :   Declaration of standard C++ libraries
     #  include <stdio.h>           // Example 1
     #  include <math.h>            // Example 2
// Section S2 - Declaration of specialized C++ libraries
       #  include <windows.h>        // Example 1
       #  include "mex.h"            // Example 2
//  Section S3 -  Definitions of types of objects:
//     a) Variables, pointers and data structures
//     b) Instances of driver *.dll  objects in C++ system programming
//     c) Definition of global functions


 // Section S4: Definition of access functions to a C++ driver, K8055D.dll
int  MyDll( ) //  a)  Loading of K8055.DLL in RAM
                    //  b) Instantiation of names of C++ functions
                    //  c) Opening connection to MDAQ interface
//  Section S5: Arguments of MexFunction input function
void mexFunction (int   nlhs,            //  Number of LHS arguments
                   mxArray *plhs[ ],  //   Pointer table plhs[0], plhs[1], …
                   int nrhs,                //  Number of RHS arguments
                   const mxArray *prhs[ ]   //  Pointer table prhs[0],
                                            //  plhs[1], …
                   )
//  Section S6:  Body of MexFunction input function
 {
    // 1) Declaration of variables and pointers of data to be Imported/Exported
    // 2) Test of imported data *prhs[ ] for error detection.
    // 3) Processing of imported data using global functions among which

MyDll( )
    // 4)  Call, if necessary, of MDAQ interface outputs in K8055D.DLL
    // 5) Creation of output memory for Array pointer to return to Matlab
    // 6) Calculation of Array outputs to return to Matlab
    // 7) Return of calculated Array output to Matlab program
 }
```

Figure 3.4. *Structure of a MEX-C++ program*

This relational model shows that a MEX-C++ library can contain a variety of functions for real-time interfacing between:

– a Matlab application and C++ application layer for digital processing of information;

– a Matlab application and C++ *driver*;

– a Matlab application and the two software layers: "C++ application" and "C++ driver".

3.3.2.1.2. Structure of a MEX-C++ program for real-time control

A MEX-C++ program for digital control via a MDAQ interface featuring its C++ driver (case of K8055D.dll in USB – VM110 model, for example) is structured into six sections (see Figure 3.4). Sections S1–S4 are the headers that can be found in a classical C++ program. Nevertheless, in section S2, the "mex.h" library is a requirement of MEX-C++ programming technology. Moreover, the "MyDll( )" function, declared in section S4, should contain the directives for accessing *driver* C++ of the MDAQ interface used, pointed by a program written in MEX-C++. For section S5, the "mexFunction(.)" is the input function for the MEX-C++ program.

The structure of the "mexFunction(.)" body indicated in section S6 is identical to that of a classical C++ program. It is in the body of this function that digital processing of imported data of "mxArray" type takes place, returning to Matlab application results of "mxArray" type.

3.3.2.1.3. Call syntax of a MEX-C++ function

The syntax of a MEX-C++ function is identical to that of a Matlab function. It relies on the administration of right arguments *rhs[ ] and of values returned to left *lhs[ ]. Figure 3.5 describes the syntactic structure of a MEX-C++ function named "MyMexCpp".

The symbols *rhs, nrhs, *lhs and nlhs have the following meaning:

– *rhs (*right-hand side*): pointer of right "mxArray" structures;

– nrhs (*number of right-hand side*): number of right structures of "mxArray" arguments, numbered 0, 1,…, nrhs – 1;

– *lhs (*left-hand side*): pointer of left "mxArray" structure;

– nlhs (*number of right left side*): number of "mxArray" structures returned to left, numbered 0, 1,…, nlhs – 1.

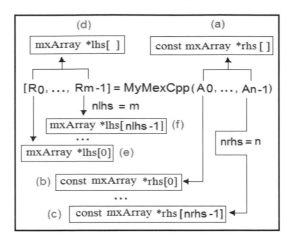

Figure 3.5. *Syntactic structure of a MEX-C++ function*

3.3.2.2. *Elements of Matlab/GUI programming technology*

3.3.2.2.1. Concept of Matlab/GUI programming

Matlab/GUI (*Graphical User Interface*) programming technology is used for the rapid development of GUI applications for the control of Matlab applications, including MEX-C++ functions.

3.3.2.2.2. Structure of a Matlab/GUI application

As shown in Figure 3.6, the structure of a Matlab/GUI application is organized into three main parts, as follows:

– GUI control panel, built with the Matlab/GUI editor. For example, in Matlab R2013a or Matlab 2014a, this editor can be opened in the command line using the command:

>> *guide*

– (*.fig) file describing the input or output visual components of the GUI control panel;

– (*.m) file constituted of codes of "callback" functions associated with event states of visual components embedded in the control panel of the GUI application.

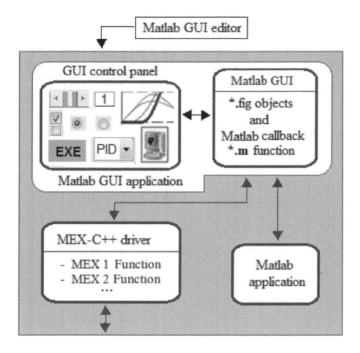

Figure 3.6. *Constituents of a Matlab/GUI application*

It is worth mentioning that the diagram in Figure 3.6 highlights that, in a Matlab/GUI application, a "callback" function can call any basic Matlab (*.m) function, as well as any function of a MEX-C++ library placed in the current folder.

3.3.2.3. *Matlab/GUI programming methodology*

Programming a Matlab/GUI application involves the following:

1) Activate the Matlab/GUI builder using the command:

>> guide

This graphics builder offers a box of parent and child visual objects organized into a hierarchy (axes, checkboxes, command buttons, option buttons, etc.), which can be used to create the GUI control panel.

2) Create the graphics interface by placing selected visual objects on the graphics editor sheet in progress. This is followed, if necessary, by the activation of the windows of properties of each object (by double clicking the object) in order to modify the default properties (color, size, etc.), as needed.

3) Save the graphic control panel built. This saving automatically creates or updates *.fig and *.m files:

- the *.fig file contains the identification data (positions and properties) of the visual components of the GUI panel. This file can be opened with "GUIDE" from the command line in order to update an existing graphic interface;

- the *.m file contains "callback" functions (visual component actions) that enable the real-time operation of the control panel created.

4) Launch the editable file *.m to insert the required modifications in the code fields of the "callback" functions.

3.4. Design of the ServoSys software application

3.4.1. *Architectural diagram of the software application*

As shown by the architectural diagram in Figure 3.7, the constituents of the ServoSys platform software application are:

– the GUI panel;

– the "ServoSys.fig" file, which contains the characteristics (nature, properties, "callback" functions, etc.) of GUI visual objects;

– the "ServoSys.m" file, which represents the software application for the automation ServoSys platform tasks;

– the range of digital images *.png;

– the layer of hardware *drivers* (drivers of peripheral devices).

The GUI panel is visible during execution by automatic opening of the "ServoSys.fig" file when launching the "ServoSys.m" application.

The "ServoSys.fig" file contains the characteristics and properties of the virtual components of the application (command buttons, checkboxes, option buttons, text area, graphic containers, selection, image and video box).

The "ServoSys.m" file designates the Matlab application constituted of:

– "callback" procedures associated with visual input components. For example: GUI data capture, operating modes administration, etc.;

– standard procedures that are accessible using "callback" procedures.

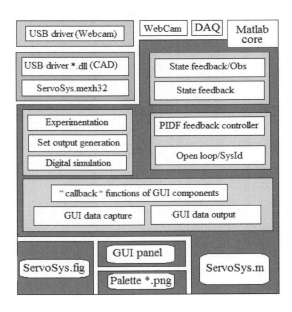

Figure 3.7. *Architectural diagram of the ServoSys platform*

Images in the *.png range are displayed at the GUI as per operator's choice. The C++ driver (K8055D.DLL) of the MDAQ interface and the MEX-C++ interfacing driver of Matlab/K8055D.DLL are found in the *drivers* layer. The previously developed [MBI 15] commands of this MEX-C++ *driver* are presented in Table 3.1.

3.4.2. *SFC of the ServoSys multimedia platform*

The ServoSys multimedia platform is a sequential automation technique whose discrete events are generated by a console or internally, with a control part aided by computer via a Matlab/GUI/MEX-C++ application. Figure 3.8 corresponds to the main SFC for the design of virtual instrumentation software of this ServoSys platform.

There are three distinct operating modes:

– parametric identification;

– speed control;

– position control.

K8055.DLL for C++	MEX-C++ library MexServoSys.mexh32
OpenDevice	State = *open_usb_card* (0)
CloseDevice	*close_usb_card* ( )
SetDigitalChannel	*ddcout* (*ddCh, Val*)
ClearDigitalChannel	ddCh = 1 to 8 → Bit Number
SetAllDigital	= 9 → Output word = 10 → All output bits
ClearAllDigital	Val = 0 – 254 if *ddCh* = 9
WriteAllDigital	= implicit (otherwise).
ReadDigitalChannel	Val = *ddcinp* (*ddCh*)
ReadAllDigitalChannel	*ddCh* = 1-8 for single bit select = 9 for reading a word
ReadAnalogChannel	N = *adcoutcode* (*Ch_Dac*)
ReadAllAnalog	N: 0-253
OutputAnalogChannel	*dacinpcode* (*dac_Ch, N1, N2*)
OutputAllAnalog	*dac_Ch* = 1, 2 or 3 (for 1 & 2)
SetAnalogChannel	*N1, N2*: 0 - 253;
SetAllAnalog	
	Val = *ddc* (*dir, Ch, State*) *dir* = 0 (output), 1 (input) *Ch* = 1-8 (bit), 9 (word), 10 (All) *State* = 0 or 1 if *dir* =0 = implicit (otherwise)
	dacout (*dac_Ch, U*) *dac_Ch* = 1, 2 and $0 \le U \le 4.7$ V
	U = *adcinp* (adc_Ch) *adc_Ch* = 1, 2 or 3 (for 1 & 2); $0 \le U \le 4.7$ V
	Y=oploco(*dacCh, Uc, adcCh, Nms*)
	Uk_1 = *UpidMat* (*Args*)
	Uk_1 = *UpidMex* (*Args*)

Table 3.1. *Commands of the K8055.DLL driver for C++ and MEX-C++*

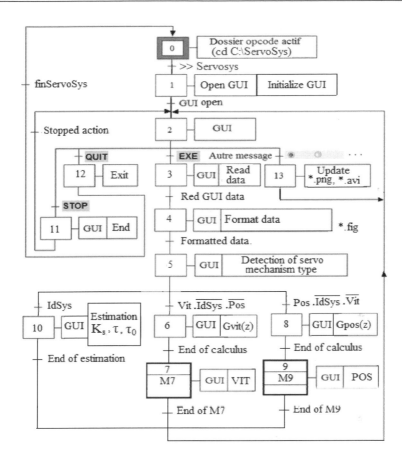

Figure 3.8. *Main SFC of the ServoSys control part*

Moreover, the M7 and M9 macro-steps expansion SFC (see Figure 3.8) are presented in Figures 3.9 and 3.10, respectively.

The M7 (speed servomechanism) and M9 (position servomechanism) macro-steps expansion SFC presented in Figures 3.9 and 3.10, respectively, are constituted of simple steps and subprogram steps. It is worth noting that, for each type of selected servomechanism, the operator can operate in simulation mode or in experimentation mode, according to one's preferences. Moreover, he/she can decide to launch the open-loop command in each mode, the PIDF controller or the state feedback control without or with observer.

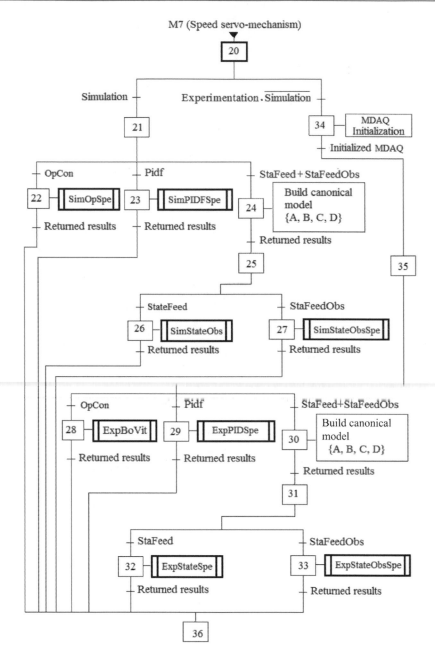

Figure 3.9. *M7 macro-step expansion SFC*

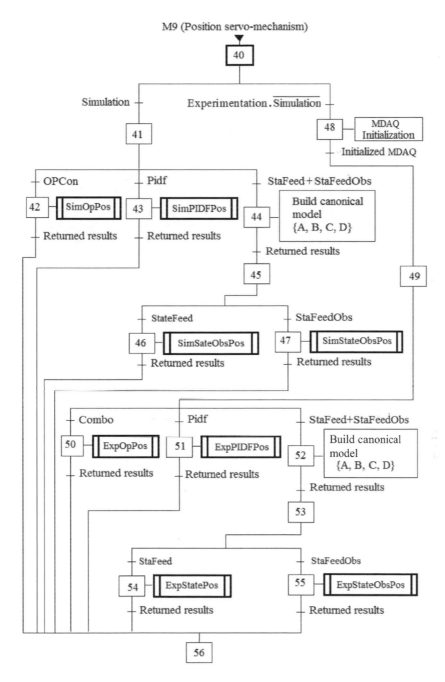

Figure 3.10. *M9 macro-step expansion SFC*

3.5. Implementation of the ServoSys multimedia platform

3.5.1. *Hardware implementation*

A shot of the hardware environment of the Matlab/GUI/MEX-C++ platform is presented in Figure 3.11.

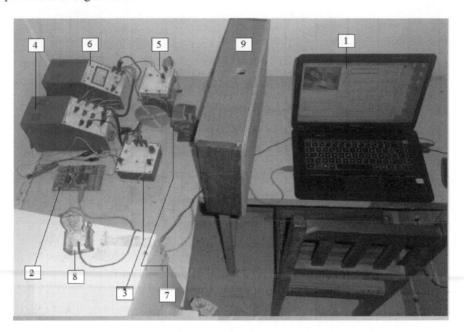

Figure 3.11. *Shot of the Matlab/GUI/MEX-C++ platform*

The numbered hardware constituents are:

1) PC/laptop;

2) MDAQ interface (VM110/USB model with 8 bits DAC and ADC);

3) PA 150C voltage preamplifier with a static gain of 2 and a command range [2.2 V 4.5 V] imposed by the CAD-embedded DAC characteristics; SA 150D power amplifier;

4) power amplifier module;

5) MT 150F servomotor with embedded tachometer with continuous output from 0 to 5 V;

6) regulated power supply module (± 15 V) PS 150D;

7) magnetic load LU 150F with adjustable graded position;

8) USB webcam;

9) wooden visual barrier that separates the operational part from the operator seated at his/her workstation.

3.5.2. *Software implementation*

The design diagrams previously presented in Figures 3.8, 3.9 and 3.10 have been implemented and tested using combined technologies of Matlab/GUI visual development and advanced MEX-C++ programming.

The operating modes effectively offered by this multimedia test bench are:

– preliminary settings: language and set point;

– data update and default operating conditions;

– automatic identification of the model of open-loop servomechanism;

– virtual simulation in speed or position mode for a set point quantity with adjustable parameters (waveform, magnitude and frequency);

– real-time tests in position or speed mode;

  stop of current mode and system initialization;

– exit from the ServoSys application.

The digital control laws offered are:

– automatic identification of the in-service servomechanism parameters;

– open-loop command;

– PIDF controller;

– state feedback controller with set point tracking;

– state feedback controller with observer;

– state feedback controller with set point tracking and observer.

The events triggered by the operator on the visual components are sources for launching "callback" functions programmed for this purpose.

The Matlab/GUI syntax of a "callback" function for the administration of properties of an input visual component named "ObjName" is the following:

```
function    ObjName1_Callback(hObject,  eventdata,  handles)
```

   % a) *Recovery with get( ) of data of GUI input components*
   Val = *get*(handles.CheckCna, 'Value'); % Value to be converted by DAC
      % b) *Modification with set( ) of the properties of GUI input components*
            set(handles.TextCanN1, 'String', num2str(N1Can)) ;   % Display
word 1
      %   c) Call if needed of standard Matlab functions, personalized
            % Malab functions, or precompiled MEX-C++ functions.
      %   d) Call of precompiled MEX-C++ functions
end

The "get(.)" and "set(.)" commands used in the code of a "callback" function
allow for writing and modifying, respectively, the properties of the component
specified in the argument(s) part of the command. For illustration purposes, several
examples will be presented, which will facilitate a better grasp of the programming
principle of the Matlab/GUI "callback" function.

EXAMPLE 1.– The "VideoPreview_callback" function of the "VideoPreview"
command button allows the real-time visualization on a video container called
"VideoAxe" of the video image generated by the current multimedia source. For a
USB webcam, a video source supported by the ServoSys platform, the
"VideoPreview_callback" function is implemented by the following Matlab program.

No.	"VideoPreview_Callback" Function
1	function VideoPreview_Callback(hObject, eventdata, handles)
2	vid = videoinput('winvideo', 4, 'RGB24_640x480') ;
3	if get(handles.VideoMode,'Value') == 1
4	src = getselectedsource(vid); vid.FramesPerTrigger = 1;
5	vidRes = get(vid, 'VideoResolution');
6	imWith = vidRes(1); imHeight = vidRes(2);
7	nBanks = get(vid,'NumberOfBands');
8	VideoHandle = image(zeros(imHeight, imWith, nBanks), . . . 'parent', handles.VideoAxe);
9	preview(vid, VideoHandle); % Display of video
10	Else
11	End

EXAMPLE 2.– A second example is the "callback" procedure, which is presented in
Figure 3.12. It allows the display in the "VideoPreview" image container of a diagram

of the (*.png) image corresponding to the operating mode selected by the operator simply by clicking on the specific option button ("RadOpId", "RadModOpl", "RadPidSim", "RadStatesSim", "RadStatesSimObs", "RadOpdCon", "RadPidfCon" and "RadStatesCon") of the "UiPansimTests" configuration group.

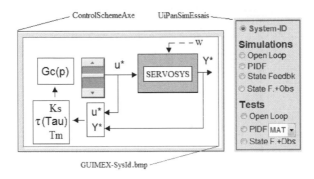

Figure 3.12. *Illustration of a second example of the "callback" function*

Thus, the Matlab program which allows the implementation of this "UiPanSimTests_SelectionChangeFcn" function is presented below.

No.	UiPanSimTests_SelectionChangeFcn Function
	function UiPanSimTests_SelectionChangeFcn (hObject, ... eventdata, handles)
1	axes(handles.ControlSchemeAxe) ;
2	if (hObject = = handles.RadBoId)
3	imshow('GUIMEX-SysId.bmp');
4	elseif (hObject = = handles.RadModSim || hObject = = handles.RadOpl)
5	imshow('GUIMEX-OPL.bmp');
6	elseif (hObject = = handles.RadPidfSim || hObject ... = = handles.RadPidfCon)
7	imshow('GUIMEX-PIDF.bmp');
8	elseif (hObject = = handles.RadStatesSim)
9	imshow('GUIMEX-SFB-SPT.bmp');
10	elseif (hObject = = handles.RadStateSimObs || hObject ... = = handles.RadStatesCon)
11	imshow('GUIMEX-SFB-SPT-OBS.bmp');
12	end

Figure 3.13 shows a screenshot of the Matlab/GUI control panel taken in run mode. This Matlab/GUI panel is organized into six main areas of virtual and interactive control numbered from 3.1 to 3.6 and identified in the caption of Figure 3.13.

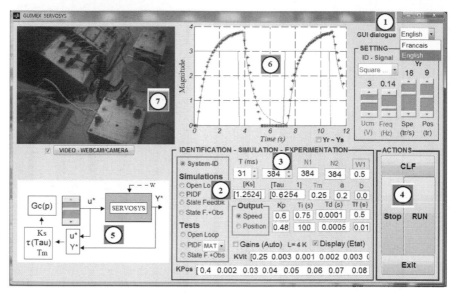

1 — set points; 2 — activities; 3 — setting of parameters; 4 — action control; 5 — image (chosen configuration) ; 6 – display; 7 – real-time video of the controlled servomechanism.

Figure 3.13. *Screenshot of the multimedia control panel. For a color version of this figure, see www.iste.co.uk/mbihi/regulation.zip*

3.6. Overall tests of the platform

3.6.1. *Commissioning and procedures*

It is worth remembering that all available modular servomechanisms are installed and connected to the MDAQ interface/USB in place.

Moreover, a PC/laptop to be used for the automation of testing sessions features Matlab R0213a application software, the "guimexservosys.m" application installed in a working folder of the C++ (*.DLL) driver of MDAQ interface/USB, as well as the MEX-C++ library copied in the same folder.

Under these conditions, platform commissioning involves the following steps:

1) turn on PC/laptop;

2) launch Matlab;

3) specify in command lines the current folder of the "mexguiservo" application;

4) open the "mexguiservo*.m" file visible in the window of the Matlab file explorer;

5) initialize "mexguiservo*.m" by clicking the "RUN" button of the editor;

6) connect the USB cable of the MDAQ to the PC/laptop;

7) turn on the servomechanism by pushing the button of the supply module.

Furthermore, the procedure of a test session involves:

1) choice of language for operator dialogue;

2) choice of mode and type of tests to be conducted;

3) setting of input data;

4) setting of output parameters;

5) clicking the "EXE" button for automatic processing of the chosen task with automatic update of multimedia display areas.

3.6.2. Samples of results displayed on the Matlab/GUI panel

The results displayed on the Matlab/GUI panel during tests are presented in Figures 3.13–3.21, for example:

– identification of dynamic models (Figure 3.13);

– PIDF control (Figures 3.14, 3.15 and 3.16);

– robustness test of PID control (Figure 3.17);

– state feedback with observer (Figure 3.18);

– robustness of state feedback with observer (Figure 3.19);

– other types of test results obtained (Figures 3.20 and 3.21).

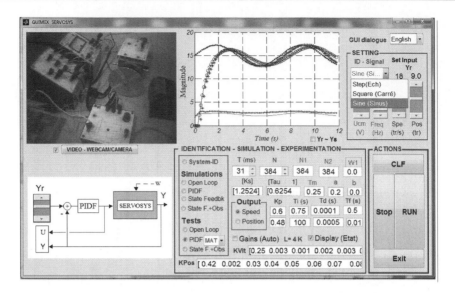

Figure 3.14. *PIDF control with "sine" speed set point. For a color version of this figure, see www.iste.co.uk/mbihi/regulation.zip*

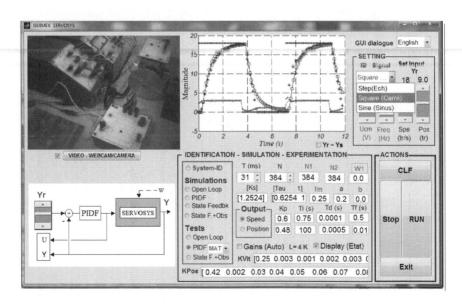

Figure 3.15. *PIDF control under "square" speed set point. For a color version of this figure, see www.iste.co.uk/mbihi/regulation.zip*

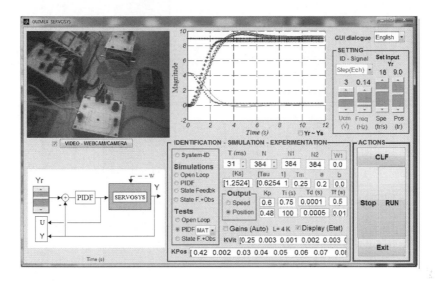

Figure 3.16. *Position control using the PIDF controller. For a color version of this figure, see www.iste.co.uk/mbihi/regulation.zip*

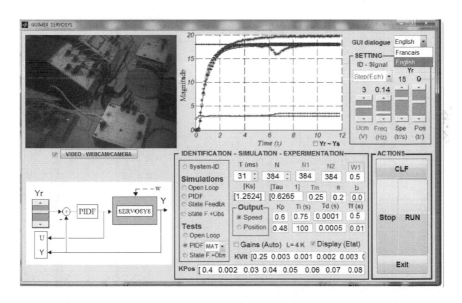

Figure 3.17. *Robustness of PIDF speed control under perturbation. For a color version of this figure, see www.iste.co.uk/mbihi/regulation.zip*

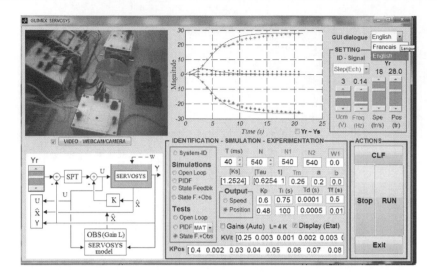

Figure 3.18. *Position state feedback control with observer. For a color version of this figure, see www.iste.co.uk/mbihi/regulation.zip*

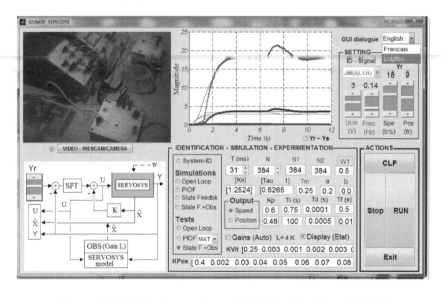

Figure 3.19. *Robustness of speed state feedback control with observer under perturbation. For a color version of this figure, see www.iste.co.uk/mbihi/regulation.zip*

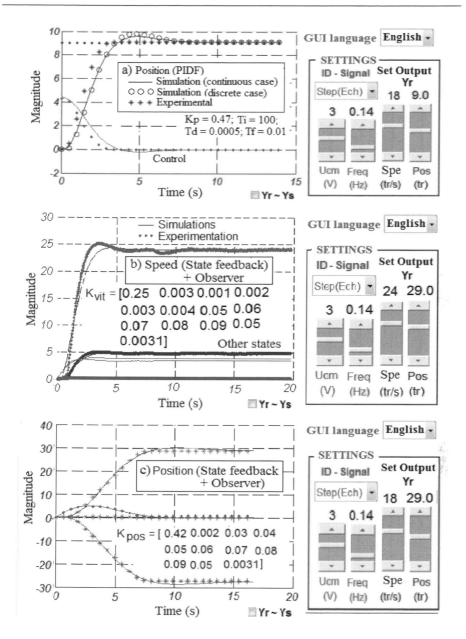

Figure 3.20. *Other obtained results. For a color version of this figure, see www.iste.co.uk/mbihi/regulation.zip*

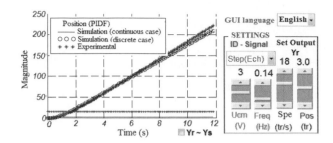

Figure 3.21. *Other obtained results(continuation). For a color version of this figure, see www.iste.co.uk/mbihi/regulation.zip*

Considering these results, it can be noted that the proposed platform effectively offers a user friendly and multimedia environment for operator dialogue. It also offers a wide range of advanced tools for the organization of laboratory sessions aimed at simulating and experimenting most of the fundamental automation concepts with minimum time effort.

3.7. Exercises and solutions

Exercise 3.1.

The default dynamic processes of the ServoSys platform, presented in this chapter, are servomechanisms.

a) What is a servomechanism?

b) What are the main fields of application of servomechanisms?

Solution – Exercise 3.1.

a) A servomechanism is a device that drives mechanical parts or subsystems with adjustable speed/position.

b) The main fields of application of servomechanisms are:

  - computer hard disks;

  - machine tools;

  - powered conveyers;

  - textile cutter machines;

  - industrial robots;

  - vehicle steering devices (car, boat, aircraft, spacecraft, etc.).

Exercise 3.2.

What are the digital control strategies provided by the ServoSys platform for dynamic processes modeled in the frequency domain?

Solution – Exercise 3.2.

The digital control strategies for dynamic processes modeled in the frequency domain are:

– open-loop command;

– PIDF controller command.

Exercise 3.3.

What are the digital control strategies provided by the ServoSys platform for dynamic processes modeled in the state space?

Solution – Exercise 3.3.

The digital control strategies for dynamic processes modeled in the state space are:

– control without observer;

  control with observer.

Exercise 3.4.

The ServoSys platform is a multimedia teaching tool. What are the multimedia elements that constitute this platform?

Solution – Exercise 3.4.

The ServoSys constitutive elements are:

– virtual elements: signal generator and input/output components;

– image;

– video.

Exercise 3.5.

What are the tools used for the design of ServoSys platform operating modes?

Solution – Exercise 3.5.

The tools used for the design of ServoSys platform operating modes are:

– main SFC;

– SFC for macro-steps expansion;

– subprogram SFC.

Exercise 3.6.

MEX-C++ programming has proved essential for the digital control of a real servomechanism using the ServoSys platform.

a) What is the general interest of MEX-C++ programming?

b) What is the specific interest of MEX-C++ programming for the data acquisition boards delivered with the C++ *driver*?

c) Interpret the constitutive programming elements of the following MEX-C++ function:

$$\text{void } mexFunction \text{ (int nlhs, mxArray } *plhs[\,], \quad prhs[1], \text{ int } nrhs,$$
$$\text{const mxArray } *prhs[\,]$$
$$) \ \{ \ \}$$

Solution – Exercise 3.6.

a) The general interest of MEX-C++ programming: it allows the development of libraries of C++ functions executable using Matlab applications.

b) The specific interest of MEX-C++ programming for data acquisition boards delivered with the C++ *driver*: it allows the development of a Matlab *driver* using functions of the basic C++ *driver*, delivered by the producer of the data acquisition board.

c) Interpretation of constitutive elements of:

$$void\ mexFunction\ (\ int\ nlhs,\ mxArray\ *plhs[\ ],\quad prhs[1],\ int\ nrhs,$$
$$const\quad mxArray\quad *prhs[\ ]$$
$$)$$
$$\{\ \}$$

- "mexFunction": input point of a "mex" function;

- int nlhs: number of left arguments to be returned;

- mxArray *plhs[ ]: table of structure pointers of left elements to be returned;

 int nrhs: number of right arguments to be used as data to be processed;

- const mxArray *prhs[ ]: table of structure pointers of right elements to be processed.

Exercise 3.7.

An MMMI-oriented Matlab/GUI application is constituted of at least three types of files. Specify these types of files.

Solution – Exercise 3.7.

The three types of files of an MMMI-oriented Matlab/GUI application are:

– *.fig;

– *.m;

– *.png, *.jpeg, etc.

Exercise 3.8.

What are the constitutive modules of the *.m file of the Matlab/GUI application of the ServoSys platform?

Solution – Exercise 3.8.

The constitutive modules of the *.m file of the Matlab/GUI application of the ServoSys platform are:

– system modules for default initialization;

– "callback( )" modules created by the programmer;

– programmer-defined functions, which can be called by "callback" functions.

Exercise 3.9.

Figure 3.22 shows the aspect of an MMMI area of the flexible ServoSys platform for the response of a step speed set point.

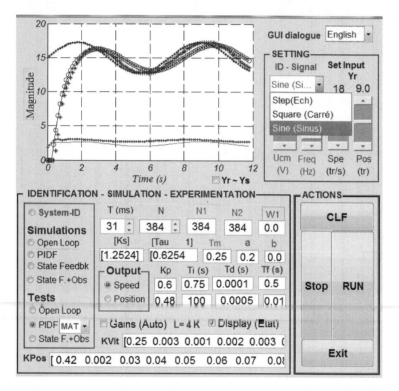

Figure 3.22. *Aspect of an MMMI area of the ServoSys platform. For a color version of this figure, see www.iste.co.uk/mbihi/regulation.zip*

a) Provide an interpretation of the simulated (or real) output between 0 and 2.25 s.

b) What are the MMMI elements that justify its flexibility?

Solution – Exercise 3.9.

a) Interpretation of the simulated (or real) output between 0 and 2.25 s:

Between 0 and 2.25 s, the response converges towards the set point; it is the transient state of the closed-loop delayed system.

b) The MMMI elements that justify its flexibility:

- nature and modifiable parameters of the set point source;

- dynamic model of the modifiable servomechanism with parameter identification possibility;

- optional speed or position servomechanisms;

- structure and modifiable parameters of control laws;

- real-time simulations or control;

- bilingual MMMI (in French or English).

Part 2

Deterministic and Stochastic Optimal Digital Feedback Control

4

Deterministic Optimal Digital Feedback Control

4.1. Optimal control: context and historical background

4.1.1. *Context*

The process control techniques studied in the first part of this book (PIDF controllers, state feedback with or without observer) enable good control performances for deterministic dynamic processes. However, with regard to highly demanding application fields, the need to reach the best performance, as measured by a fixed functional control criterion, becomes an ultimate priority. Under these conditions, a control technique that yields the best value of the criterion in a defined class of admissible control laws is called the "optimal regulation or optimal feedback control law".

4.1.2. *Historical background*

Modern optimal control of dynamic processes draws on dynamic optimization theory, whose origin dates back to ancient times. If it exists, the solution to a dynamic optimization problem is an optimal trajectory (series of points) such that between two points (initial and final) it provides the best value for a fixed functional criterion, with or without constraint.

Table 4.1 summarizes the main events that have marked the history of dynamic optimization theory. More detailed historical aspects of this theory are available in the literature [LEW 92, BEN 96, BIS 09]. There are three approaches to the research of optimal trajectories:

– variational calculus;

– maximum principle;

– dynamic programming.

The common aim of these approaches is to transform the functional formulation, with or without constraint, of an optimization problem into a structure of ingenious equations to be solved in order to get the solution to the original problem.

The variational calculus approach involves the transformation of the original functional formulation into Euler equations (cases without constraint) or into Euler–Lagrange equations (cases with constraint), to be solved while taking into account the associated transversality conditions. If possible, the resolution of these equations leads to an open-loop global solution.

Pontryagin's maximum principle involves putting the original functional structure into the form of maximization equations with respect to the control quantity of Pontryagin's function (similar to the Hamiltonian). If it exists, the optimal trajectory resulting from this maximization leads to an open-loop global solution.

Bellman's dynamic programming, drawing on Bellman's principle of optimality, involves putting the functional structure into the form of a sequence of Hamilton–Jacobi–Bellman (H–J–B) equations to be solved in a regressive direction, from a fixed final condition. In this case, if the optimal solution exists, it leads to a closed-loop recursive solution. Thus, dynamic programming is, in the state space, a valuable tool for the synthesis of closed-loop optimal control laws for deterministic and stochastic dynamic processes, whether or not subjected to state and control constraints.

In summary, Bellman's dynamic programming approach, which will be used in this chapter as a tool for the synthesis of optimal control laws, differs from variational calculus and from Pontryagin's maximum principle in that it offers two significant advantages:

– it conveniently takes into account (state or control) constraints and the stochastic nature of the dynamic process under study, which allows a wider area of application;

– it produces closed-loop optimal control, therefore it is naturally more robust and reliable under the uncertain operating conditions of real dynamic processes.

Date	Names	Events
814 BC	Dido, Queen of Carthage	Initiation and intuitive resolution of the isoperimetric problem, which involves determining a figure of the largest possible area whose boundary has a fixed length, given that it is bounded by a straight line.
1669	Newton	Creation of the derivative, published in 1687.
1675	Leibniz	Creation of the derivative, drawing on Pascal's infinitesimal theory.
1694	Newton	Creation of variational calculus and resolution of the problem of the solid of revolution, which opposes minimum resistance to fluid advancement.
1696	Jacob Bernoulli	The cycloid: solution to the problem of the brachistochrone – a thread on which a ring can slide from point A to point B within a maximum time period.
1720	Riccati	Formulation of Riccati matrix equations.
1728	Johann Bernoulli	Problem of geodesics submitted to Euler.
1736	Euler (student of Johann Bernoulli)	Creation of partial derivative and publication of Euler equation.
1744	Euler	Publication of the first variational calculus book.
1788	Lagrange (Euler's collaborator)	Creation of Lagrangian concept and publication of Euler–Lagrange equation.
19th Century	Hamilton and Poisson	Creation of Hamiltonian concept.
1837	Jacobi	Second order optimality condition for weak variations.
1870–1880	Weierstrass	– Second-order sufficient optimality condition for strong variations. – Theory of minimum of the Hamiltonian in any point of an optimal trajectory.
20th Century	Bolza	Bolza problem.
1928–1942	Von Neumann	Creation of static game theory.
1940	Bellman	Creation of the concept of dynamic programming.
1948	Von Neumann	Creation of the theory of sequential computers.
1950	Raggazini	Creation of the z-transform and of digital control.
1950	Franklein, Ragazzini	Creation of the theory of sampled systems.
1954–1955	Isaacs	Development of the theory of dynamic games.
1955	Radner and Marschack	Development of the theory of team coordination.
1955	Kalman	Kalman filter, concept of controllability.
1957	Bellman	First book on dynamic programming.
1958	Ragazzini et al.	Publication of a book on sampled systems.
1958	Jury	Publication of a book on sampled systems.
1960	Kalman	Resolution of discrete LQR problem.
1960	Pontryagin	Creation of the maximum principle.
1963	Kalman	Publication of discrete Kalman filter.
1964	Jury	Publication of a book on the theory and applications of z-transform.

Table 4.1. *Landmarks in the history of dynamic optimization*

A general mathematical formulation of a discrete-time optimal control problem will be provided in section 4.2 of this chapter. Then, a detailed case study related to the *Linear Quadratic Regulator* (LQR) will be presented. Thus, the term LQR designates the optimal control law obtained when considering a quadratic functional criterion in the class of deterministic linear dynamic processes. A simple technique for the discretization of the continuous mathematical structure of an optimal control problem will be presented in section 4.3. Finally, section 4.4 will provide an introduction to predictive optimal control.

4.2. General problem of discrete-time optimal control

4.2.1. *Principle*

Optimal control is an advanced technique for the synthesis of dynamic systems control laws, following a profile that minimizes (or maximizes) a functional criterion. As shown in Figure 4.1, this criterion is generally defined in a space of admissible trajectories (states and associated controls), having P_0 as the initial point and P_1 as the final point.

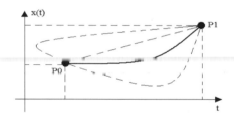

Figure 4.1. *Space of admissible trajectories*

4.2.2. *Functional formulation*

The functional formulation of a discrete-time optimal control problem is given by [4.1]:

$$\underset{u_k}{Min}\, J(x_0) = \left(\sum_{k=0}^{N-1} \left(g(x_k, u_k) \right) \right) + \varphi(x_N) \qquad \text{(a)}$$

$$x_{k+1} = f(x_k, u_k) \qquad \text{(b)}$$

[4.1]

where the term [4.1a] describes the functional criterion and the term [4.1b] is the state equation (or dynamic constraint). Under these conditions, applying to [4.1]

Bellman's dynamic programming principle leads to H–J–B (Hamilton–Jacobi–Bellman) equations given by [4.2], where $V(x_k, u_k)$ designates the value function at stage k, knowing the optimal value $V(x_{k+1}, u_{k+1}) = V(f(x_k, u_k), u_{k+1})$ calculated at stage $k + 1$, $u^*(k)$ being the optimal control applicable at stage k, resulting from the minimization of $V(x_k, u_k)$ with respect to u_k:

$$x_{k+1} = f(x_k, u_k)$$
$$V(x_k, u_k) = g(x_k, u_k) + V(f(x_k, u_k), u_{k+1}^*)$$
$$u_k^* = \underset{u(k)}{Min}\left(V(x_k, u_k)\right), \text{ or to solve: } \frac{\partial\{V(x_k, u_k\}}{\partial u_k} = 0 \qquad [4.2]$$
$$\text{with: } V(x_N, u_N) = \varphi(x_N), \ u_k = 0$$

Optimal control of dynamic processes is nevertheless a very broad topic, whose exhaustive study would require an entire book. Readers who are interested in detailed aspects of deterministic optimal control theory can refer to the work of Lewis and Syrmos [LEW 95]. This chapter focuses on the study of two optimal control topologies, as follows:

– optimal LQR (linear quadratic regulator);

– predictive optimal controller.

Univariate dynamic systems will be considered in both cases, described by linear discrete models that are time-invariant.

4.3. Linear quadratic regulator (LQR)

4.3.1. *Definition, formulation and study methods*

An LQR (*Linear Quadratic Regulator*) is an optimal feedback control law, allowing a deterministic linear dynamic process to pass from the initial state x_0 to a final state x_N while minimizing a quadratic functional criterion. In this case, the mathematical formulation given by [4.1] can then be written in the following form:

$$\underset{\Omega_u}{Min}\left(J(x_0) = \sum_{k=0}^{N-1} \left(\frac{1}{2}x_k^T Q_k x_k + \frac{1}{2}u_k^T R_k u_k \right) + \frac{1}{2}x_N^T Q_N x_N \right) \qquad [4.3]$$

with:

$-\; x_{k+1} = A\, x_k + B\, u_k;$

$-\, x_k \in \mathfrak{R}^n ;$

$-\, u_k \in \mathfrak{R}^m ;$

$-\, k = 0, 1,..., N-1.$

In [4.3], it is assumed that $Q_k \geq 0$ and $R_k > 0$, while A and B are matrices whose dimensions are n x n and n x 1, respectively.

4.3.2. H–J–B equations

4.3.2.1. Structure

Knowing [4.3], H–J–B equations [4.2] are written as:

$$x_{k+1} = A\, x_k + B\, u_k$$

$$V(x_k, u_k) = \frac{1}{2}x_k^T Q_k x_k + \frac{1}{2}u_k^T R_k u_k + V\left(Ax_k + Bu_k, \mathrm{u}_{k+1}^*\right)$$

$$\mathrm{u}_k^* = \underset{u_k}{Min} V(x_k, u_k) \;\; \text{or to solve: } \frac{\partial\{V(x_k, u_k)\}}{\partial u_k} = 0 \qquad [4.4]$$

$$\text{with: } V(x_N, u_N) = \frac{1}{2}x_N^T Q_N x_N, \;\; u_N = 0$$

4.3.2.2. Resolution of H–J–B equations and Riccati equation

H–J–B equations [4.4] can be solved step by step for $k = N, N-1,..., 2, 1, 0$, as follows:

$-\, k = N, \;\; \mathrm{u}_N^* = 0$

$$V(\mathrm{x}_N, \mathrm{u}_N^*) = \frac{1}{2}x_N^T S_N\, x_N$$

$$= \frac{1}{2}\left(Ax_{N-1} + Bu_{N-1}\right)^T S_N\, \left(Ax_{N-1}\right) + Bu_{N-1}\right) \qquad [4.5]$$

with $S_N = Q_N$.

   $- k = N - 1$

$$V(x_{N-1}, u_{N-1}) = \frac{1}{2} x_{N-1}^T Q_{N-1} \, x_{N-1} + \frac{1}{2} u_{N-1}^T R_{N-1} \, u_{N-1} + V(x_N, u_N^*)$$

$$= \frac{1}{2} x_{N-1}^T Q_{N-1} \, x_{N-1} + \frac{1}{2} u_{N-1}^T R_{N-1} \, u_{N-1} + \frac{1}{2} x_N^T S_N x_N \qquad [4.6]$$

$$= \frac{1}{2} x_{N-1}^T Q_{N-1} \, x_{N-1} + \frac{1}{2} u_{N-1}^T R_{N-1} \, u_{N-1}$$
$$+ \frac{1}{2} (A x_{N-1} + B u_{N-1})^T S_N \, (A x_{N-1}) + B u_{N-1})$$

$$\frac{\partial V(x_{N-1}, u_{N-1})}{\partial u_{N-1}} = R_{N-1} \, u_{N-1} + B^T S_N (A x_{N-1} + B u_{N-1}) = 0 \qquad [4.7]$$

$$\rightarrow u_{N-1}^* = - \left(R_{N-1} + B^T Q_N B \right)^{-1} B^T S_N A \, x_{N-1} = - K_{N-1} \, x_{N-1}$$

$$\rightarrow V(x_{N-1}, u_{N-1}^*) = \begin{cases} \frac{1}{2} x_{N-1}^T Q_{N-1} \, x_{N-1} + \frac{1}{2} x_{N-1}^T Q_{N-1}^T R_{N-1} \, Q_{N-1} \, x_{N-1} \\ \\ + \frac{1}{2} x_{N-1}^T (A - B K_{N-1})^T S_N \, (A - B K_{N-1}) \, x_{N-1} \end{cases} \qquad [4.8]$$

$$\rightarrow V(x_{N-1}, u_{N-1}^*) = \frac{1}{2} x_{N-1}^T \left(Q_{N-1} + K_{N-1}^T R_{N-1} \, K_{N-1} \right.$$
$$\left. + (A - B K_{N-1})^T S_N \, (A - B K_{N-1}) \right) x_{N-1} = \frac{1}{2} x_{N-1}^T S_{N-1} x_{N-1} \qquad [4.9]$$

with:

$$P_{N-1} = Q_{N-1} + K_{N-1}^T R_{N-1} \, K_{N-1} + (A - B K_{N-1})^T S_N \, (A - B K_{N-1}) \qquad [4.10]$$

After similar calculations, the following recurrence relations are obtained, for $k = N - 1, N - 2, \ldots$:

$$K_k = \left(R + B^T P_{k+1} B\right)^{-1} B^T P_{k+1} A : \text{Kalman gain} \qquad [4.11]$$

$$u_k^* = - K_k (x_k - x_{ref}) : \text{optimal state feedback} \qquad [4.12]$$

$$P_k = Q_k + K_k^T R\, K_k + (A - BK_k)^T P_{k+1} (A - BK_k): \qquad [4.13]$$

$$V(x_k, u_k^*) = \frac{1}{2} x_k^T P_k x_k \qquad [4.14]$$

Considering $S_N = Q_N$, Kalman gains K_k in [4.11] can be calculated *off-line* with the following algorithm, for $k = N - 1, N - 2, N - 3, \ldots, 1, 0$:

$$K_k = \left(R + B^T P_{k+1} B\right)^{-1} B^T S_{k+1} A \qquad [4.15]$$

$$P_k = Q_k + K_k^T R\, K_k + (A - BK_k)^T P_{k+1} (A - BK_k) \qquad [4.16]$$

They can subsequently be used in real time for implementing the optimal control law defined by [4.12].

It is worth mentioning at this stage that nonlinear matrix equations [4.15] and [4.16] are coupled. Therefore, if this coupling is omitted, for example when a sequence of arbitrary gains $K(k)$ is considered in [4.16], then equation [4.16] becomes simply the Lyapunov equation, which depends on a known parameter, in which case the dynamic process resulting from the resolution of [4.16] would be suboptimal. This remark will later be useful for the understanding of LQR behavior.

Coupled equations [4.15] and [4.16] can be combined in one equation in P_k and P_{k+1}. Indeed, if K_k is replaced in [4.16] with its expression yielded by [4.15], the following is obtained:

$$
\begin{aligned}
S_k &= Q + K_k^T R_k\, K_k + (A - BK_k)^T P_{k+1} (A - BK_k) \\
&= Q_k + K_k^T R_k\, K_k + (A - (K_k)^T B^T) P_{k+1} (A - BK_{k+1}) \\
&= Q_k + K_k^T R_k\, K_k + (A^T S_{k+1} - (K_k)^T B^T P_{k+1}) (A - BK_{k+1}) \qquad [4.17] \\
&= Q_k + K_k^T R_k\, K_k + A^T S_{k+1}\, A - A^T P_{k+1} BK_{k+1} \\
&\quad - (K_k)^T B^T P_{k+1}\, A - (K_k)^T B^T P_{k+1}\, BK_k)
\end{aligned}
$$

Subsequent expansions yield:

$$P_k = Q_k + A^T P_{k+1} A$$

$$+\left(\left(R_k + B^T S_{k+1} B\right)^{-1} B^T P_{k+1} A\right)^T \left(R_k + B^T P_{k+1} B\right)\left(\left(R_k + B^T P_{k+1} B\right)^{-1} B^T P_{k+1} A\right)$$

$$= Q_k + A^T P_{k+1}) A + A^T P_{k+1}) B \left(R_k + B^T P_{k+1} B\right)^{-1} B^T P_{k+1} A$$

$$- A^T P_{k+1} B \left(R_k + B^T P_{k+1} B\right)^{-1} B^T P_{k+1} A$$

$$- A^T P_{k+1} B \left(R_k + B^T P_{k+1}) B\right)^{-1} B^T P_{k+1} A$$

$$= Q_k + A^T P_{k+1} A - A^T P_{k+1} B \left(R_k + B^T P_{k+1}) B\right)^{-1} B^T P_{k+1} A$$

[4.18]

Thus, with respect to variable P_k, a Riccati equation is obtained, which is given by [4.19]:

$$P_k = Q_k + A^T P_{k+1} A - A^T P_{k+1} B \left(R_k + B^T P_{k+1} B\right)^{-1} B^T P_{k+1} A$$

[4.19]

Through step-by-step resolution of Riccati equation [4.19] having S_k (for $k = N$, $N-1$, $N-2$,...) as variable, it is still possible to find the sequence of optimal Kalman gains obtained by [4.20], as well as the corresponding optimal controls:

$$K_k - \left(R_k + B^T P_{k+1} B\right)^{-1} B^T P_{k+1} A \;, \quad u_k^* - - K_k x_k$$

[4.20]

4.3.2.3. LQR structure

Since LQR gains can be pre-calculated and memorized for subsequent use, the resulting dynamic optimization diagram is presented in Figure 4.2.

The structure of the optimal solution of an LQR requires several comments:

– optimal gain is a function of time, even though the considered system is linear and steady (time-invariant);

– in the case of convergence of the solution of Riccati equation, the limit solution $S = S_\infty$ corresponds to the root of stationary Riccati equation [4.21]:

$$P = Q + A^T P A - A^T P B \left(R + B^T PB\right)^{-1} B^T P A$$

[4.21]

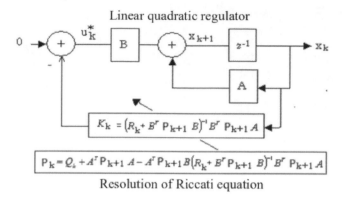

Figure 4.2. *Diagram of LQR dynamic optimization*

4.3.2.4. Linear quadratic regulator over infinite horizon ([0 ∞])

The control law entirely relying on [4.21] is suboptimal and characterized by constant gain equal to:

$$K = \left(R + B^T P B\right)^{-1} B^T P A \qquad\qquad [4.22]$$

For certain practical problems, this suboptimal control law is preferred, because it helps saving memory space for the storage of pre calculated gain sequences.

NOTE.– The calculation of P = P∞ in [4.21] and of K in [4.22] is rendered easier by the Matlab® "dlqr" command.

4.4. Translation in discrete time of continuous LQR problem

When an LQR problem is formulated in continuous time, this can be solved using the corresponding continuous Riccati equation:

$$J(0) = \int_0^{t_1} (x^T(t)\, Q_c\, x(t) + u^T(t)\, R_c\, u(t))\, dt$$

$$\text{with} \qquad\qquad [4.23]$$

$$\frac{dx(t)}{dt} = A_c\, x(t) + B_c\, u(t)$$

On the contrary, the approach presented in this section involves discretizing [4.23] then solving the resulting equivalent discrete LQR problem.

4.4.1. *Discretization of state equation*

Applying the results of dynamic model discretization, the discrete dynamic equation in [4.23] can be written in the following form:

$$x_{k+1} = A\,x_k + B\,u_k$$
$$\text{with}$$
$$A = e^{A_c T},\; B = \left(\int_0^T e^{A_c \eta} d\eta \right) B_c$$

[4.24]

where T is the sampling period.

4.4.2. *Discretization of the cost function*

The Riemann series of cost J(0), calculated considering a sufficiently short sampling period T, can be written in the following form:

$$J(0) = \sum_{k=0}^{N-1} \int_{kT}^{(k+1)T} (x^T(\tau)\,Q_c\,x(\tau) + u^T(\tau)\,R_c\,u(\tau))\,dt$$

[4.25]

Applying the principle of zero-order holder approximation to [4.25] leads to [4.26]:

$$\int_{kT}^{(k+1)T} (x^T(\tau)\,Q_c\,x(\tau) + u^T(\tau)\,R_c\,u(\tau))\,d\tau$$
$$= T\,\left(x^T(kT)\,Q_c\,x(kT) + u^T(kT)\,R_c u(kT) \right)$$

[4.26]

In this case, [4.25] becomes:

$$J(0) = \sum_{k=0}^{N-1} x^T(kT)\,T\,Q_c\,x(kT) + u^T(kT)\,T\,R_c\,u(kT)$$

[4.27]

Thus, the formulation of the continuous LQR problem in discrete time takes the following form:

$$J(0) = \sum_{k=0}^{N-1} x^T(kT)\;Q\,x(kT) + u^T(kT)\;R\,u(kT)$$
$$\text{with}$$
$$x_{k+1} = A\,x_k + B\,u_k$$
$$\text{and}$$
$$A = e^{A_c T},\; B = \left(\int_0^T e^{A_c \eta} d\eta \right) B_c,\; Q = T\,Q_c,\; R = T\,R_c$$

[4.28]

4.4.3. *Case study of a scalar LQR problem*

4.4.3.1. *Data*

The process to be controlled by LQR is a speed servomechanism described by the following transfer function:

$$G(s) = \frac{\omega(s)}{\omega_r(s)} = \frac{K_m}{1+\tau s}$$

with:

– $K_m = 0.375$;

– $\tau = 0.29$ s.

Considering the state $x(t) = \omega(t)$, the following scalar state model is obtained:

$$dx(t)/dt = a_c\, x(t) + b_c\, u_c(t) \tag{4.29}$$

with:

– $a_c = -1/\tau$;

– $b_c = K_m/\tau$.

The continuous cost parameters are assumed to be $q_c = 2000$ and $r_c = 80$.

4.4.3.2. *Solution of discrete LQR with T = 5 ms (sampling period)*

After discretization of [4.29] using a sampling period T = 0.005 ms, the resulting equivalent scalar discrete model can be written in the following form:

$$x_{k+1} = a\, x_k + b\, u_k \tag{4.30}$$

with:

– $a = e^{a_c T}$;

– $b = K_m\left(1 - e^{a_c T}\right)$.

According to [4.28], the costs in discrete time are:

– $q = q_c$;

– $T = 10$;

– $r = r_c$;

– $T = 0.4$.

Thus, knowing [4.19] and [4.20], the solution to a scalar discrete LQR problem over a finite time horizon (N T) is:

$$
\begin{cases}
K_k = \dfrac{a\, b\, P_{k+1}}{r + b^2\, P_{k+1}}, \\[4mm]
P_k = \dfrac{a}{b}\, r\, K_k + q\, ;
\end{cases}
\qquad\qquad [4.31]
$$

for $k = N - 1, N - 2, \ldots, 0$.

Knowing the successive values of $K(k)$ given by [4.31] for any $k = N, N - 1, N - 2, \ldots, 2, 1, 0$, then the optimal control law in discrete time is given by:

$$- u(k) = - K(k)\,(x(k) - x_r) \text{ for optimal LQR} \qquad\qquad [4.32]$$

$$- u(k) = - K_\infty(x(k) - x_r) \text{ for suboptimal LQR} \qquad\qquad [4.33]$$

where the suboptimal gain $K_\infty = \dfrac{a\, b\, P}{(r + b^2\, P)}$ in [4.33], P being the solution of the following stationary Riccati equation:

$$P = a^2\, r\, \dfrac{P}{(r + b^2\, P)} + q \qquad\qquad [4.34]$$

If the solution to [4.34] exists, it can be found using the Matlab "dlqr(a, b, q, r)" command.

The Matlab program in Table 4.2 allows the calculation and simulation of the behavior of a discrete optimal LQR, as well as of a suboptimal LQR with constant gain over an infinite time horizon.

Numerical application

$T = 0.005$ s, $K_m = 0.375$, $\tau = 0.29$ s, $N = 200$;

$q = 20$, $r = 0.4$ (in discrete time), $s(N) = 5$ and $x_{Ref} = 3$.

In these conditions, $a = 0.9829$, $b = 0.0064$ and $K_\infty = 2.9453$ are obtained and the discrete state model becomes:

$$x(k + 1) = 0.9829\, x(k) + 0.0064\, u(k)$$

4.4.3.3. *Resolution using Matlab program*

The following "LqrScalaire.m" program in Table 4.2 allows the simulation and graphic representation of the characteristics of optimal control using scalar LQR.

No.	"LqrScalaire.m" program
1	Km = 0.375; tau = 0.29 ; % Parameter of continuous process
2	Ref = 3 ; N=200; N1=N-1 ; % References and number of samples
3	c = 1 ; d = 0 ; q = 10; r = 0.4; ac = -1/tau; bc= Km/tau ; % Parameters
4	P(N) = 5; Pinf(N) = P(N) ; % Initial conditions
5	a = exp(ac*T) ; b = (1/ac)*(exp(ac*T)-1)*bc ; % Other parameters
6	T = 0.005 ; sysd = c2d(sysc, T) ; % Same model of discrete state
7	[Kinf, Pinf,Ei] = dlqr(a, b, q, r) ; % LQR∞
8	kk(N) = N ; % Discrete time vector
9	K(N) = 0; u(N) =0; x(1) = 0 ; % Initialization of optimal LQR
10	uinf(N) = 0; xinf(1) = x(1) ; % Initialization of suboptimal LQR∞
11	xref = Ref; % Voltage reference
12	for k = N1:-1:1
13	kk(k) = k ; K(k) = a * b * P(k+1) / (r+b^2*P(k+1)) ; % optimal K
14	P(k) = (a/b) * r * K(k) + q ; % Case of LQR
15	Pinf(k) = (a-b*Kinf)^2 * Pinf(k+1) + r * Kinf^2 +q; % Case of LQR∞
16	End
17	for k=1:N1
18	u(k) = -K(k) * (x(k) - xref) ; % Optimal control
19	x(k+1) = a * x(k) + b * u(k) ; % Dynamic equation
20	uinf(k) = -Kinf * (xinf(k) - xref) ; % Suboptimal control
21	xinf(k+1) = a*xinf(k) + b*uinf(k) ;
22	end
23	uinf(N) = -Kinf * (xinf(N) - xref) ; % Suboptimal control
24	Figure 9.1 ; plot(kk*T, K, kk * T, Kinf*ones(1,N),'.') ;
25	title(' AssVit(RQL)- Gains K(k): --- Optimal ... Suboptimal');
26	figure 9.2 ; plot(kk(1:50) * T, u(1:50), kk(1:50) * T, uinf(1:50),'.') ;
27	title(' AssVit(RQL)- u(k): --- Optimal ... Suboptimal')
28	Figure 9.3 ; plot(kk(1:50)*T, x(1:50), kk(1:50) * T, xinf(1:50), '.')
29	title('AssVit(RQL) - Etats x(k): --- optimal ... Suboptimal')
30	Figure 9.4 ; plot(kk * T, P, kk * T, Pinf,'.')
31	title('AssVit(RQL)- P(k) : --- optimal ... Suboptimal')

Table 4.2. *Matlab program "LqrScalaire.m" for the resolution*

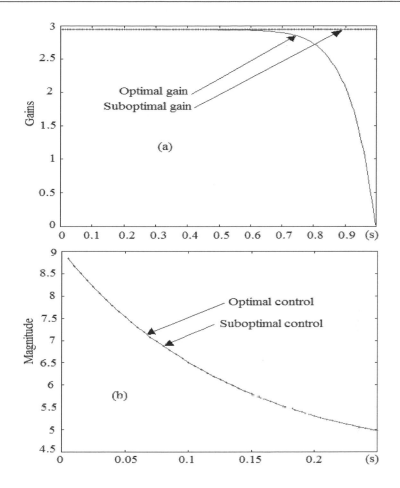

Figure 4.3. *Gains, controls and costs generated by the "LqrScalaire.m" program*

The obtained simulation results are presented in Figure 4.3, which shows the profiles of optimal and suboptimal characteristics (gains, commands and costs). Figure 4.4 presents the graphs of controls and gains obtained. It is worth noting that, in these two figures, the error between suboptimal and optimal characteristics becomes negligible if the time horizon = N × T is sufficiently large.

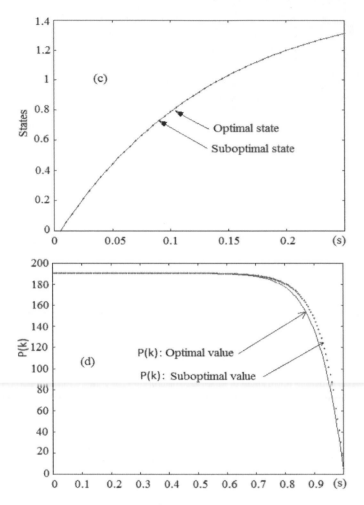

Figure 4.4. *States and values generated by the "LqrScalaire.m" program*

4.5. Predictive optimal control

4.5.1. *Basic principle*

The optimal control, which has been studied earlier using LQR, applies specifically to processes modeled by state equations. On the contrary, predictive control is applicable to dynamic processes modeled by state equations and discrete transfer functions. It also allows the optimization of critical dynamic systems, subjected to:

– great delay;

– strong oscillations or instabilities;

– nonlinearities;

– wide uncertainty margins.

Several predictive control structures are mentioned in the literature. The type presented in this section is MPC (*Model Predictive Control*). The corresponding block diagram is shown in Figure 4.5.

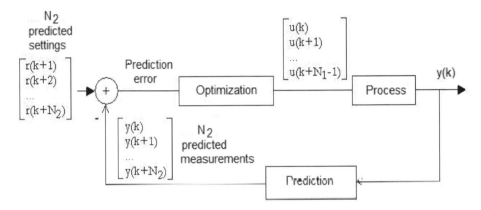

Figure 4.5. *Block diagram of MPC*

The diagram of a predictive control law functions as follows:

1) at stage k, N_2 predicted outputs are calculated, knowing the measure $y(k)$, as well as the digital model of the dynamic process;

2) a sequence of N_1 commands $\{u(k), u(k+1), u(k+2),..., u(k+N_1-1)\}$ is calculated using an algorithm for the cost optimization of prediction errors;

3) the first value $u(k)$ of the sequence of predicted commands is applied to the process;

4) at stage $(k+1)$, the calculations are repeated from stage 1.

4.5.2. *Recurrence equation of a process based on* q^{-1} *operator*

Let us consider a discrete dynamic process, described by the discrete transfer function:

$$G(z) = \frac{Y(z)}{U(z)} = \frac{b_0 z^M + b_1 z^{-(m-1)} + \ldots + b_m}{z^N + a_1 z^{n-1} + \ldots + a_n} = z^{-(N-M)} \left(\frac{b_0 + b_1 z^{-1} + \ldots + b_m z^{-M}}{1 + a_1 z^{-1} + \ldots + a_n z^{-N}} \right) \qquad [4.35]$$

or alternatively:

$$\left(1 + a_1 z^{-1} + \ldots + a_n z^{-N} \right) Y(z) = z^{-(N-M)} \left(b_0 + b_1 z^{-1} + \ldots + b_m z^{-M} \right) U(z) \qquad [4.36]$$

According to the properties of z-transform, z^{-i} notation represents a delay operator of i steps. On the contrary, if an equivalent operator denoted q^{-1} is considered in space-time, such that $z^{-i} Y(z) \equiv q^{-i} y(k) = y(k-i)$, then [4.36] becomes:

$$\left(1 + a_1 q^{-1} + \ldots + a_n q^{-N} \right) y(k) = q^{-(N-M)} \left(b_0 + b_1 q^{-1} + \ldots + b_m q^{-M} \right) u(k) \qquad [4.37]$$

Now, considering:

$$\begin{cases} A(q^{-1}) = 1 + a_1 q^{-1} + \ldots + a_N q^{-N} \\ B(q^{-1}) = b_0 + b_1 q^{-1} + \ldots + b_M q^{-M} \\ d = N - M \text{ (relative degree)} \end{cases} \qquad [4.38]$$

this yields:

$$A(q^{-1}) y(k) = q^{-d} B(q^{-1}) u(k) \qquad [4.39]$$

4.5.3. *General formulation of a prediction model*

In the general case, the formulation of a prediction model with d steps of a dynamic process (where d is the relative degree of the process or a fixed appropriate integer) involves finding the functions $F(q^{-1})$ and $G(q^{-1})$ of the form:

$$\begin{cases} F(q^{-1}) = 1 + f_1 q^{-1} + \ldots + a_{d-1} q^{-(d-1)} \\ G(q^{-1}) = g_0 + g_1 q^{-1} + \ldots + g_{N-1} q^{-(N-1)} \end{cases} \qquad [4.40]$$

so that for any q:

$$A(q^{-1}) F(q^{-1}) + q^{-d} G(q^{-1}) = 1 \qquad [4.41]$$

Or, knowing [4.40], the expanded expressions of the two terms contained in [4.41] can be written in the following form:

$$\begin{cases} A(q^{-1}) F(q^{-1}) = 1 + \sum_{m=1}^{N+d-1} \left\{ \left(\sum_{j=0}^{m} a_j f_{m-j} \right) q^{-m} \right\} & \text{with} \begin{cases} a_0 = f_0 = 1 \\ a_j = 0 \ \ si \ \ N < N+d-1 \\ f_j = 0 \ \ si \ \ d-1 < j \leq N+d-1 \end{cases} \\ q^{-d} G(q^{-1}) = g_0 q^{-d} + g_1 q^{-d-1} + \ldots + g_{N-1} q^{-d-(N-1)} = \sum_{m=d}^{d+N-1} \left(g_{m-d} q^{-m} \right) \end{cases} \quad [4.42]$$

therefore [4.41] becomes:

$$1 + \sum_{m=1}^{d-1} \left\{ \left(\sum_{j=0}^{m} a_j f_{m-j} \right) q^{-m} \right\} + \sum_{m=d}^{N+d-1} \left\{ \left(g_{m-d} + \left(\sum_{j=0}^{m} a_j f_{m-j} \right) \right) q^{-m} \right\} = 1 \qquad [4.43]$$

Thus, the condition $A(q^{-1}) F(q^{-1}) + q^{-d} G(q^{-1}) = 1$ for any q^{-1} leads to the following equations:

$$\begin{cases} 0 = \sum_{j=0}^{m} \{ a_j f_{m-j} \}, \quad m = 1, 2, \ldots, d\text{-}1 & \rightarrow (d\text{-}1) \text{ equations} \\ 0 = \sum_{j=0}^{m} \{ a_j f_{m-j} + g_{m-d} \}, \quad m = d, d+1, \ldots, N & \rightarrow (N-d+1) \text{ equations} \\ 0 = \sum_{j=0}^{m} \{ a_j f_{m-j} + g_{m-d} \}, \quad m = N+1, N+2, \ldots, N+d\text{-}1 & \rightarrow (d\text{-}1) \text{ equations} \end{cases} \qquad [4.44]$$

which gives a total of $N + d - 1$ equations required in order to determine $(d-1)$ coefficients $(f_1, \ldots, f_{d-1})$ of $F(q^{-1})$ and N coefficients $(g_0, g_1, \ldots, g_{N-1})$ of $G(q^{-1})$.

Thus, combining the two equations [4.45]:

$$\begin{cases} A(q^{-1}) y(k) = q^{-d} B(q^{-1}) u(k) \\ A(q^{-1}) F(q^{-1}) + q^{-d} G(q^{-1}) = 1 \end{cases} \qquad [4.45]$$

leads to:

$$
\begin{cases}
q^d \; y(k) = B(q^{-1})\left(\dfrac{1}{A(q^{-1})}\right)u(k) \\[2mm]
\dfrac{1}{A(q^{-1})} = F(q^{-1}) + q^{-d}\dfrac{G(q^{-1})}{A(q^{-1})}
\end{cases}
\Rightarrow y(k+d) = B(q^{-1})\left(F(q^{-1}) + q^{-d}\dfrac{G(q^{-1})}{A(q^{-1})}\right)u(k)
\qquad [4.46]
$$

The previous equation is equivalent to:

$$
y(k+d) = B(q^{-1})\,F(q^{-1})\,u(k) + G(q^{-1})\left(q^{-d}\dfrac{B(q^{-1})}{A(q^{-1})}\right)u(k)
\qquad [4.47]
$$

The predictive formulation of the process is therefore given by the equation:

$$
y(k+d) = B(q^{-1})\,F(q^{-1})\,u(k) + G(q^{-1})\,y(k)
\qquad [4.48]
$$

This equation is the prediction law at stage k of the system's response to a future stage of d steps.

4.5.4. Solution and structure of predictive optimal control

Knowing the system's predictive model, the optimization problem involves, at this stage, finding a control law that minimizes the prediction cost. For example, let us consider the following cost:

$$
\begin{aligned}
J(k) &= \left(P(q^{-1})y_{k+d} - Q(q^{-1})\,y_{Ref}\right)^2 + \left(R(q^{-1})u(k)\right)^2 \\[2mm]
&= \left(P(q^{-1})\left(B(q^{-1})F(q^{-1})\,u(k) + G(q^{-1})\,y(k)\right) - Q(q^{-1})\,y_{Ref}\right)^2 + \left(R(q^{-1})u(k)\right)^2 \\[2mm]
&= \left(P(q^{-1})\underbrace{B(q^{-1})}_{b_0 + b_1 q^{-1}+\dots}F(q^{-1})\,u(k) + G(q^{-1})\,y(k) - Q(q^{-1})\,y_{Ref}\right)^2 \\[2mm]
&\quad + \left(\underbrace{R(q^{-1})}_{r_0 + r_1 q^{-1}+\dots}u(k)\right)^2
\end{aligned}
\qquad [4.49]
$$

The partial derivative of J(k) with respect to $u(k)$ is written as:

$$\frac{\partial J(k)}{\partial u(k)} = 2\left(P(q^{-1}) \left(B(q^{-1}) F(q^{-1}) u(k) + G(q^{-1}) y(k) \right) - Q(q^{-1}) y_{\text{Re}f} \right) b_0$$

$$+ 2\, R(q^{-1})\, u(k)\, r_0$$ [4.50]

Thus, after nullification of the partial derivative given by [4.50], the structure of the resulting predictive optimal control law u^* is written as:

$$\left(P(q^{-1})\, F(q^{-1})\, B(q^{-1}) + \frac{r_0}{b_0}\, R(q^{-1}) \right) u_k^* = -P(q^{-1})\, G(q^{-1})\, y(k) + Q(q^{-1})\, y_{ref}$$ [4.51]

Relation [4.51] shows that the predictive optimal control law is characterized by a closed-loop structure (Figure 4.6) with output feedback. Therefore, it meets the robustness condition for set output tracking.

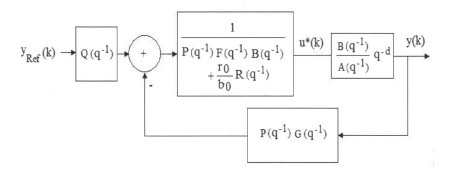

Figure 4.6. *Structure of predictive optimal control*

4.6. Exercises and solutions

Exercise 4.1.

When solving a dynamic optimization problem, what are the advantages of dynamic programming compared to variational approach and maximum principle?

Solution – Exercise 4.1.

Compared to the variational approach and the maximum principle, dynamic programming has three important advantages:

– it conveniently takes into account the state and control constraints that are manifest in real processes;

– it conveniently takes into account the stochastic aspect of the studied process, which enables covering a wider field of application;

– it produces a closed-loop optimal solution and, consequently, the robustness required by a reliable real-time implementation.

Exercise 4.2.

Let us explicitly solve the LQR problem in the scalar case, where matrices A, B, Q, R, N and S_N are real numbers: $a = 1.06$; $b = 0.01$; $q = 1$; $r = 2$; $N = 100$ and $P_N = 5$, respectively.

a) Write the Riccati equation associated with the optimal solution.

b) Propose a Matlab program, allowing the numerical calculation of the solutions to LQR and suboptimal LQR problems.

c) Generate and interpret the graphs of the obtained results

Solution – Exercise 4.2.

a) The Riccati equation associated with the optimal solution is:

$$\begin{cases} K_k = \dfrac{abP_{k+1}}{r + b^2 P_{k+1}} \\[3mm] P_k = \dfrac{a^2 r\, P_{k+1}}{r + b^2 P_{k+1}} + q \end{cases}$$

with:

– N = 100;

– $P_N = 5$.

b) The Matlab program presented in Figure 4.7 allows the simulation of the solutions of LQR and suboptimal LQR, using the "dlqr" command.

```
                    % Matlab program
clear
a = 1.05;  b=0.01;  a=1.06;  b=0.01;  % Process parameters
q = 1; r = 2;                          % Cost parameters
N = 100; N1 = N-1;                     % Number of samples
kk(N)=N;                               % discrete time vector
K(N)=0; u(N)=0; x(1)=10; % Initialization of optimal LQR
uinf(N)=0;  xinf(1)=10;      % Initialization of suboptimal LQR
P(N)=5;                      % Terminal cost parameter

% Numerical resolution:  optimal LQR over infinite horizon
[Kinf, Pinf, Ei] = dlqr(a,b,q,r) ;
% Resolution of: optimal LQR, suboptimal LQR (with Kinf)
for k = N1:-1:1
  kk(k) = k;
  P(k) = ((a^2*r*P(k+1))/(r+b^2*P(k+1)))+q;  % Optimal LQR
  K(k) = a*b*P(k+1)/(r+b^2*P(k+1));
  Pinf(k) = (a-b*Kinf)^2*Pinf(k+1)+r*Kinf^2+q;  % LQRinf
% Application  of regulators to the process
for k=1:N1
   u(k) = -K(k)*x(k);            x(k+1) = a*x(k) + b*u(k);
   uinf(k) = - Kinf*xinf(k) ;   xinf(k+1) = a*xinf(k)+b*uinf(k);
end
subplot(211), plot(kk,K,'*',kk,x, '.',kk,Kinf*ones(1,N), kk, xinf,'k')
subplot(212);   plot(kk,s,'.',kk, Pinf)
```

Figure 4.7. *Simulation program for LQR and suboptimal LQR*

c) The obtained simulation results are presented in Figure 4.8. It can be noted that a suboptimal LQR over an infinite horizon is asymptotically optimal for the same problem studied in the case of a finite horizon for $k \ll N$.

Exercise 4.3.

Let us once again consider the LQR problem in the scalar case, when a and b are scalar and $b = 1$, $q = 1$, $r = 2$. Find the expression of the characteristics of the suboptimal solution over an infinite time horizon, if it exists. Then, draw these characteristics within the range $-1/2 \leq a \leq 1/2$.

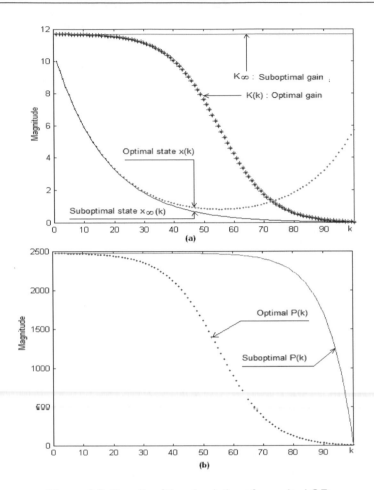

Figure 4.8. *Results of the simulation of a scalar LQR*

Solution – Exercise 4.3.

Let P_∞ be the solution to the scalar LQR problem over an infinite horizon (if it exists), then the two following equations can be written:

$$
\begin{cases}
P_\infty = \dfrac{a^2 r\, P_\infty}{r + b^2 s_{\infty 1}} + q & \text{(solution of stationary Riccati equation)} \\[3mm]
K_\infty = \dfrac{ab P_\infty}{r + b^2 P_\infty} & \text{(suboptimal gain)}
\end{cases}
$$

The first relation leads to the following second degree equation:

$$b^2 P_\infty^2 + (r(1-a^2) - q\, b^2)\, P_\infty - q\, r = P_\infty^2 + (2(1-a^2)-1)\, P_\infty - 2 = 0$$

The theoretical solution to this equation is given by:

$$P_\infty(a) = \frac{2\,a^2 - 1}{2} \pm \frac{\sqrt{(2a^2 - 1)^2 + 8}}{2}\ ,\quad K_\infty = \frac{ab P_\infty}{r + b^2 P_\infty}$$

This analytical solution exists for any value of a that provides a solution $S_\infty(a) > 0$. The graph of $S_\infty(a)$ for $-1/2 \le a \le 1/2$ is presented in Figure 4.9.

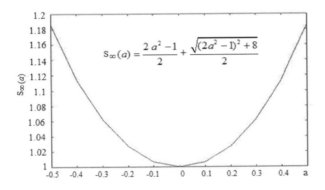

$$S_\infty(a) = \frac{2\,a^2 - 1}{2} + \frac{\sqrt{(2a^2 - 1)^2 + 8}}{2}$$

Figure 4.9. Graph of $S_\infty(a)$ for $-1/2 \le a \le 1/2$

Exercise 4.4.

What are the specific properties of a predictive optimal control law?

Solution – Exercise 4.4.

A predictive optimal control law has the following specific properties:

– it is adapted to the optimization of dynamic systems modeled by discrete transfer functions, without the need for an equivalent state realization;

– it is applicable to critical dynamic systems: unstable, with non-minimal phase difference, uncertain, nonlinear, multivariable, etc.;

– the solution structure takes the form of an output feedback loop.

Exercise 4.5.

Assign names to the signals and subsystems contained by the structural diagram of predictive optimal control, using the same terminology applicable to the block diagram.

Solution – Exercise 4.5.

The signals and subsystems of the structural diagram of predictive optimal control are designated in Figure 4.10.

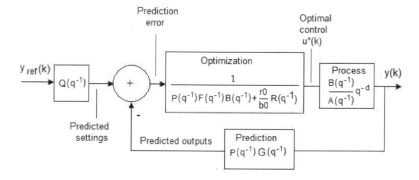

Figure 4.10. *Structural diagram of predictive control*

Exercise 4.6.

Let us consider a dynamic process described by the following discrete model:

$$H(z) = \frac{Y(z)}{U(z)} = \frac{0.01\,z^2 - 0.01z}{z^2 - 2.002\,z + 1.002}$$

Establish the predictive model of this process considering a prediction step $d = 2$.

Solution – Exercise 4.6.

Prediction model of the process:

The following can be written:

$$H(z) = \frac{Y(z)}{U(z)} = \frac{0,01 - 0,01\,z^{-1}}{1 - 2,002\,z^{-1} + 1,002\,z^{-2}}$$

therefore:

$$\begin{cases} A(q^{-1}) = 1 + a_1 q^{-1} + a_2 q^{-2} \\ B(q^{-1}) = b_0 + b_1 q^{-1} \\ d = 2 \end{cases} \quad with \quad \begin{cases} a_1 = -2.002 \ et \ a_2 = 1.002 \\ b_0 = 0.01 \ and \ b_1 = -0.01 \end{cases}$$

The objective is to find the functions $F(q^{-1})$ and $G(q^{-1})$ of the following form:

$$\begin{cases} F(q^{-1}) = 1 + f_1 \ q^{-1} \\ G(q^{-1}) = g_0 + g_1 \ q^{-1} \end{cases}$$

Solving the following system of equations:

$$\begin{cases} 0 = f_1 + a_1; & (d-1) = 1 \ \text{equation} \\ g_0 = -a_1 \ f_1 - a_2; & (N-d+1) = 1 \ \text{equation} \\ 0 = a_2 \ f_1 + g_1 & (d-1) = 1 \ \text{equation} \end{cases}$$

leads to:

$$f_1 = - a_1 = 2.002;$$

$$g_0 = - a_1 f_1 - a_2 = (a_1)^2 - a_2 = (2.002)^2 - 1.002 - 3.006;$$

$$g_1 = - a_2 f_1 - a_3 = - 1.002 \ \text{x} \ 2.002 = - 2.006.$$

hence:

$$\begin{cases} F(q^{-1}) = 1 + 2.002 \ q^{-1} \\ G(q^{-1}) = 3.006 - 2.006 \ q^{-1} \end{cases}$$

Finally, the predictive model of the discrete process can be written as:

$$y(k+2) = \underbrace{(3.006 \ -2{,}006 \ q^{-1})}_{G} \ y(k) + \underbrace{(0.01 \ - \ 0.01 \ q^{-1})}_{B} \ \underbrace{(1 \ + \ 2.002 \ q^{-1})}_{F} \ u(k)$$

Expansion and arrangement of terms finally leads to:

$$y(k+2) = 3.006y(k) - 2.006y(k-1) + 0.01u(k) + 0.01u(k-1) - 0.02u(k-2)$$

Exercise 4.7.

Using $J(k) = y^2(k+d) + 0,1\left(u(k) - u(k-1)\right)^2$ as the cost function, calculate the predictive optimal control law of the process in Exercise 4.6.

Solution – Exercise 4.7.

The characteristic polynomials of the predictive control law are:

$-P(q^{-1}) = 1;$

$-Q(q^{-1}) = 0;$

$-R(q^{-1}) = 0.1 - 0.1\ q^{-1}.$

therefore $r_0 = 0.01$.

Predictive optimal control is then given by:

$$\left(P(q^{-1})\ F(q^{-1})\ B(q^{-1}) + \frac{r_0}{b_0}\ R(q^{-1}) \right) u_k^* = -P(q^{-1})\ G(q^{-1})\ y(k) + Q(q^{-1})\ y_{ref}$$

or:

$$\left((1 + 2.002\ q^{-1})\ (0.01 \quad 0.01\ q^{-1}) + \frac{0.1}{0.01} \right) u_k^* = (3.006 \quad 2.006\ q^{-1})\ y_k$$

Expansion and arrangement of terms yields:

$$\left(-0.0200\ q^{-2} \quad -0.9900\ q^{-1} + 1.0100 \right) u_k^* = -(3.006 - 2.006\ q^{-1})\ y_k$$

which leads to the recurrence equation:

$$(1.0100)\ u_k^* = 0.0200\ u(k\text{-}2) + 0.9900\ u(k\text{-}1) - 3.006\,y(k) + 2.006\ \ y(k-1)$$

The sought-for optimal control law is written as follows:

$$u_k^* = 0.0198\ u(k\text{-}2) + 0.9802\ u(k\text{-}1) - 2.9762\,y(k) + 1.9861\ \ y(k-1)$$

5

Stochastic Optimal
Digital Feedback Control

5.1. Introduction to stochastic dynamic processes

Unlike exact models of deterministic processes, models of stochastic processes are probabilistic. The class of stochastic dynamic processes includes:

– Markov chains $\{\xi(t)\}$ with M-dimensional discrete state space. These are commonly used in various scientific domains, such as:

- study of failure modes of simple or composite dynamic structures,

- analysis of random queuing systems,

- theory of random dynamic games, etc.;

– Markov jump processes. In this case, the state is a hybrid vector, which is constituted of a physical quantity $x(t)$ and a Markov chain $\{\xi(t)\}$;

– semi-deterministic processes, shown in Figure 5.1. These are normally deterministic physical processes, which, on the contrary, are contaminated by unpredictable noise $\{v(t), w(t)\}$, resulting from operating conditions.

The stochastic processes considered in this book are semi-deterministic and linear. Thus, their characteristic quantities (state $x(t)$ and output $y(t)$) are probabilistic by contamination, and are consequently more difficult to accurately control. Nevertheless, the assumption is made that the probability laws of noise $\{v(t), w(t)\}$ are known.

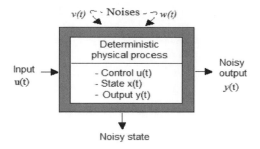

Figure 5.1. *Illustrative diagram of semi-deterministic processes*

This chapter aims at providing a synthesis of algorithmic diagrams of the fundamental constituents of the implementation of stochastic optimal control systems. These include:

– the stochastic LQR (linear quadratic regulator), operational if state measurements are available;

– the Kalman filter;

– the Linear Quadratic and Gaussian (LQG) regulator.

Readers who are willing to gain wider knowledge on these broad topics are invited to refer to the books of Siouris [SIO 96] and Bagchi [BAG 93].

5.2. Stochastic LQR

5.2.1. *Formulation*

Let us consider a discrete dynamic process described by:

$$x(k+1) = A(k) x(k) + B(k) u(k) + F(k) v(k) \qquad [5.1]$$

with:

– $k = 0, 1, \ldots, N-1$;

– $x(k) \in \mathfrak{R}^n$: state quantity;

– $u(k) \in \mathfrak{R}^m$: control quantity;

– $v(k) \in \mathfrak{R}^q$: zero-mean white noise;

– $A(k)$, $B(k)$ and $F(k)$: matrices of appropriate dimension.

Under these conditions, let us note that, in the absence of noise, the state $x(k)$ of the process is a deterministic quantity for any k, while the state $x(0)$ is fixed. Moreover, the hypothesis $v(k) \in \mathfrak{R}^q$ implies that F(k) in [5.1] is a matrix of order $n \times q$.

The problem of stochastic LQR involves finding a strategy of control $u^*(x_k)$ of the dynamic process [5.1] that minimizes the cost function:

$$J(x(0)) = E_v \left\{ \sum_{i=0}^{N-1} \left(\frac{1}{2}x^T(i)Q(i)x(i) + \frac{1}{2}u^T(i)R(i)\,u(i) \right) + \frac{1}{2}x^T(N)Q\,(N)x(N) \right\} \quad [5.2]$$

with:

- $Q_i > 0$ (positive definite symmetric matrix);

- $R_i > 0$ (positive semi-definite symmetric matrix);

- E(.): symbol of mathematical expectation of white noise $v(k)$.

For reasons of clarity, the following notations will be considered in further expansions:

- A(k) ≡ A$_k$; B(k) ≡ B$_k$; Q(k) ≡ Q$_k$; R(k) ≡ R$_k$; F(k) ≡ F$_k$; v(k) ≡ v$_k$;

- x(k) ≡ x$_k$; u(k) ≡ u$_k$; v(k) ≡ v$_k$ [5.3]

Following the application of the dynamic programming principle to the optimization process described by relations [5.1] and [5.2], the stochastic Hamilton–Jacobi–Bellman (H–J–B) equation at instant k is obtained, in the following form:

$$V(x_k, u_k) = E_v \left(\frac{1}{2}x_k^T Q_k\,x_k + \frac{1}{2}u_k^T R_k\,u_k + V(Ax_k + Bu_k + F_k v_k,\, u_{k+1}^*) \right)$$

with $V(x_N, u_N^*) = \frac{1}{2}x_N^T Q_N\,x_N$, $u_N^* = 0$.   [5.4]

5.2.2. Resolution of the stochastic H–J–B equation

A step-by-step approach can be adopted in order to solve the previously obtained H–J–B equation, for $k = N, N - 1, N - 2, \ldots$:

- $k = N$, $J^*(x_N) = \frac{1}{2}x_N^T Q_N\,x_N$, $u_N = 0$ [5.5]

- $k = N - 1$,

$$V(x_{N-1}, u_{N-1}) = \underset{v}{E} \left\{ \frac{1}{2} x_{N-1}^T Q_{N-1} x_{N-1} + V(x_N, u_N) \right\}$$

$$\underset{u(N-1)}{}$$

$$= \underset{v}{E} \left\{ \begin{array}{l} \frac{1}{2} x_{N-1}^T Q_{N-1} x_{N-1} + \frac{1}{2} u_{N-1}^T R_{N-1} u_{N-1} \\ + \frac{1}{2} \left(A x_{N-1} + B\, u_{N-1} + F_{k-1} v_{N-1} \right)^T Q_N \left(A x_{N-1} + B\, u_{N-1} + F_{N-1} v_{N-1} \right) \end{array} \right\} \qquad [5.6]$$

or:

$$\underset{v}{E} \left\{ \begin{array}{l} \frac{1}{2} x_{N-1}^T Q_{N-1} x_{N-1} + \frac{1}{2} u_{N-1}^T R_{N-1} u_{N-1} \\ + \frac{1}{2} \left(A_k x_{N-1} + B_{N-1}\, u_{N-1} + F_{N-1} v_{N-1} \right)^T Q_N \left(A_{N-1} x_{N-1} + B_{N-1}\, u_{N-1} + F_{N-1} v_{N-1} \right) \end{array} \right\}$$

$$= \frac{1}{2} x_{N-1}^T Q_{N-1} x_{N-1} + \frac{1}{2} u_{N-1}^T R_{N-1} u_{N-1}$$

$$+ \frac{1}{2} x_{N-1}^T A_{N-1}^{\ T} Q_N A_{N-1}\, x_{N-1} + \frac{1}{2} 2 x_{N-1}^T A_{N-1}^{\ T} Q_N B_{N-1}\, u_{N-1} \qquad [5.7]$$

$$+ \frac{1}{2} u_{N-1}^T B^T Q_N B_{N-1}\, u_{N-1} + \frac{1}{2} E\left(v_{N-1}^T F_{N-1}^T Q_N F_{N-1} v_{N-1}^T \right)$$

$$+ \frac{1}{2} x_{N-1}^T A_{n-1}^{\ T} Q_N A_{N-1} \underbrace{E(F_{N-1} v_{N-1})}_{0} + \frac{1}{2} u_{N-1}^T R_{N-1}^{\ T} Q_N \underbrace{F(F_{N-1} v_{N-1})}_{0}$$

$$+ \frac{1}{2} \underbrace{E\left(v_{N-1F}^T F_{N-1}^T \right)}_{0} Q_N \left(A_{N-1} x_{N-1} + B_{N-1}\, u_{N-1} \right)$$

therefore:

$$V(x_{N-1}, u_{N-1}) = \frac{1}{2} x_{N-1}^T Q_{N-1} x_{N-1} + \frac{1}{2} x_{N-1}^T A_{N-1}^{\ T} Q_N A_{N-1}\, x_{N-1}$$

$$+ E\left(v_{N-1}^T F_{N-1}^T Q_N F_{N-1}^T v_{N-1} \right) \qquad [5.8]$$

$$+ \frac{1}{2} \left\{ \begin{array}{l} u_{N-1}^T R_{N-1} u_{N-1} + 2 x_{N-1}^T A_{N-1}^{\ T} Q_N B_{N-1}\, u_{N-1} \\ + u_{N-1}^T B_{N-1}^{\ T} Q_N B_{N-1}\, u_{N-1} \end{array} \right\}$$

The optimal control law of the process can then be found by solving the following equation:

$$\frac{\partial\left\{V(u_{N-1}, u_{N-1})\right\}}{\partial u_{N-1}} = 0$$

or   [5.9]

$$\frac{\partial\left\{u_{N-1}^T R_{N-1} u_{N-1} + 2x_{N-1}^T A_{N-1}{}^T Q_N B_{N-1}\ u_{N-1} + u_{N-1}^T B_{N-1}{}^T Q_N B_{N-1}\ u_{N-1}\right\}}{\partial u_{N-1}} = 0$$

The resolution of the previous equation requires knowledge on the properties of scalar fields. This resolution yields:

$$u_{N-1}^* = -\left(R_{N-1} + B_{N-1}^T Q_N B_{N-1}\right)^{-1} B_{N-1}^T Q_N A_{N-1} x_{N-1}$$ [5.10]

Replacing the previous expression of u_{N-1}^* in [5.10] yields:

$$V(x_{N-1}, u_{N-1}) = \frac{1}{2} x_{N-1}^T Q_{N-1} x_{N-1} + \frac{1}{2} x_{N-1}^T A_{N-1}{}^T Q_N A_{N-1}\ x_{N-1}$$
$$+ E\left(v_{N-1}^T F_{N-1}^T Q_N F_{N-1} v_{N-1}\right) + \frac{1}{2}\left(u_{N-1}\right)^T R_{N-1} u_{N-1}$$ [5.11]
$$+ \frac{1}{2} 2x_{N-1}^T A_{N-1}{}^T Q_N B_{N-1}\ u_{N-1} + \frac{1}{2}\left(u_{N-1}^T\right) B_{N-1}{}^T Q_N B_{N-1}\ u_{N-1}$$

After regrouping the similar terms, relation [5.11] becomes:

$$V(x_{N-1}, u_{N-1}) = \frac{1}{2} x_{N-1}^T \left(Q_{N-1} + A_{N-1}{}^T Q_N A_{N-1}\right) x_{N-1} + E\left(v_{N-1}^T F_{N-1}^T Q_N F_{Nk-1} v_{N-1}\right)$$
$$+ \frac{1}{2}\left(u_{N-1}\right)^T \left(R_{N-1} + B_{N-1}{}^T Q_N B_{N-1}\right) u_{N-1} + x_{N-1}^T A_{N-1}{}^T Q_N B_{N-1}\ u_{N-1}$$ [5.12]

Moreover, replacing [5.10] in [5.12], this yields:

$$V(x_{N-1}, u_{N-1}^*) = \frac{1}{2} x_{N-1}^T \left(Q_{N-1} + A_{N-1}^T Q_N A_N\right) x_{N-1} + E(v_{N-1}^T F_{N-1}^T Q_N F_{N-1} v_{N-1})$$
$$+ \frac{1}{2} x_{N-1}^T A_{N-1}^T Q_N B_{N-1}\left(R_{N-1} + B_{N-1}^T Q_N B_{N-1}\right)^{-1}$$ [5.13]
$$\times\ \left(R_{N-1} + B_{N-1}^T Q_N B_{N-1}\right)\left(R_{N-1} + B_{N-1}^T Q_N B_{N-1}\right)^{-1} B_{N-1}^T Q_N A_{N-1} x_{N-1}$$
$$- x_{N-1}^T A_{N-1}^T Q_N B_{N-1}\left(R_{N-1} + B_{N-1}^T Q_N B_{N-1}\right)^{-1} B_{N-1}^T Q_N A_{N-1} x_{N-1}$$

Regrouping of terms of [5.13] leads to:

$$V(x_{N-1}, u_{N-1}) =$$

$$\frac{1}{2} x_{N-1}^T \left(Q_{N-1} + A_{N-1}^T Q_N A_N - A_{N-1}^T Q_N B_{N-1} \left(R_{N-1} + B_{N-1}^T Q_N B_{N-1} \right)^{-1} B_{N-1}^T Q_N A_{N-1} \right) x_{N-1} \quad [5.14]$$

$$+ E(v_{N-1}^T F_{N-1}^T Q_N F_{N-1} v_{N-1})$$

Finally, considering:

$$P_N = Q_N$$

$$P_{N-1} = Q_{N-1} + A_{N-1}^T Q_N A_{N-1} - A_{N-1}^T Q_N B_{N-1} \left(R_{N-1} + B_{N-1}^T P_N B_{N-1} \right)^{-1} B_{N-1}^T P_N A_{N-1} \qquad [5.15]$$

the following can be written at instant $N - 1$:

$$K_{N-1} = \left(R_{N-1} + B_{N-1}^T P_N B_{N-1} \right)^{-1} B_{N-1}^T P_N A_{N-1}$$

$$V(x_{N-1}, u_{N-1}^*) = \frac{1}{2} x_{N-1}^T \left[Q_{N-1} + A_{N-1}^T \overbrace{\left[\underbrace{Q_N}_{P_N} - \underbrace{Q_N}_{P_N} A_{N-1}^T B_{N-1} \left(R_{N-1} + B_{N-1}^T \underbrace{Q_N}_{P_N} B_{N-1} \right)^{-1} B_{N-1}^T \underbrace{Q_N}_{P_N} \right]}^{P_{N-1}} A_{N-1} \right] x_{N-1}$$

$$+ E(v_{N-1}^T F_{N-1}^T P_N F_{N-1} v_{N-1}) \qquad [5.16]$$

$$= \frac{1}{2} x_{N-1}^T P_{N-1} x_{N-1} + E(v_{N-1}^T F_{N-1}^T P_N F_{N-1} v_{N-1})$$

Thus, the gain and cost of stochastic LQR at stage $N - 1$ can be written as:

$$K_{N-1} = \left(R_{N-1} + B_{N-1}^T P_N B_{N-1} \right)^{-1} B_{N-1}^T P_N A_{N-1} \qquad [5.17]$$

$$V(x_{N-1}) = \frac{1}{2} x_{N-1}^T P_{N-1} x_{N-1} + E\left(v_{N-1}^T F_{N-1}^T P_N F_{N-1} v_{N-1} \right) \qquad [5.18]$$

where matrix P_{N-1} corresponds at stage $N - 1$ to the solution of Riccati equation:

$$P_{N-1} = Q_{N-1} + A_{N-1}^T \left(P_N - P_N B_{N-1} (R_{N-1} + B_{N-1}^T P_N B_{N-1})^{-1} B_{N-1}^T P_N \right) A_{N-1} \qquad [5.19]$$

with $P_N = Q_N$.

Using an analog reasoning for $k = N - 2, N - 3, ..., 3, 2, 0$, leads to the following similar relations characterizing the stochastic LQR law at stage k:

$$K_k = \left(R_k + B_k^T P_{k+1} B_k \right)^{-1} B_k^T P_{k+1} A_k \qquad [5.20]$$

$$u_k^* = -\left(R_k + B_k^T P_{k+1} B_k \right)^{-1} B_k^T P_{k+1} A_k x_k \qquad [5.21]$$

$$P_k = Q_k + A_k^T \left(P_{k+1} - P_{k+1} B_k (R_k + B_k^T P_{k+1} B_k)^{-1} B_k^T P_{k+1} \right) A_k \qquad [5.22]$$

with $P_N = Q_N$:

$$V(x_k, u_k) = \frac{1}{2} x_k^T P_k \, x_k + \sum_{i=k}^{N-1} v_i^T F_i^T P_{i+1} F_i v_i \qquad [5.23]$$

5.2.3. *Block diagram of stochastic LQR*

The block diagram of the stochastic linear regulator, considering full availability of the state measurements for feedback, is represented in Figure 5.2.

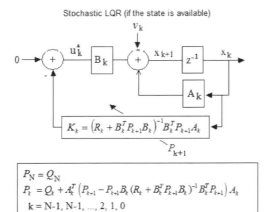

Figure 5.2. *Algorithmic diagram of the stochastic LQR*

This diagram illustrates the Certainty Equivalent Principle, according to which the stochastic LQR control law of a linear dynamic process subjected to Gaussian white noise is certainly equivalent to that of the same deterministic process controlled by LQR. Nevertheless, according to relation [5.23], it is worth mentioning that the cost incurred in the case of stochastic LQR is higher than that occasioned by a deterministic LQR. Therefore, the additive component $\sum_{i=k}^{N-1} v_i^T F_i^T P_{i+1} F_i v_i$ represents the total additive cost due to the stochasticity effect.

5.2.4. Properties of stochastic LQR

Given the dynamic equation [5.1] and knowing the structure of stochastic LQR provided by [5.20] to [5.23], the following can be written:

$$
\begin{aligned}
x_{k+1} &= \left(A_k - B_k \left(R_k + B_k^T P_{k+1} B_k \right)^{-1} B_k^T P_{k+1} A_k \right) x_k + F_k v_k \\
&= A_k^f x_k + F_k v_k
\end{aligned}
$$

[5.24]

with:

$$
A_k^f = A_k - B_k \left(R_k + B_k^T P_{k+1} B_k \right)^{-1} B_k^T P_{k+1} A_k
$$

[5.25]

5.2.4.1. Solution of open-loop system

Given relation [5.24], the following can be written:

$$
\begin{aligned}
x_{k+1} &= A_k^f x_k + B_k u_k + F_k v_k \\
&= A_k^f \left(A_{k-1}^f x_{k-1} + B_{k-1} u_{k-1} + F_{k-1} v_{k-1} \right) + F_k v_k \\
&= A_k^f A_{k-1}^f x_{k-1} + A_k^f A_{k-1}^f B_{k-1} u_{k-1} + F_{k-1} v_{k-1} + F_k v_k \\
&= A_k^f A_{k-1}^f \left(A_{k-2}^f x_{k-2} + B_{k-2} u_{k-2} + F_{k-2} v_{k-2} \right) + A_k^f F_{k-1} v_{k-1} + F_k v_k \\
&= A_k^f A_{k-1}^f A_{k-2}^f x_{k-2} + A_k^f A_{k-1}^f B_{k-2} u_{k-2} \\
&\qquad + A_k^f A_{k-1}^f F_{k-2} v_{k-2} + A_k^f F_{k-1} v_{k-1} + F_k v_k
\end{aligned}
$$

[5.26]

The general structure of [5.26], which is obtained by continuing the expansion of the previous expression for all $k > k_0$, has the following form:

$$
x(k) = \Phi(k, k_0) \ x(k_0) + \sum_{i=k_0}^{k-1} \left\{ \Phi(k, i+1) \left(B_i u_i + F_i v_i \right) \right\}
$$

[5.27]

with $\Phi(k, k_0) = A_{k-1}^f A_{k-2}^f \cdots A_{k0}^f$ and $\Phi(k,k) = I$

For a stationary system (parameters A_f, A, B and F constant):

$$x_k = A_f^{k-k_0} x_{k_0} + \sum_{j=k_0}^{k-1} A^{k-(j+1)} \left(B u_j + F v_j \right)$$ [5.28]

5.2.4.2. *Propagation of statistic means if v_k is a white noise*

If in [5.24] the statistic mean of a quantity χ is denoted by $\overline{\chi}$, then (case of deterministic control) the following can be written:

$$\overline{x_{k+1}} = A_k^f \, \overline{x_k} + B_k u_k$$ [5.29]

5.2.4.3. *Propagation of variances if v(k) is a white noise*

If in [5.24] the covariance matrix of xk is denoted by P_k, then (case of deterministic control) the following can be written:

$$P_{k+1}^x \underset{x,v}{E} \left[A_k^f \left(x_k - \overline{x_{k+1}} \right) + F_k v_k \right]\left[A_k^f \left(x_k - \overline{x_{k+1}} \right) + F_k v_k \right]^T$$
$$= A_k^f P_k^x (A_k^f)^T + F_k \, P_k^v F_k^T$$ [5.30]

5.2.4.4. *Asymptotic behavior*

For a stationary process that has to be optimized over an infinite time horizon, relation [5.22] converges toward a stationary value P that can be obtained by solving (for example, using the Matlab® "ric" command) the following equation:

$$P = Q + A^T \left(P - PB \left(R + B^T P B \right)^{-1} B^T P \right) A$$ [5.31]

In this case, the corresponding optimal gain can be written as:

$$K = \left(R + B^T PB \right)^{-1} B^T P A$$ [5.32]

The solution of [5.31], which exists in the space of positive semi-definite symmetric matrices, is unique and corresponds to $P = \underset{k \to \infty}{Lim} P_k$. Moreover, the corresponding state matrix [5.33] obtained in closed loop is stable:

$$A_k^f = A - B \left(R + B^T P B_k \right)^{-1} B^T P A$$ [5.33]

5.3. Discrete Kalman filter

The implementation of a stochastic LQR, studied in the previous section, requires full knowledge of the measurements of state x. Otherwise, a discrete Kalman filter can be used for real-time generation of the optimal estimated state, which can be used by a stochastic LQR. This section focuses on the presentation of the scientific context and algorithmic diagram of the Kalman filter, as originally developed in the work by Kalman [KAL 58, KAL 60a, KAL 60b], and Kalman and Bucy [KAL 61].

5.3.1. *Scientific context and hypotheses*

Let us consider a linear stochastic dynamic process described by:

$$\begin{cases} x_{k+1} = A_k\, x_k + F_k\, v_k \\ y_k = C_k\, x_k + w_k \end{cases} \tag{5.34}$$

where processes $\{v_k, k\}$ and $\{w_k, k\}$ are assumed:

– white (neither auto-correlated nor cross-correlated), with $(E(v_k) = 0$ and $E(w_k) = 0)$;

– Gaussian, with the respective covariance matrices $Rv_k = E(v_k\ v_k^{\mathrm{T}}) \geq 0$ and $Rw_k = F(w_k\ w_k^{\mathrm{T}}) > 0$.

Moreover, the optimal estimation criterion being considered involves minimizing the variance of the estimation error samples of state x_k of the system described by [5.34], knowing the observations $y_0, y_1, \ldots, y_k$.

5.3.2. *Notations*

The new notations that will be used frequently in this section are:

– $x_{k/k}$: best estimate of x_k at stage k, knowing the measurements $y_0, y_1, \ldots, y_k$:

$x_{k/k} = E(X_k\,/\,y_0, y_1, \ldots, y_k)$;

– $x_{k+1/k}$: best estimate of x_{k+1}, knowing the measurements $y_0, y_1, \ldots, y_k$:

$x_{k+1/k} = E(x_{k+1}\,/\,y_0, y_1, \ldots, y_k)$. It is a value predicted at one step;

– $P_{k/k}$: covariance matrix of the estimation error $x_k - x_{k/k}$:

$P_{k/k} = E[(x_k - x_{k/k})\,(x_k - x_{k/k})^{\mathrm{T}}]$;

– $P_{k+1/k}$: covariance matrix of the prediction error $x_k - x_{k+1/k}$:

$$P_{k+1/k} = E[(x_{k+1} - x_{k+1/k}) (x_{k+1} - x_{k+1/k})^T];$$

– R_{vk}: covariance matrix for any process $\{v_k, k\}$:

$$R_{vk} = E[(v_k - E(v_k)) (\omega_k - E(v_k))^T];$$

– R_{wk}: covariance matrix for any process $\{w_k, k\}$:

$$R_{wk} = E[(w_k - E(w_k)) (w_k - E(w_k))^T].$$

5.3.3. *Closed-loop algorithmic diagram*

The recursive equations of the discrete Kalman filter, established by Kalman and Bucy [KAL 61], are the following:

$$
\begin{cases}
x_{k+1/k} = A_k x_{k/k} & \text{(a)} \\
P_{k+1/k} = A_k P_{k/k} A_k^T + F_k R_v F_k^T & \text{(b)} \\
L_{k+1} = P_{k+1/k} C_{k+1}^T (C_{k+1} P_{k+1/k} C_{k+1}^T + R_w)^{-1} & \text{(c)} \\
x_{k+1/k+1} = x_{k+1/k} + L_{k+1} \left(y_{k+1} - C_{k+1} x_{k+1/k} \right) & \text{(d)} \\
P_{k+1/k+1} = P_{k+1/k} - L_{k+1} C_{k+1} P_{k+1/k} & \text{(e)}
\end{cases}
\qquad [5.35]
$$

with given initial conditions $x_{0/0} = x_{(0)}$, $P_{0/0}$, $R_{v(0)}$, $R_{w(0)}$.

The closed-loop algorithmic diagram of the discrete Kalman filter, established from [5.34] and [5.35], is represented in Figure 5.3. It can be noted that the parameters of this discrete filter vary in time, despite the fact that the parameters of the dynamic process and those of noises might be constant.

It can readily be verified that if in [5.35c] and [5.35e] the common term $P_{k+1/k}$ is replaced by its expression resulting from [5.35b], then (if the process and noise parameters are constant) expressions [5.36] and [5.37] are obtained, and they only depend on homogeneous terms $P_{k+1/k+1}$ and $P_{k/k}$:

$$
\begin{aligned}
P(k+1) = &(A\,P(k)\,A^T + F\,R_v\,F^T) \\
& -\left(A\,P(k)\,A^T + F\,R_v\,F^T\right) C^T \left(R_w + C\,(A\,P(k)\,A^T + F\,R_v\,F^T)\,C^T\right)^{-1} \\
& \qquad C\,\left(A\,P(k)\,A^T + F\,R_v\,F^T\right)
\end{aligned}
\qquad [5.36]
$$

$$
L^*(k+1) = (A\,P(k)\,A^T + F\,R_v\,F^T)\,C^T \begin{pmatrix} R_w + C\,(A\,P(k)\,A^T \\ + F\,R_v\,F^T)\,C^T \end{pmatrix}^{-1}
\qquad [5.37]
$$

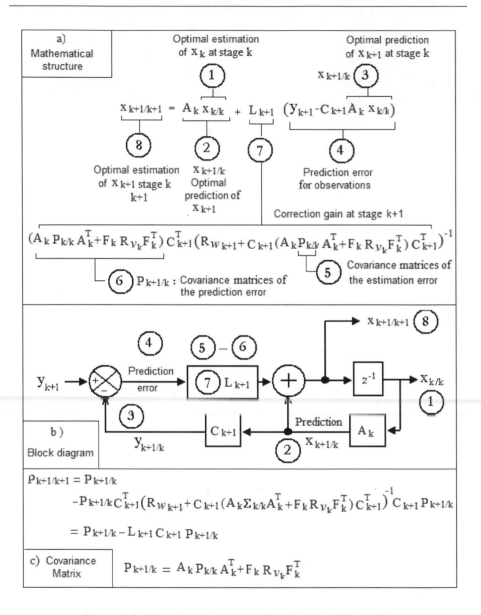

Figure 5.3. *Algorithmic diagram of the discrete Kalman filter*

Thus, even assuming that process and noise parameters are constant in equations [5.35] to [5.37], the rigorous structure of Kalman filter preserves its time-variant nature. Nevertheless, if under these conditions there are asymptotic solutions of [5.36] and [5.37] when k tends towards infinity, then they can be calculated from stationary equations [5.38] and [5.39]:

$$P\infty = (A\ P\infty\ A^T + F\ R_v\ F^T)$$
$$-\left(A\ P\infty\ A^T + F\ R_v\ F^T\right)\ C^T \left(R_w + C\ (A\ P\infty\ A^T + F\ R_v\ F^T)\ C^T\right)^{-1} \quad [5.38]$$
$$C\ \left(A\ P\infty\ A^T + F\ R_v\ F^T\right)$$

$$L\infty\ =\ (A\ P\infty\ P\ A^T + F\ R_v\ F^T)\ C^T \begin{pmatrix} R_w + C\ (A\ P\infty\ A^T \\ + F\ R_v\ F^T)\ C^T \end{pmatrix}^{-1} \quad [5.39]$$

A rigorous proof of the existence of stationary solutions P∞ and L∞, which are asymptotically optimal over an infinite horizon, has been established by Bagchi [BAG 93] and Siouris [SIO 96].

A simple and concrete example of convergence of the parameters of a Kalman filter towards an asymptotically optimal solution over a sufficiently long/wide time horizon will be the object of a corrected exercise.

5.4. Linear Quadratic Gaussian regulator

5.4.1. *Context*

A linear stochastic regulator with the Kalman filter is, by definition, the solution to the optimal control problem with quadratic criterion of a linear stochastic dynamic process characterized by:

– Gaussian process input noise;

– Gaussian measurement noise;

– incomplete information on the state, which means that at any discrete instant only measurements or observations $y(k)$ are available.

The LQG algorithm's mission is to calculate, given the incomplete information on the state and knowing the observations y_0, y_1, y_2,..., an optimal control law that minimizes the criterion:

$$J(x_0) = \sum_{k=0}^{N-1} \left(\frac{1}{2} x_k^T Q_k x_k + \frac{1}{2} u_k^T R_k u_k \right) + \frac{1}{2} x_N^T Q_N x_N \qquad [5.40]$$

under the dynamic constraint:

$$\begin{cases} x_{k+1} = A_k\, x_k + B_k\, u_k + F_k v_k \\ y_k = C_k\, x_k + w_k \end{cases} \qquad [5.41]$$

with:

$- x_k \in \mathfrak{R}^n$;

$- u_k \in \mathfrak{R}^m$, $v_k \in \mathfrak{R}^q$, $w_k \in \mathfrak{R}$ (case of univariate process);

$- k = 0, 1,..., N-1$

where v_k and w_k are noises of process and of measurement, respectively, assumed to be white and Gaussian, with positive definite covariance matrices R_{vk} and R_{wk}, respectively.

5.4.2. Separation principle

According to the separation theorem, the solution to optimal stochastic control defined by [5.40] and [5.41] has two constituents that function in cascade, namely:

– a stochastic linear regulator with state feedback of the estimated:

$$u_k^* = - K_k x_{k/k} \qquad [5.42]$$

with:

- $K_k = \left(R_k + B_k^T P_{k+1} B_k \right)^{-1} B_k^T P_{k+1} A_k$,

- $P_k = Q_k + A_k^T \left(P_{k+1} - P_{k+1} B_k (R_k + B_k^T P_{k+1} B_k)^{-1} B_k^T P_{k+1} \right) A_k$, and $P_N = Q_N$,

- $x_{k/k}$ = best estimate of x_k at stage k;

– a Kalman estimator filter having control u_k and output y_k as quantities for input and output, respectively, and which generates the best estimate $x_{k/k}$ of the state satisfying the dynamic model:

$$x_{k+1/k+1} = A_k\, \hat{x}_{k/k} + B_k\, u_k + L_k(y_k - C_k\, x_{k/k}),\ k = 0,\ 1,...,\ N-1 \quad [5.43]$$

where L_k is a gain that varies in time, which is pre-calculated from [5.36] and [5.37].

5.4.3. *Algorithmic diagram of LQG regulator*

Figure 5.4 describes the algorithmic diagram of the complete system over a finite time horizon resulting from the application of the superposition theorem, known as the Linear Quadratic and Gaussian regulator.

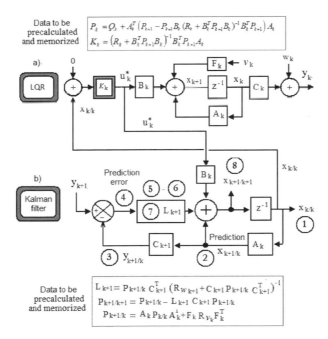

Figure 5.4. *Block diagram of the LQG regulator*

This block diagram is constituted of a LQR (Figure 5.4(a)), whose gains K_k can be pre-calculated by solving the corresponding Riccati equation, and a Kalman filter (Figure 5.4(b)) that provides the best estimate $x_{k/k}$ (of state x_k) required for state feedback.

5.5. Exercises and solutions

Exercise 5.1.

What are the basic hypotheses when studying the stochastic linear regulator?

Solution – Exercise 5.1.

The hypotheses for the study of stochastic linear regulator are:

– a linear dynamic system, with states available for state feedback control;

– uncorrelated noises;

– cost matrices Q_i and R_i are symmetric and positive definite.

Exercise 5.2.

Compare the solution of a stochastic linear regulator to that of a linear quadratic regulator, which is studied in Chapter 3.

Solution – Exercise 5.2.

For the same data (parameters of the dynamic system, cost matrices), the optimal control laws are identical in both cases; however, the cost of control using the stochastic linear regulator is greater than that occasioned by linear quadratic control.

Exercise 5.3.

What are the hypotheses underlying the Kalman filter study?

Solution – Exercise 5.3.

The basic hypotheses underlying the Kalman filter study are:

– a linear dynamic system;

– uncorrelated noises;

– Gaussian and Markovian noises;

– autocovariance matrices of noises $E(v_k\ v_k^{\mathrm{T}})$ and $E(w_k\ w_k^{\mathrm{T}})$ being symmetric and positive definite.

Exercise 5.4.

Let us consider a scalar Kalman filter whose parameters are real numbers such as:

$$A_k = a,\ F_k = f,\ C_k = c$$

$$P_{k+1/k} = \sigma^2_{k+1/k},\ P_{k+1/k+1} = \sigma^2_{k+1/k+1},\ R_{v(k)} = \sigma^2_v,\ R_{w(k)} = \sigma^2_w$$

a) Under these conditions, generate the filter equations as a function of a, f, c, $\sigma^2_{k+1/k}$, $\sigma^2_{k+1/k+1}$, σ^2_v and σ^2_w.

b) Given the values of $a = 1$, $b = 1$, $c = 1$, $\sigma^2_v = 20$, $\sigma^2_w = 10$ and $\sigma^2_{0/0} = 60$, create a Matlab program allowing the simulation of this filter.

c) Generate the table of the first values of parameters $\sigma^2_{k+1/k}$, $\sigma^2_{k+1/k+1}$ and L_{k+1} (filter gain) allowing the observation of filter convergence.

Solution – Exercise 5.4.

a) Equations of the filter:

$$\begin{cases} \sigma^2_{k+1/k} = a^2\ \sigma^2_{k/k} + f^2\ \sigma^2_v \\[2mm] L_{k+1} = c\ \dfrac{\left(a^2\ \sigma^2_{k/k} + f^2\ \sigma^2_v\right)}{\sigma^2_w + c^2\ a^2\ \sigma^2_{k/k} + c^2 f^2\ \sigma^2_v} \\[2mm] \sigma^2_{k+1/k+1} = \sigma^2_{k+1/k} - L_{k+1}\ c\ \sigma^2_{k+1/k} \end{cases}$$

b) Matlab program for filter simulation with $a = 1$, $b = 1$, $c = 1$, $\sigma^2_v = 20$, $\sigma^2_w = 10$ and $\sigma^2_{0/0} = 60$

In the proposed program (see Figure 5.5), the following notations are used:

$\mathrm{sv} \to \sigma^2_v$, $\mathrm{sw} \to \sigma^2_w$, $\mathrm{sxe(k+1)} \to \sigma^2_{k+1/k+1}$ and $\mathrm{sxp(k+1)} \to \sigma^2_{k+1/k}$.

```
% Scalar and stationary Kalman filter
clear
a=1; f=1; c=1;
sxe(1)=60; %
sv=20;
sw=10;
for i=2:10
  k(i)=i
sxp(i)=a^2*sxe(i-1)+f^2*sv;
L(i)=(c*a^2*sxe(i-1)+c*f^2*sv)/(sw+c^2*a^2*sxe(i-1)+c^ 2*f^2*sv);
sxe(i)=sxp(i)-L(i)*c*sxp(i);
end
[k' sxp' L' sxe']
```

Figure 5.5. *Proposed program*

c) The results of the filter simulation are presented in Table 5.1.

k	$\sigma_{k+1/k}$	L_k	$\sigma_{k/k}$
−1	0	0	60.000
1.0000	80.0000	0.8889	8.8889
2.0000	28.8889	0.7429	7.4286
3.0000	27.4286	0.7328	7.3282
4.0000	27.3282	0.7321	7.3211
5.0000	27.3211	0.7321	7.3205
6.0000	27.3205	0.7321	7.3205
7.0000	27.3205	0.7321	7.3205
8.0000	27.3205	0.7321	7.3205
9.0000	27.3205	0.7321	7.3205

Table 5.1. *Results of the filter simulation*

6

Deployed Matlab/GUI Platform for the Design and Virtual Simulation of Stochastic Optimal Control Systems

6.1. Introduction to OPCODE (*Optimal Control Design*) platform

6.1.1. *Scientific context*

The OPCODE (*Optimal Control Design*) platform, presented in this chapter, is the result of revisions and major expansions of the descriptive elements of a research product that has been briefly presented in [MBI 16, MBI 17]. It provides a simple and user-friendly environment for the design and rapid virtual simulation of a variety of digital deterministic and stochastic optimal control strategies over finite or infinite time horizons. This platform has been created and implemented with Matlab®, and then successfully shifted for 32/64-bit Windows runtime targets, using the Matlab 2016b "deploytool".

6.1.2. *Detailed presentation methodology*

In this chapter, section 6.2 provides a summary of the fundamental design elements of the OPCODE platform for deterministic and stochastic processes. In section 6.3, the techniques for the design of operating modes of the said tool according to the approach of macro-representations by main SFC and subprogram SFC [MBI 05] are revealed. Software implementation elements are detailed in section 6.4 and section 6.5 presents case studies of graphic design using the OPCODE tool. Finally, the technique for producing a first deployed version of OPCODE is described in section 6.6.

6.2. Fundamental OPCODE design elements

6.2.1. *Elements of deterministic optimal control*

6.2.1.1. *Diagrams of deterministic optimal control*

The diagrams of deterministic optimal control embedded in OPCODE are summarized in Figure 6.1.

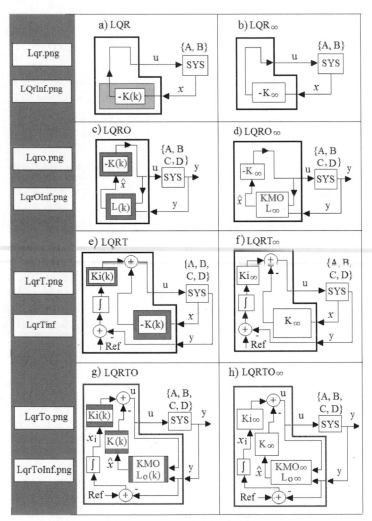

*.png are image components to be managed with OPCODE

Figure 6.1. *Diagrams of deterministic optimal control of OPCODE*

The wide palette of constitutive deterministic optimal regulators that can be parameterized by the user is comprised of:

– LQR (*Linear Quadratic Regulator*) with finite optimization time (Figure 6.1(a));

– LQR∞ or LQR with infinite optimization time (Figure 6.1(b));

– LQRO (*LQR with Observer*) with finite optimization time (Figure 6.1(c));

– LQRO∞ or LQRO with infinite optimization time (Figure 6.1(d));

– LQRT (*LQR with Tracking*) with finite optimization time (Figure 6.1(e));

– LQRT∞ or LQRT with infinite optimization time (Figure 6.1(f));

– LQRTO (*LQRT with Observer*) (Figure 6.1(g));

– LQRTO∞ or LQRTO with infinite optimization time horizon (Figure 6.1(h)).

6.2.1.2. *Generic formulation of deterministic optimal control problems*

Deterministic optimal control problems can be formulated using the basic LQR/LQRO configuration given by [6.1]. This formulation can readily be expanded or reduced in order to reconstruct other types of configuration:

$$
\begin{cases}
\text{(a)} \quad \text{Min} \quad J(x_0) = \dfrac{1}{T_f} \int_0^{T_f} \left(x^T(t)\, Q_c\, x(t) + u^T(t)\, R_c\, u(t) \right) dt \\[2mm]
\qquad \text{with} \\[2mm]
\text{(b) if LQR :} \quad \begin{cases} \dot{x}(t) = A_c\, x(t) + B_c\, u(t) \\ u(t) = -K(t)\, x(t) \end{cases} \\[4mm]
\text{(c) if LQRO :} \quad \begin{cases} \dot{x}(t) = A_c\, x(t) + B_c\, u(t) \\ y(t) = C_c\, x(t \\ \dot{\hat{x}}(t) = A_c\, \hat{x}(t) + B_c\, u(t) + L_c(t)\, (y(t) - \hat{y}(t)) \\ \hat{y}(t) = C_c\, \hat{x}(t) \\ u(t) = -K(t)\, \hat{x}(t) \end{cases}
\end{cases}
\qquad [6.1]
$$

Moreover, the discretization of [6.1] using the step invariance discretization method has led to the discrete structure [6.2]:

$$\left\{ \begin{array}{l} \text{(a)} \quad \text{Min} \quad J(x_0) = \dfrac{1}{N} \sum_{k=0}^{N-1} \left(x^T(k) \; Q(k) \; x(k) + u^T(k) \; R \; u(k) \right) \\[2mm] \qquad \qquad \text{with} \\[2mm] \text{(b) if LQR:} \quad \begin{cases} x_{k+1} = A \, x_k + B \, u_k \\ u_k \quad = -K_k x_k \end{cases} \\[4mm] \text{(c) if LQRO:} \quad \begin{cases} x_{k+1} = A \, x_k + B \, u_k \\ y_k \quad = C \; x_k \\ \hat{x}_{k+1} = A \, \hat{x}_k + B \, u_k + L_{k+1}(y_{(k+1)} - \hat{y}_{k+1}) \\ \hat{y}_k \quad = C \, \hat{x}_k \\ u_k \quad = -K_k \hat{x}_k \end{cases} \end{array} \right. \qquad [6.2]$$

with:

$$\begin{cases} Q = T \, Q_c, \quad R = T \, R_c & \text{(a)} \\[2mm] A = e^{A_c \, T}, \quad B = \left(\displaystyle\int_0^T e^{A_c \, \tau} d\tau \right) B_c & \text{(b)} \end{cases} \qquad [6.3]$$

At this development stage, it is worth noting that the passage from LQR/LQRO problems [6.1] to more complex LQRT/LQTRO problems is possible if in [6.1] or [6.2], x, Q, A, B and K quantities are replaced with the equivalent augmented new quantities, as follows:

$$x \equiv \begin{bmatrix} x \\ x_i \end{bmatrix}, \qquad \text{(a)}$$

$$Q \equiv \begin{bmatrix} Q & 0 \\ 0 & q_i \end{bmatrix}, \qquad \text{(b)} \qquad [6.4]$$

$$A \equiv \begin{bmatrix} A_c & 0 \\ C_c & 0 \end{bmatrix}, \quad B \equiv \begin{bmatrix} B \\ 0 \end{bmatrix}, \qquad \text{(c)}$$

$$K \equiv \begin{bmatrix} K & K_i \end{bmatrix} \qquad \text{(d)}$$

with:

$$\begin{cases} x_i(t) = \displaystyle\int_0^t \left(y(\tau) - y_r(\tau) \right) d\tau \quad \Rightarrow \quad \dot{x}_i(t) = y(t) - y_r(t) \quad \text{(a) (continuous case)} \\[4mm] x_i(k+1) = x_i(k) + \left(y(k) - y_{ref}(k) \right) \qquad\qquad \text{(b) (discrete case)} \end{cases} \qquad [6.5]$$

It should be noted that [6.5b] results from the discretization of [6.5a] using the pole(s) and zero(s) transformation method.

6.2.1.3. *Algorithms for numerical optimization of LQR/LQRO problems*

Riccati equations to be implemented for the preliminary calculus of optimal gains K*(k), to be used in deferred time for the simulation of deterministic optimal control systems, are defined by [6.6] and [6.7] [LEW 95]:

$$S(k) = Q + A^T S(k+1) A$$
$$- A^T S(k+1) B \left(R + B^T S(k+1) B \right)^{-1} \left(B^T S(k+1) A \right)$$

[6.6]

$$K^*(k) = (R + B^T S(k+1) B)^{-1} B^T S(k+1) A$$

[6.7]

where S(k) corresponds to the matrix of associated costs at the discrete instant kT.

In the asymptotic case of LQR∞/LQRT∞ problems, equations [6.6] and [6.7] become:

$$S_\infty = Q + A^T S_\infty A - A^T S_\infty B \left(R + B^T S_\infty B \right)^{-1} \left(B^T S_\infty A \right)$$

[6.8]

$$K^*_\infty = (R + B^T S_\infty B)^{-1} B^T S_\infty A$$

[6.9]

6.2.2. *Elements of stochastic optimal control*

6.2.2.1. *Diagrams of stochastic optimal control*

On the contrary, the strategies for stochastic optimal control being considered, summarized in Figure 6.2, are:

– KMF (*Kalman Filter*) with finite optimization time (Figure 6.2(a));

– KMF∞ or KMF with infinite optimization time (Figure 6.2(b));

– LQG (*Linear Quadratic and Gaussian*) or stochastic linear and Gaussian regulators with finite optimization time horizon (Figure 6.2(c));

– LQG∞ or LQR with infinite optimization time horizon (Figure 6.2(d));

– LQGT or LQG with set output tracking loop and finite optimization time horizon (Figure 6.2(e));

– LQGT∞ or LQGT with set output tracking and infinite optimization time horizon (Figure 6.2(f)).

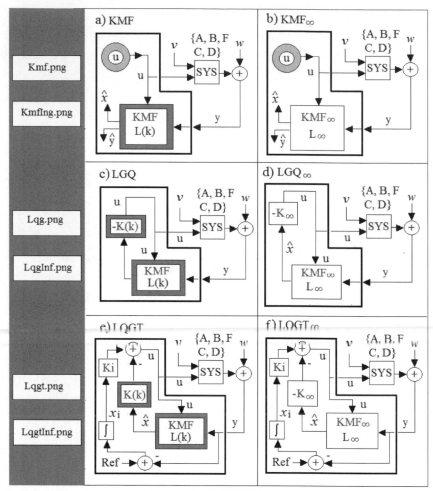

*.png are image components to be managed with OPCODE

Figure 6.2. *Palette of stochastic optimal control diagrams*

6.2.2.2. *Formulation of stochastic optimal control problems*

The generic formulation of stochastic optimal control problems given by [6.10] is established using a basic LQG/LQGT configuration:

$$\begin{cases} \text{Min} \quad J(x_0) = E\left(\displaystyle\int_0^{Tf} x^T(t)\, Q\, x(t) + u^T(t)\, R\, u(t)\, dt\right) & \text{(a)} \\[2mm] \text{with} \\[2mm] \begin{cases} \dot{x}(t) = A\, x(t) + B\, u(t) + F\, v(t) & \text{(b)} \\ y(t) = C\, x(t) + w(t) & \text{(c)} \\ \hat{\dot{x}}(t) = A\, \hat{x}(t) + B\, u(t) + L(t)\, (y(t) - \hat{y}(t)) & \text{(d)} \\ \hat{y}(t) = C\, \hat{x}(t) & \text{(e)} \\ u(t) = -K(t)\, \hat{x}(t) & \text{(f)} \end{cases} \end{cases} \qquad [6.10]$$

It can be readily modifiable automatically, as needed, for the numerical reconstruction of other types of configurations.

In [6.10], the E(.) operator designates the mathematical expectation of the stochastic quantity used as argument, and supposed to be stationary (convergence of trajectories for any initial condition) and ergodic (sample mean is equal to statistical mean).

Moreover, the discretization of [6.10] based on the step invariance principle leads to [6.11] and [6.12]:

$$\begin{cases} \text{Min} \quad J(x_0) = E\left(\displaystyle\sum_{k-0}^{N-1} \left(x^T(k)\, Q(k)\, x(k) + u^T(k)\, R\, u(k)\right)\right) & \text{(a)} \\[2mm] \text{with} \\[2mm] \begin{cases} x(k+1) = A\, x(k) + B\, u(k) + Fv(k) \\ y(k) = C\, x(k) + w(k) & \text{(b)} \\ \hat{x}(k+1) = A\, \hat{x}(k) + B\, u(k) + L(k+1)\, (y(k+1) - \hat{y}(k+1)) \\ \hat{y}(k) = C\, \hat{x}(k) & \text{(c)} \\ u(k) = -K(k)\, \hat{x}(k) & \text{(d)} \end{cases} \end{cases} \qquad [6.11]$$

with:

$$\begin{cases} Q = T\, Q_c, \quad R = T\, R_c & \text{(a)} \\ A = e^{A_c T}, \quad B = \left(\int_0^T e^{A_c \tau}\, d\tau\right) B_c, \; F = \left(\int_0^T e^{A_c \tau}\, d\tau\right) F_c & \text{(b)} \end{cases} \qquad [6.12]$$

6.2.2.3. *Algorithms for the numerical optimization of LQG/LQGT problems*

According to the development results in the previous chapter, the nonlinear matrix equations to be implemented in OPCODE for the automatic numerical calculus over finite or infinite time horizon of the optimal gains of LQR and Kalman filter are summarized here by [6.13] to [6.16]:

$$\begin{aligned} P(k+1) = &(A\, P(k)\, A^T + F\, R_v\, F^T) \\ &- \left(A\, P(k)\, A^T + F\, R_v\, F^T\right) C^T \left(R_w + C\, (A\, P(k)\, A^T + F\, R_v\, F^T)\, C^T\right)^{-1} \qquad [6.13] \\ &\quad C\, \left(A\, P(k)\, A^T + F\, R_v\, F^T\right) \end{aligned}$$

$$L^*(k+1) = (A\, P(k)\, A^T + F\, R_v\, F^T)\, C^T \left(\begin{array}{c} R_w + C\,(A\, P(k)\, A^T \\ + F\, R_v\, F^T)\, C^T \end{array}\right)^{-1} \qquad [6.14]$$

$$\begin{aligned} P_\infty = &(A\, P_\infty\, A^T + F\, R_v\, F^T) - \left(A\, P_\infty\, A^T + F\, R_v\, F^T\right) \\ &\quad C^T \left(R_w + C\,(A\, P_\infty\, A^T + F\, R_v\, F^T)\, C^T\right)^{-1} \qquad [6.15] \\ &\quad C\, \left(A\, P_\infty\, A^T + F\, R_v\, F^T\right) \end{aligned}$$

$$L_\infty^* = (A\, P_\infty\, A^T + F\, R_v\, F^T)\, C^T \left(R_w + C\,(A\, P_\infty\, A^T + F\, R_v\, F^T)\, C^T\right)^{-1} \qquad [6.16]$$

6.3. Design of OPCODE using SFC

6.3.1. *Architectural diagram*

The architectural diagram of OPCODE corresponds to Figure 6.3. This diagram has been established by assembling the individual construction components, which have been each described in section 6.2. The significant constitutive subsystems of this architectural diagram are:

– visual part of OPCODE GUI, which during run time corresponds to the virtual panel of operator dialogue;

– "Opcode.fig" file, containing characteristic information (nature, properties, "callback" functions, etc.) on GUI visual objects;

– "Opcode.m" file, which represents the software application for the automation of GUI-aided OPCODE operation;

– palette of *.png images displayable at GUI depending on the diagram of optimal control to be designed or that is being designed.

The design of automation tasks executable in the OPCODE application relies on the macro-representation approach using SFC.

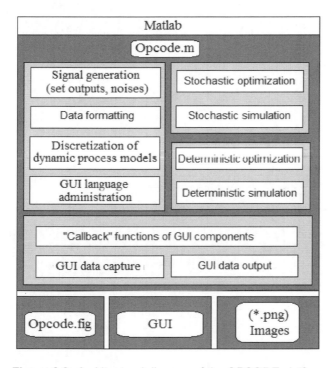

Figure 6.3. *Architectural diagram of the OPCODE platform*

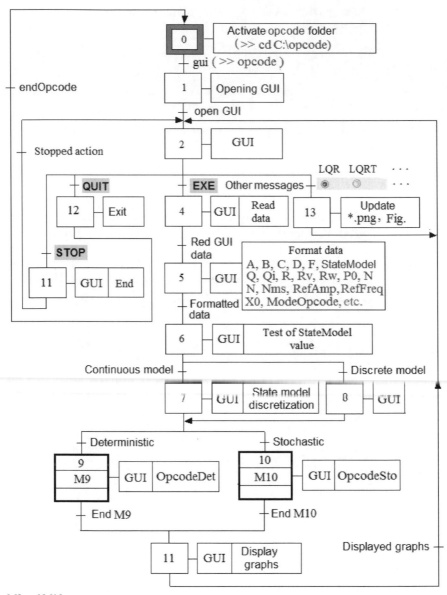

M9 and M10 are macro-steps

Figure 6.4. *Main SFC of the OPCODE software platform*

6.3.2. *Implementation of SFC*

From the MMMI (Multimedia Man–Machine Interface) perspective, the OPCODE software tool can be perceived as a programmable sequential controller for the digital processing of discrete events generated by the console and internally. Indeed, it is in charge of:

1) gathering data from GUI input visual components;

2) processing according to the specifications of the required tasks;

3) execution of the tasks programmed for this purpose, depending on the processing results obtained;

4) updating the visual state of MMMI.

Under these conditions, the MMMI represents the virtual console part of the programmable controller implemented in the software core of OPCODE.

For easier understanding, implementation and future expansion possibilities, the complete SFC of OPCODE is divided into three parts, as follows:

– Main SFC of OPCODE software platform (Figure 6.4), constituted of simple stages, as well as of macro-steps M9 and M10;

– SFC for the expansion of macro-step M9 (see Figure 6.5), constituted of simple stages and subprogram macro-steps;

– SFC for the expansion of macro-step M10 (see Figure 6.6), also constituted of simple stages and subprogram macro-steps.

It can be noted that in the main SFC, at stage 0, the OPCODE folder is initially assumed active under the Matlab control window. Then, "gui" transition remains validated until the command:

>> opcode,

opens the OPCODE application. For an easier recognition of responsiveness sources, GUI commands are marked by the corresponding visual symbols. It is worth noting that GUI remains active through all stages, until the command for exiting OPCODE is launched.

It should be noted that in SFC for the expansion of macro-step M9 (Figure 6.5), four subprograms, LQR, LQR∞, KMO (*Kalman Observer*) and KMO∞, whose input data can be reconfigured upstream, are adequate for the calculus of optimal gains of LQR/LQRT, LQR∞/LQRO∞, LQRO/LQRTO and LQRO∞/LQRTO∞ problems. Similarly, KMF, KMF∞, LQR and LQR∞ subprograms are adequate for the resolution of LQG/LQGT and LQG∞/LQGT∞ problems of SFC for the expansion of macro-step M10 (Figure 6.6). Thus, the generic deterministic and stochastic optimization models developed in section 6.2 have allowed a significant decrease in the complexity of implementation of the OPCODE software core.

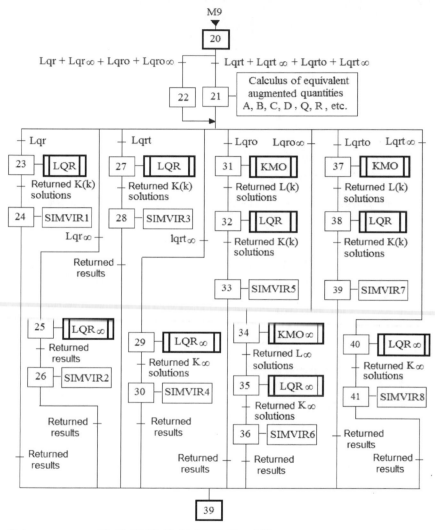

(Subprogram stages: 23, 25, 27, 29, 31, 32, 34, 37, 38 and 40)

Figure 6.5. *SFC for the expansion of macro-step M9*

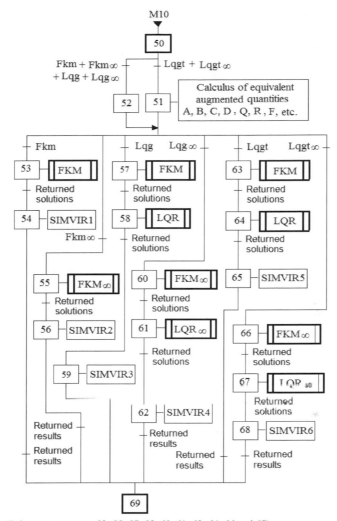

(Subprogram stages: 53, 55, 57, 58, 60, 61, 63, 64, 66 and 67)

Figure 6.6. *SFC for the expansion of macro-step M10*

6.4. Software implementation

SFC for normalized description and design of OPCODE has been implemented using the Matlab/GUI visual programming technology.

Figure 6.7 presents the display of the MMMI of the OPCODE platform after starting up. This GUI is organized into seven main administration areas, which are numbered from I to VII. The remaining areas are dedicated to graphic representation of simulation results, image visualization of the selected control system and display of numerical values of optimal gains to be returned during run time by the dynamic deterministic and stochastic optimization subprograms.

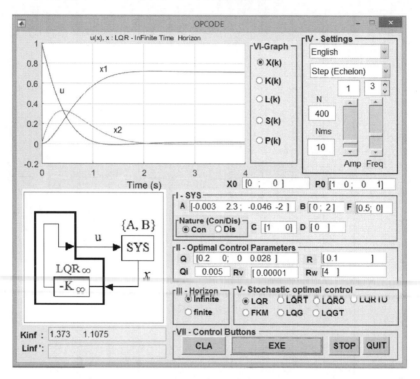

Figure 6.7. *Default options of the OPCODE GUI. For a color version of this figure, see www.iste.co.uk/mbihi/regulation.zip*

The default configuration observed in Figure 6.7 corresponds to that of an LQR∞ problem for a second-order continuous deterministic dynamic process. Going a step further, the designer can easily extend his design to an LQRT∞ and then compare the results with those obtained previously. He can also change, as desired, the other default options, including the GUI dialogue language, the parameters of set output signals, the matrices and the nature of the state model of the open-loop dynamic process, the sampling period, the cost function parameters, the initial conditions, etc.

Figure 6.7 shows that the state x_1 stabilizes quite far from the set output. Thus, even though the state feedback stabilizes the closed-loop control system, it can be noted that, in a steady state, the position quantity x_1 does not follow that of the set output (unit step).

6.5. Examples of OPCODE use

6.5.1. *Design of deterministic optimal control systems*

The examples of OPCODE use for designing deterministic optimal control systems LQR∞/LQRT∞, LQRT and LQRO are presented in Figures 6.8–6.12. Figure 6.8 shows the precision effect generated in a steady state by the extension of the original LQR∞ problem (Figure 6.7) to LQRT∞.

Figure 6.8 shows the design results with the simulation of the LQRT configuration, with automated display of optimal characteristics over a finite time horizon (optimal state trajectories and optimal gain profile).

In reality, the curves of states and those of gains have been superimposed on the graphic window by successive simulation, without erasure of the figure object content, in order to emulate the effect of a storage oscilloscope.

It is worth noting that, in the case of an LQRT for a second-order dynamic process, the optimal vector of displayed gains has three components. In fact, the third component corresponds to the gain of integral state x_i.

6.5.2. *Design of stochastic optimal control systems*

The examples of OPCODE use for the design and simulation of stochastic optimal control systems (KMF and LQGT) are presented in Figures 6.9 and 6.10. Figure 6.9 presents the response of a Kalman filter to a square wave input signal.

For a good understanding of the quality of the displayed results, it is worth noting that the stochastic dynamic process whose states are estimated using the Kalman filter is a position servomechanism that operates under a square wave open-loop control signal. Thus, there is an increase in speed and position for a positive step, followed by a slowdown state when the step shifts to 0 level, which tends towards shutdown while waiting for the next control cycle. In any case, it can be noted that the Kalman filter rigorously replicates the position estimate of x_1.

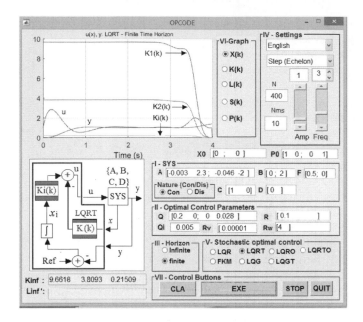

Figure 6.8. *LQRT design. For a color version of this figure, see www.iste.co.uk/mbihi/regulation.zip*

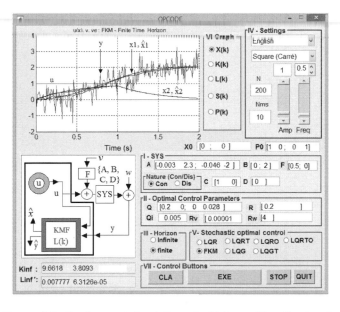

Figure 6.9. *Design and simulation of a Kalman filter. For a color version of this figure, see www.iste.co.uk/mbihi/regulation.zip*

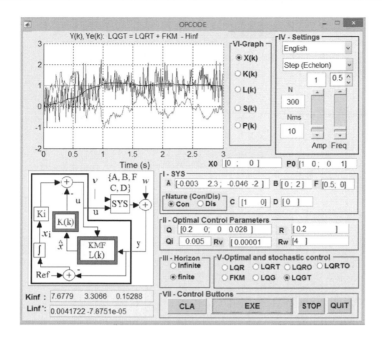

Figure 6.10. *LQGT∞ design. For a color version of this figure,*
see www.iste.co.uk/mbihi/regulation.zip

Figure 6.10 presents the results of the design and simulation of an LQGT∞ configuration under step set output. In this case, it can be noted that the closed-loop stochastic optimal control system is adequately stabilized, with quasi-perfect output tracking of the set output step. Many optimal control results published in the literature in specific contexts (for example, [RUB 12]) have been very accurately reproduced in the OPCODE platform, in the same simulation conditions.

6.6. Production of deployed OPCODE.EXE application

6.6.1. *Interest of Matlab/GUI application deployment*

The original OPCODE platform is a Matlab/GUI application that can only run under the Matlab environment. This constraint is a serious obstacle impeding the exploitation and distribution of this product. It is for these reasons that, once the Matlab/GUI version of OPCODE has been developed, it was useful to produce a first deployed version, executable under Windows without the activation of the Matlab/GUI environment. The first deployed version of OPCODE.EXE was produced and tested under Matlab 2016b for 32/64-bit Windows targets.

6.6.2. *Deployment methodology*

For reasons of user-friendliness, the deployment process requires preliminary work aimed at:

– regrouping all the files of the Matlab/GUI application (Matlab script, images, logo, etc.) to be deployed in a single folder;

– verifying the properly installed C++ compiler that will be used for deployment.

Deployment from the Matlab control window is effectively launched by typing and then validating the following command:

>> deploytool

which after a certain time activates the graphic deployment aid. Following successful deployment, three files of the deployed application are generated in the initially chosen output folder, namely:

– "OPCODE.EXE", deployed application;

– "Splash.png", for example, the customized logo (in image format) which will be displayed at the start of the deployed OPCODE.EXE application;

– "MCRInstaller.exe", which plays the role of runtime software, and can be freely installed on any computer, runtime target under 32/64-bit Windows.

Figure 6.11 shows the components of the deployed OPCODE application folder, which is generated at the end of the deployment process.

Name	Date modified	Type	Size
MCRInstaller	08-Sep-16 8:20 AM	Application	997,435 KB
OPCODEGUI	09-Feb-17 1:33 AM	Application	12,014 KB
splash	09-Feb-17 11:20 PM	PNG File	275 KB

Figure 6.11. *Folder of the deployed OPCODE.EXE application*

6.6.3. *Tests of deployed OPCODE.EXE application*

Figure 6.12 presents a screenshot of a sample of virtual simulation results of a LQG (stochastic LQR + FKM) system over a finite time horizon.

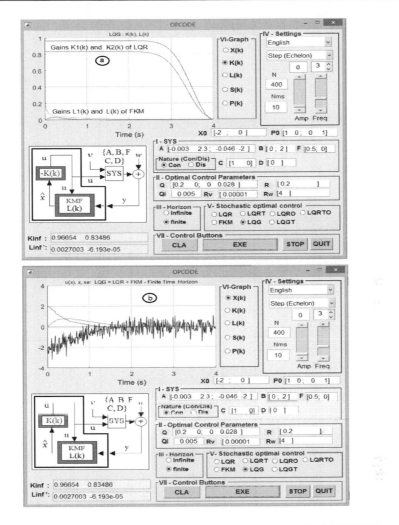

Figure 6.12. *Sample of the obtained results with deployed OPCODE.EXE. For a color version of this figure, see www.iste.co.uk/mbihi/regulation.zip*

As regards the stability of the feedback control system using LQR simulated in Figure 6.12, it is worth noting in Figure 6.12(a) and 6.12(b) that:

– the set output magnitude is null when the initial conditions of the state vector components are $x_1(0) = -2$ and $x_2(0) = 0$;

– after a dynamic state of 2.5 seconds, the optimal trajectories of $x_1(k)$ and $x_2(k)$ converge towards the equilibrium state $(0,0)$.

Moreover, Figure 6.12(a) shows the graphic profiles of optimal gains $K(k) = [K_1(k)\ K_2(k)]$ of the stochastic LQR, as well as the profiles of optimal gains $L(k) = [L_1(k)\ L_2(k)]$ of FKM. These observed graphic profiles effectively confirm that LQG = {LQR, FKM} converges towards the suboptimal regulator LGR∞ = {[LQR∞, FKM∞} whose numerical values of characteristic gains K∞ (or K_{inf}) and L∞ (or L_{inf}) are $K_{inf} = [0.98654\ 0.83496]^T$ and $L_{inf} = [0.\ 0027003 - 6.193^e - 05]$ in this case.

According to our knowledge, there is so far no deployed Matlab/GUI tool that offers such advanced and flexible possibilities for rapid design and virtual simulation of stochastic optimal control systems.

6.7. Exercises and solutions

Exercise 6.1.

What are the types of dynamic models supported by OPCODE?

Solution – Exercise 6.1.

The types of dynamic models supported by the OPCODE platform are:

– linear;

– invariant;

– deterministic;

– stochastic.

Exercise 6.2.

What are the types of diagrams of deterministic optimal control supported by the OPCODE platform?

Solution – Exercise 6.2.

The types of diagrams of deterministic optimal control supported by the OPCODE platform are:

– LQR;

– LQR∞;

– LQRO;

– LQRO∞;

– LQRT;

– LQRT∞;

– LQRTO;

– LQRTO∞.

Exercise 6.3.

What are the types of diagrams of stochastic optimal control supported by the OPCODE platform?

Solution – Exercise 6.3.

The types of diagrams of stochastic optimal control supported by the OPCODE platform are:

– KMF (Kalman filter);

– KMF∞;

– LQG;

– LQG∞;

– LQGT;

– LQGT∞.

Exercise 6.4.

What tools have been used for the design of the OPCODE platform operating modes?

Solution – Exercise 6.4.

The tools that have been used for the design of the operating modes of OPCODE are:

– main SFC;

– macro-step expansion SFC;

– subprogram SFC.

Exercise 6.5.

The OPCODE platform, which has been described in this chapter, is a virtual and flexible teaching tool.

a) Compile the list of constitutive virtual elements of this platform.

b) What elements account for the flexibility of the OPCODE platform?

Solution – Exercise 6.5.

a) The constitutive virtual elements of this platform are:

– image components;

– graph components;

– text box;

– selection box;

– checkboxes;

– panels of option buttons.

b) The elements that account for the flexibility of the OPCODE platform are:

– dynamic models of arbitrary dimension;

– adjustable set output parameters;

– optional diagrams of deterministic optimal control;

– optional diagrams of stochastic optimal control.

Exercise 6.6.

Figure 6.13 presents an area of the VMMI (Virtual Man–Machine Interface) of the OPCODE platform.

a) Identify the corresponding active control diagram.

b) Determine the corresponding mathematical formulation.

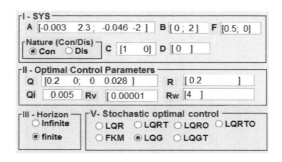

Figure 6.13. *VMMI area*

Solution – Exercise 6.6.

a) The corresponding active control diagram: LQG over a finite horizon.

b) Mathematical formulation (continuous time):

$$
\text{Min} \quad J(x_0) = E \left(\int_0^{Tf} x^T(t) \, Q \, x(t) + u^T(t) \, R \, u(t) \, dt \right) \tag{a}
$$

with

$$
\begin{cases}
\dot{x}(t) = A\,x(t) + B\,u(t) + F\,v(t) & \text{(b)} \\
v(t) - C\,x(t) + w(t) & \text{(c)} \\
\dot{\hat{x}}(t) = A\,\hat{x}(t) + B\,u(t) + L(t)\,(y(t) - \hat{y}(t)) & \text{(d)} \\
\hat{y}(t) = C\,\hat{x}(t) & \text{(e)} \\
u(t) = -K(t)\,\hat{x}(t) & \text{(f)}
\end{cases}
$$

with:

$$
A = \begin{bmatrix} -0.003 & 2{,}3 \\ -0.046 & -2 \end{bmatrix}, \quad B = \begin{bmatrix} 0 \\ 2 \end{bmatrix}, \quad C = \begin{bmatrix} 1 & 0 \end{bmatrix}, \ D = 0
$$

$$
F = \begin{bmatrix} 0.5 \\ 0 \end{bmatrix}, \ Q = \begin{bmatrix} 0{,}2 & 0 \\ 0 & 0.028 \end{bmatrix}, \ R = 0.1, \ Rv = 0.00001, \ Rw = 4
$$

Part 3

Remotely Operated Feedback Control Systems via the Internet

Elements of Remotely Operated Feedback Control Systems via the Internet

7.1. Problem statement

The control systems that were studied in the first and second part of this book are automation techniques for direct and isolated computer-aided digital control. Although these types of automation techniques may be less difficult and less expensive to implement, in certain application fields, the following technical problems may be encountered in their exploitation:

– difficulties involved in wide-scale sharing of fixed infrastructure (hardware and software) resources, installed in a remote geographic site;

– imperative physical presence of the operator at the console of the single direct-control computer;

– low service potential due to off-peak hours, as a consequence of the constraints of the institutional work timetable.

The above technical problems, and many others, have led to the creation of:

– dynamic systems operated remotely via the Internet for servomechanisms and robots for civilian applications, which emerged on the eve of the 20th Century;

– remotely operated laboratories via the Internet, which emerged in the early 20th Century.

Nowadays, the field of remotely operated control systems is very active and presents increasing global interest for technical education and scientific research. Their implementation however, requires, multidisciplinary competences in fields such as: physics, industrial electronics, mechatronics, automation, industrial computing, etc.

The elements of remotely operated control systems via the Internet studied in this chapter are especially addressed to readers who are little acquainted with infrastructural topologies and tools for implementing real dynamic processes with remote digital feedback control via a local network or the Internet.

7.2. Infrastructural topologies

7.2.1. *Basic topology*[2]

A real remotely operated control system (REOPCPS) via the Internet designates a set of distributed infrastructural means used for controlling the behavior of a real process via an Internet access terminal.

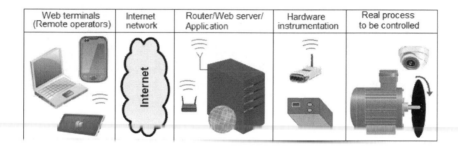

Web terminals (Remote operators)	Internet network	Router/Web server/ Application	Hardware instrumentation	Real process to be controlled

Figure 7.1. *Basic infrastructural topology of a REOPCOS*

Figure 7.1 presents the basic infrastructural topology of a REOPCOS. As can be seen, a REOPCOS is structured into five infrastructural layers, as follows:

– "Real process" layer: the input/output signals of this layer are generally analog;

– "Hardware instrumentation" layer: this is equipped with a MDAQ (multifunction data acquisition board) with a physical bus or wireless in view of the D/A conversion of the digital control signal and of the A/D conversion of the output quantity returned by the measurement mechanism;

– "Internet router/web server/application" layer, in which:

  - the application component corresponds to the digital control software based on a set output issued by a web terminal;

  - the web server is a software tool that manages the access of authorized Internet remote operators to the process;

- the router enables the communication between server and recognized web terminals;

– "Internet network" layer: this represents the set of infrastructures installed between the local router and the authenticated Internet terminals;

– "Web terminals" layer (or web clients) for Internet operators: this layer corresponds to the set of devices (e.g. PC, laptop, tablet, etc.) that remote operators who have authorized access can use for real-time control of the real process via the Internet.

7.2.2. Advanced topologies

Given the current and future state of the very rapid evolution of NICT (new information and communication technologies) and of design norms of CSEHL (computer science environment for human learning), a wide variety of REOPCOS topologies can be designed, as has been briefly presented by Pauné [PAU 16] and Pauné and Mbihi [MBI 17], and as will be detailed in the following sections.

7.2.2.1. Monoserver and multiprocess topology

Figure 7.2 corresponds to the monoserver and multiprocess topology.

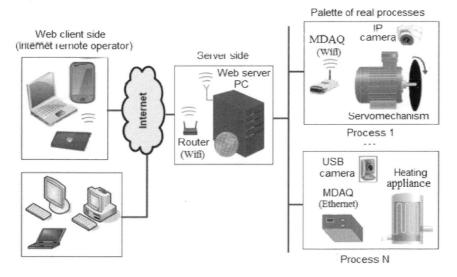

Figure 7.2. *Monoserver and multiprocess topology*

There is a palette of N real processes, state sensors and a video of the experimental arrangement, one MDAQ per process, one local PC (featuring a power backup supply that has not been represented) that plays the roles of web server and direct digital control device, a router for Internet access, and also a population of web remote operators.

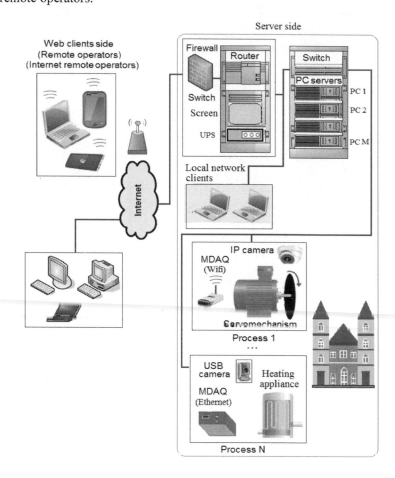

Figure 7.3. *Multiserver and multiprocess topology*

7.2.2.2. *Multiserver and multiprocess topology*

Multiserver and multiprocess topology is presented in Figure 7.3. Although its implementation is more expensive than that shown in Figure 7.2, it offers higher security and performances under the same operation constraints: same number of processes, same types of experimental activity, same online operator traffic, etc.

Indeed, it features a firewall for the Internet interface, a dedicated PC as router for Internet access, one dedicated rackable PC server for each single process to be controlled, a main *switch* for the interconnection of M rackable PC web servers and a local network for remote operators of the Intranet system of the institution hosting the real home site of REOPCOS.

7.2.2.3. *Topology of cooperative remotely operated control systems*

The topology of cooperative remotely operated control systems represented in Figure 7.4 is applicable to partner institutions, whose infrastructure is organized into REOPCOS specialized poles that are shared online.

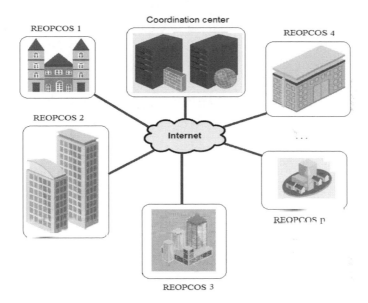

Figure 7.4. *Topology of cooperative REOPCOS*

In this case, a leader institution can host the site of the center for general coordination of the traffic of experimental activities via Internet.

7.2.2.4. *Universal topology*

The universal topology presented in Figure 7.5 results from the global scale integration of a composite mega-infrastructure, formed of REOPCOS specialized poles shown in Figure 7.4 and of poles of virtual remotely operated systems (VIREOPCOS). A VIREOPCOS is, for example, a combination of classical digital campuses for distance learning and multimedia libraries.

It is, in fact, a futuristic topology, since an actual implementation would involve insuperable technical problems related to traffic administration and lack of sufficient bandwidth required for coordinating all of the participants.

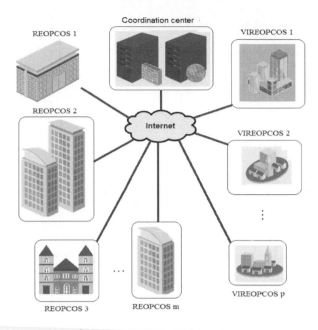

Figure 7.5. Universal topology

7.3. Remotely operated laboratories via the Internet

A remotely operated laboratory via the Internet is a type of REOPCOS specifically designed for remote operation of experimental activities in a real platform, equipped with devices to be controlled in real time from an authorized web terminal that can be connected to the Internet irrespective of its location.

7.3.1. *Comparison between classical and remotely operated laboratories*

In a classical laboratory, the organization of practical activities that support the acquisition of technical knowledge in a discipline encounters many limitations, the most important of which are the following:

– constraint represented by the permanent physical presence of support staff (laboratory coordinators and technicians) for starting and monitoring laboratory work;

– constraints of absolute physical presence of the students during practice assignments;

– restriction of practical activities to working hours, according to the institutional work schedule;

– high risk of breakdown, maladjustment and especially damage of specialized and expensive equipment (precision instruments, machines) caused by their direct manipulations;

– long downtime due to lengthy commissioning sequences, improper adjustments of equipment, maneuvering errors, possible actions occasioned by material storage upon completion of practice assignments;

– reduced hosting capacity, in terms of workstations available in the operation time unit;

– wide variability of experimental results from one workstation to another.

Unlike classical laboratories, remotely operated laboratories via the Internet have a variety of advantages, such as:

– automated services (commissioning, changes of procedure and decommissioning), without permanent trainer(s) or technician(s). This minimizes downtime per active workstation. Moreover, service availability can reach 24/24 h if the real site has a backup power supply source;

– quasi-unlimited service capacity per unit time per remotely operated workstation. The concept of a remotely operated laboratory equipped with a single workstation is therefore justified, since during a fixed period of time a large number of student remote operators can each engage in part-time overall management of a session of practice assignments;

– real-time accessibility at the regional, national, continental and global scales for any authorized remote operator who is connected to the Internet;

– easy online sharing of equipment by students enrolled with partner institutions;

– significant time gain per workstation and per student;

– high security of handled hardware and of the student remote operators, since there is no direct maneuver of the real equipment handled.

Nevertheless, certain advantages of remotely operated laboratories are also sources of shortcomings in terms of the efficiency of the learning environment. Several examples of such shortcomings are:

– lack of face-to-face collaboration among the participants in a single learning experimental platform;

– insufficient level of acquisition of technical competences related to the effective use of instruments and of real dynamic targets handled;

– lack of acquisition of competences for effective use of the tools for creating virtual instrumentation applications.

Besides these learning-related shortcomings, several technical problems can be mentioned:

– time lag between data transmitted by one side and received by the other, due to the time required for data to propagate through the Internet;

– decrease in reliability of measurements and observations when the client–server process global chain of communication behaves as a strongly time-variant mega system.

Since from both technical and learning perspectives, both classical laboratories and those remotely operated via the Internet have advantages and shortcomings, the best strategy would highlight their complementary aspects. This would involve a classical laboratory context featuring several special remotely operated workstations, allowing local students as well as those of partner institutions to conduct experimental research activities via the Internet.

7.3.2. *Infrastructures on the server side of a remotely operated laboratory*

7.3.2.1. *Experimental platform*

The experimental device to be controlled designates a variety of equipment installed on the real platform. Each workstation requires a minimum amount of equipment, as follows:

– target digital control machine, equipped with at least the following constitutive elements:

   - actuator(s);

   - power interface(s) supplied with controllable energy;

   - output quantities state sensor(s);

   - video camera (USB, Ethernet or WiFi, programmable or not);

– MDAQ (multifunction data acquisition interface) with standard bus (USB, Ethernet, PCI, PCI-X, PCI-E) or WiFi (radio), used as a hardware interface between the process to be controlled and the local computer;

– multifunction local PC equipped with specialized software tools.

It is worth mentioning that rigorous design of a digital control strategy on an experimental platform is not necessarily a simple problem. Indeed, if possible, it should take into account several real factors, some of which are:

– structure and parameters of the dynamic model of the process to be controlled;

– unpredictable time delay of propagation of set output quantities coming from the remote control terminals distributed over the Internet.

7.3.2.2. *Software applications*

On the server side, the minimum requirement is a MMMI (multimedia man–machine interface), a distributed database web server and a software tool for the interface between the web server and the Internet.

Even though the software applications can be implemented by network programming in a standard language (JavaApplet, AJAX, Visual C++, Visual C#, etc.), the advanced tools, which are most commonly used in practice, without low-level programming and which offer significant time gains for building MMMI and web applications, are:

– Labview;

– Matlab;

– TeamViewer.

Table 7.1 describes the basic characteristics of these popular tools.

Tool	Specific resources (server side)	Elements of host PC deployed to the client	Resources (client side)
Labview	– Labview MMMI Application – Labview Server – Aid in generating Labview web application	MMMI Instances	– Labview runtime software – Web browser
Matlab	– Matlab MMMI Application – Matlab Builder NE (aid in generating Matlab web application)	MMMI Instances	– Matlab runtime software – Web browser
TeamViewer	– C++/C#/VB Application – TeamViewer Server	Local PC screen (host)	– Client TeamViewer – Web browser

Table 7.1. *Tools for rapid production of web and MMMI applications*

7.3.2.3. *Network equipment*

The minimum network equipment includes:

– a switch for the local network;

– a router featuring a firewall for Internet access.

7.3.3. *Criteria for the creation of a remotely operated laboratory*

There are many criteria to be considered when creating a remotely operated laboratory. The focus here will be on the following high-priority criteria:

– technical use framework: teaching, experimental research or commercial platform;

– relevant discipline: applied physics, mechatronics, robotics, hydraulics, industrial automation and process engineering;

– study level (Bachelor, Master and PhD);

– experimental sessions: sequential, simultaneous or combined;

– operating modes: open loop, automated experimental modeling of the dynamic process to be controlled, control with or without disturbance, etc.;

– user friendliness and comfort: GMMI (Graphical Man–Machine Interface), video of the experimental arrangement;

– strategy for web client queue control based on the type of experiment;

– online evaluation of learning elements;

– operational performances: availability, service capacity per experiment and remote operator and factor of impact on learning efficiency;

– security level: hardware security and trained access security;

– budget constraints: costs of implementation, maintenance and system administration.

7.4. Exercises and solutions

Exercise 7.1.

What are the main aspects that are common to classical laboratories and remotely operated via Internet laboratories?

Solution – Exercise 7.1.

The main common aspects of classical laboratories and remotely operated via Internet laboratories are:

– the purpose of practical training in a technical field;

– experimental sites equipped with hardware instruments and real dynamic processes or procedures.

Exercise 7.2.

The first generations of remotely operated laboratories via the Internet created at the beginning of the 21st Century were a single station and had a single dynamic target to control. Why then should they be called "remotely operated laboratories" and not "remotely operated workstations or test benches"?

Solution – Exercise 7.2.

The reasons for designating a single workstation as a remotely operated laboratory are the following:

– this single workstation can be shared online, for a fixed period of time by a significant number of students;

– on the contrary, a similar classical laboratory, equipped with many similar workstations, would service a smaller number of students.

Exercise 7.3.

Despite the interest presented by remotely operated laboratories, what are their main shortcomings when compared to classical laboratories?

Solution – Exercise 7.3.

The main shortcomings of remotely operated laboratories are the following:

– lack of collaboration among participants on the same learning platform;

– lack of acquisition of competences on the effective use of instruments and real dynamic targets to be handled;

– lack of skill in using tools for the development of virtual instrumentation applications, etc.;

– limitation to experimental procedures with low level of complexity.

Exercise 7.4.

List, in ascending order of use complexity, examples of development tools for MMMI and web applications for remotely operated laboratories.

Solution – Exercise 7.4.

The tools for developing MMMI and web applications are listed below in ascending order of use complexity:

– JavaApplet;

– AJAX;

– Visual C++;

– Visual C#;

– Matlab;

– Labview;

– TeamViewer.

Exercise 7.5.

Is it possible to use, in a remotely operated laboratory via the Internet, different web server technologies for MMMI applications? Give a concrete example in support of your answer.

Solution – Exercise 7.5.

In a remotely operated laboratory via the Internet, it is possible to use different web server technologies for MMMI applications. For example, a Labview MMMI application can be managed by a TeamViewer web server.

Exercise 7.6.

What types of hardware terminals can a remote operator use in order to access a remotely operated laboratory via the Internet?

Solution – Exercise 7.6.

The types of personal hardware terminals that a remote operator can use in order to access a remotely operated laboratory via the Internet are:

– PC;

– laptop;

– tablet;

– iPhone.

Exercise 7.7.

What are the essential selection criteria for the nature of a dynamic experimental process in a remotely operated automated laboratory?

Solution – Exercise 7.7.

The essential selection criteria for the nature of a dynamic experimental process considered when designing a remotely operated automated laboratory are:

– learning categories: general knowledge of automation or knowledge of a specialized field of automation (e.g. robotics);

– types of exciting product effects: visual, audio and video effects;

– practical applications· home or industrial automation, social or professional use;

– implementation cost.

Exercise 7.8.

The PID controller is extensively used in the implementation of most existing remotely operated automated laboratories, which enable the practical strengthening of general knowledge. What are the reasons that justify this fact?

Solution – Exercise 7.8.

The reasons justifying this fact are:

– its simplicity of implementation;

– the high level of its static and dynamic performances when the parameters are properly calculated.

Exercise 7.9.

Figure 7.6 represents a topological configuration of a block diagram of a remotely operated laboratory via the Internet, in which the digital controller is implemented on the web client side. List the problems generated by this type of configuration.

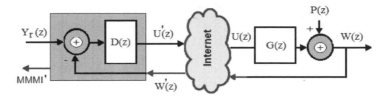

Figure 7.6. *Topology featuring a controller on the web client side*

Solution – Exercise 7.9.

The problems generated by this block diagram of the configuration of a remotely operated automated laboratory via the Internet are:

– the closed-loop system is fundamentally uncertain and time-invariant, as the Internet network is a constitutive part of the loop;

   the non distributed controller;

– the risks of unpredictable instability;

– the poor performances due to the scarcity of knowledge available on the dynamic model of the Internet network between two access points.

Exercise 7.10.

Figure 7.7 represents an instance of a MMMI image of a remotely operated automated laboratory. This image is transmitted at instant zero by the local server to the terminal of a remote operator.

Knowing that the transmission path delay over the Internet is two time units, reconstruct the MMMI image received on the client side within the same time scale and under the hypothesis of time-invariance of the dynamic behavior of the Internet network.

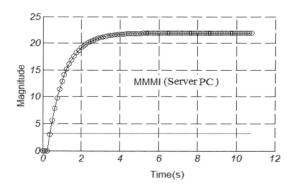

Figure 7.7. *MMMI image of a remotely operated laboratory*

Solution – Exercise 7.10.

The MMMI image received on the client side after a delay of two time units is represented in Figure 7.8.

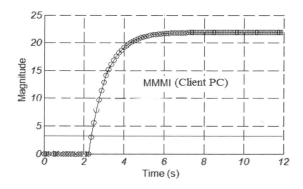

Figure 7.8. *Image received after two time units*

8

Remotely Operated Automation Laboratory via the Internet

8.1. Introduction to remotely operated automation laboratory

8.1.1. *Creation context*

Automation is a transversal discipline in engineering schools, which are increasingly overcrowded with students. Thus, the lack of sufficient didactic equipment required for high quality competence-oriented education poses a difficult problem wherever equipment renewal involves high costs and when higher student enrollment capacity is costly.

Thus, given the limits of classical automation laboratories, REOPAULAB technology (REmotely OPerated AUtomation LABoratory) enables the creation of flexible workstations that offer students, remote operators via the Internet, the huge advantage of remote sharing of didactic equipment, as well as quasi unlimited service capacity for a small number of installed workstations.

REOPAULAB for dynamic power lighting systems for work sites, presented in this chapter, is therefore a logical illustration of CSEHL (Computer Science Environment for Human Learning) products. It allows a globally spread student population to have real-time experience of fundamental concepts of automation.

The original prototype of this REOPAULAB has been created and implemented at the ENSET campus of the University of Douala, within the framework of an ambitious PhD research project [PAU 16] initiated and directed by the author of this book, with the active participation of other researchers [PAU 14, PAU 16, PAU 17].

8.1.2. *Didactic context*

REOPAULAB, presented in this chapter, enables authorized remote operators to experiment with the basic concepts of industrial automation on a dynamic target that is controllable via the Internet.

The controllable dynamic process being considered is a power lighting system of a work environment. The choice of this specific type of dynamic process to be controlled relies on the following considerations:

– power lighting is a permanent social need, manifesting wherever daylight is not available or is insufficient for human visual comfort. Moreover, power lighting systems are noisy dynamic processes, with significant input delay and uncertain rated parameters. Therefore, they present high teaching interest as regards to the practice of automation concepts;

– the generated luminous flux is a captivating visual quantity in the context of automation laboratories;

– the automated control of work environment lighting helps to maintain a level of visual comfort that is in compliance with the thresholds required by worker safety standards defined by types of activity [LUX 04, AFN 11]. For example, the average lighting of an industrial design hall is 750 Lux, while that of a conference hall is 500 Lux;

– power lighting system control in a site accessible to ambient lighting can generate significant energy savings.

8.1.3. *Specifications*

From a technical point of view, the creation specifications are:

– low implementation cost;

– user friendliness and comfort with MMMIs (multimedia man–machine interface), with no permanent lab technician(s) or trainer(s);

– flexible exploitation conditions, with or without domain name (DNS).

From a didactic point of view, experimental works conducted remotely via the Internet network should allow remote operators, i.e. students enrolled in Bachelor and Master 1 and 2 programs of study, to simulate and experiment with the fundamental elements of basic automation.

Table 8.1 summarizes the palette of automation experiments and concepts that have been properly integrated in REOPAULAB, which will be presented in detail in the following sections.

No.	EXPERIMENTS	ASSOCIATED CONCEPTS
\multicolumn3 Experiments and concepts to be tested		
1	Open-loop tests without disturbance	Properties of an open-loop system
2	Open-loop tests with disturbance	Shortcomings of open-loop setting
3	PID control without disturbance	Effects of closed-loop control: stability, rapidity, static accuracy (lighting quality), etc.
4	PID control under light disturbance of the work station	Robustness, energy savings at the main lighting source
5	Variation of PID parameters	Complementarity of PID parameters
6	Variation of sampling period T	Effect of sampling period

Table 8.1. *Automation experiments and concepts of the REOPAULAB*

8.2. Design and implementation of the experimental system

8.2.1. *Descriptive diagrams*

The descriptive diagrams of the experimental system for local PC-aided control of the dynamic power lighting system of REOPAULAB are shown in Figure 8.1. Figure 8.1(a) corresponds to the local infrastructural diagram that shows:

– local PC, equipped with a digital control application, aided by basic MMMI;

– MDAQ (multifunction data acquisition) interface with Ethernet bus, equipped with at least an ADC (analog-to-digital converter) and a DAC (digital-to-analog converter);

– source of power lighting (block of 2 lamps with dimmable electronic ballast);

– source of light disturbance, in the form of a controlled on/off light lamp;

– work site with controllable lighting flux aided by a local computer;

– light sensor (photosensitive resistance).

Figures 8.1(b) and 8.1(c) represent, respectively, the sampled and discrete block diagrams of the computer-aided complete system of light control. Two important parts can be noted:

– dynamic system for digital control of power lighting;

– MMMI-aided PC controller.

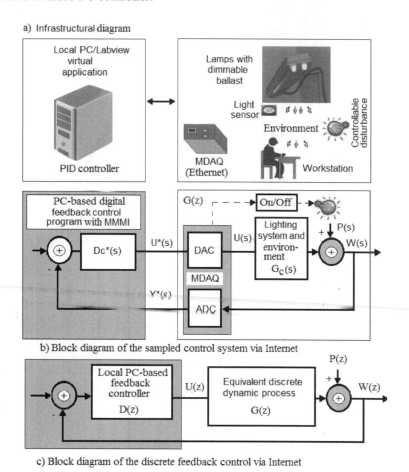

a) Infrastructural diagram

b) Block diagram of the sampled control system via Internet

c) Block diagram of the discrete feedback control via Internet

Figure 8.1. *Diagrams of the experimental system for lighting control*

8.2.2. *Dynamic model of the real power lighting system*

The transfer functions for the lighting system with lighted environment and working area, which have been determined using the Strejc method based on the experimental open-loop step response, are given by [8.1] and [8.2]:

$$G(s) = \frac{W(s)}{U(s)} = \frac{K_w}{(1+T_w s)^2} \; e^{-a s} \; \text{ with } K_w = k_y \, k_W \qquad [8.1]$$

$$G(z) = z^{-m} \left(\frac{z-1}{z} \right) Z \left(\frac{K_w}{s \,(1+\tau_w s)^2} \right) \qquad [8.2]$$

with:

- $K_y = 0.87$;
- $k_w = 0.5648$;
- $K_W = 0.4914$;
- $T_w = 0.035$ s;
- $a \approx 0.005$;
- K_y: static gain of the source device;
- k_W: static gain of the lighting environment;
- m: order required for the rationalization of the z-transform of [8.1].

After the expansion and simplification, relation [8.2] becomes:

$$G(z) = K_w \frac{(1 - e^{-aT} - aT \, e^{-aT}) \, z + (e^{-2aT} - e^{-aT} + aT \, e^{-aT})}{z^m \, (z - e^{-aT})^2} \qquad [8.3]$$

8.2.3. *Dynamic model of the PID controller for power lighting*

Let us remember that the transfer function $D_c(s) = U(s)/E(s) = K_p + 1/(T_i s) + T_d s$ of the PID controller, which is discretized using the Tustin method, can be written as:

$$D(z) = K_p \frac{\left(1 + \dfrac{T}{2\,T_i} + 2\dfrac{T_d}{T}\right) z^2 + (\dfrac{T}{T_i} - 4\dfrac{T_d}{T}) \, z + \left(\dfrac{T}{2\,T_i} + 2\dfrac{T_d}{T} - 1\right)}{z^2 - z} \qquad [8.4]$$

Thus, the digital feedback control law for lighting using the input data K_p, T_i and T_d captured by the MMMI corresponds to [8.5]:

$$u(k) = u(k-1) + a_0 e(k) + a_1\ e(k-1) + a_2 e(k-2)$$

$$\text{with}\ \begin{cases} a_2 = K_p\ \left(1 + 2\dfrac{T_d}{T} + \dfrac{T}{2\,T_i}\right), \\[2ex] a_1 = K_p\ \left(\dfrac{T}{T_i} - 4\dfrac{T_d}{T}\right), \\[2ex] a_0 = K_p\ \left(\dfrac{T}{2\,T_i} + 2\dfrac{T_d}{T} - 1\right) \end{cases}$$

[8.5]

8.2.4. *MMMI-aided Labview application*

Figure 8.2 presents a screenshot of the MMMI of the Labview client/server application for the automation of experimental tasks launched by any online remote operator.

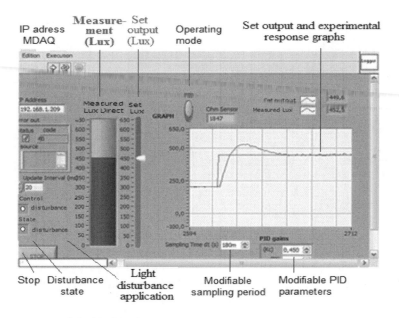

Figure 8.2. *MMMI of the Labview client/server application. For a color version of this figure, see www.iste.co.uk/mbihi/regulation.zip*

This figure shows the required strategic data, which have been used during the construction phase for the validation of the experimental digital control system of power lighting in a remote working site.

8.3. Topology of the remotely operated automation laboratory

Figure 8.3 presents the diagrams of the new REOPAULAB for power lighting control in a work site. It shows the infrastructural diagram (Figure 8.3(a)), as well as the diagram of the discrete closed-loop control system via the Internet (Figure 8.3(b)).

It is worth noting that the set output quantity $Y_r'(z)$ coming from the other end of the world via the Internet could arrive at the local PC server with a certain time delay $T_r = \alpha T$, where T is the sampling period. If α is an integer quantity, then $Y_r(z) = z^{-\alpha}Y_r'(z)$. The same applies to MMMIs that could experience a delayed display with respect to its locally originated image. Nevertheless, if α is slightly time-variant, the quantities received via the Internet will be simply shifted in time, no morphological change being involved.

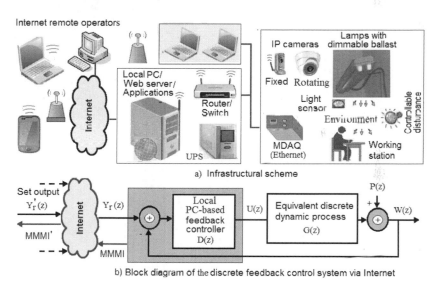

a) Infrastructural scheme

b) Block diagram of the discrete feedback control system via Internet

Figure 8.3. *Diagrams of the REOPAULAB for lighting control. For a color version of this figure, see www.iste.co.uk/mbihi/regulation.zip*

8.3.1. *Hardware infrastructure*

As it can be noted in Figure 8.3(a), the experimental power lighting control system on the local server PC side is equipped with supplementary instrumentation hardware, among which a fixed IP camera, a rotating IP camera, a router/WiFi *switch* and a backup power source. Figure 8.4 presents a snapshot of the remotely operated experimental platform installed in a specialized site of lecture hall 300 of ENSET at the University of Douala.

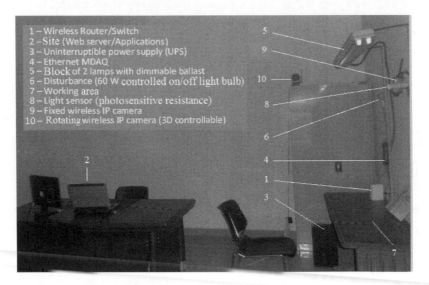

1 – Wireless Router/Switch
2 – Site (Web server/Applications)
3 – Uninterruptible power supply (UPS)
4 – Ethernet MDAQ
5 – Block of 2 lamps with dimmable ballast
6 – Disturbance (60 W controlled on/off light bulb)
7 – Working area
8 – Light sensor (photosensitive resistance)
9 – Fixed wireless IP camera
10 – Rotating wireless IP camera (3D controllable)

Figure 8.4. *Snapshot of the remotely operated experimental platform [PAU 16]*

8.3.2. *Specialized infrastructure on the server side*

8.3.2.1. *Software applications*

The server PC is equipped with two specialized software applications, as follows:

– MMMI-aided Labview application, developed for real-time digital control of the power lighting system, with experimental data monitoring. An example of MMMI display of this remotely operated automation laboratory is presented in Figure 8.5, which shows strategic information, such as:

- display area of the name of the IP address for access to laboratory;

- video area of the lighting arrangement;

- 3D rotation control matrix of the experimental site scan camera;

- area of the site scanned by the rotating camera, etc.;

– Labview web application, in charge of collecting and applying the set outputs and setting data of any authorized web client to the experimental system, and of deploying the instances of real local MMMI to this client;

– TeamViewer (client/web server) application, which can be used, if needed, as a replacement tool for the Labview web server.

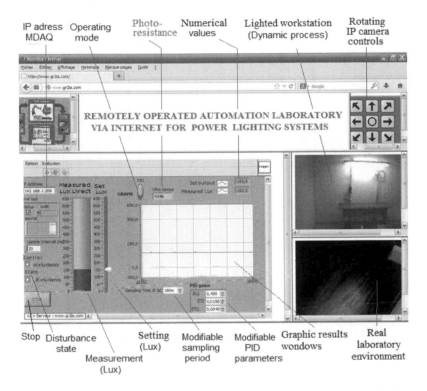

Figure 8.5. *MMMI display of the complete Labview application [PAU 16].* *For a color version of this figure, see www.iste.co.uk/mbihi/regulation.zip*

It is worth noting that on the graph observed, the unit of the time axis corresponds to the number of samples treated under the sampling period T, which the remote operator can modify, if needed. For example, for T, if N_1 and N_2

designate the respective displayed values of the left and right boundaries of the abscissa axis, then the time range corresponds to $[N_1 \times 20 \quad N_2 \times 20]$ ms, and it represents $20T(N_2 - N_1)$ ms.

8.3.2.2. Labview/TeamViewer web server(s)

Two optional web servers are considered, depending on the availability of the Domain Name Server (DNS). These are Labview and TeamViewer web servers.

The Labview server is high priority when DNS is available based on a yearly fee that can be paid to the Internet access provider. Otherwise, TeamViewer's web server can be used as a backup deployment tool.

However, already authorized web clients are duly registered in the database of each web server.

8.3.3. Infrastructure on the remote operator side

If Labview web server is active via a valid DNS, then the remote operator terminal should be equipped with:

– Labview runtime engine, compatible with Labview application version that runs on the host server side;

– web browser: Internet Explorer, Netscape, Mozilla, etc.

On the contrary, if the TeamViewer web server is active, then the remote operator terminal should also be equipped with:

– TeamViewer client compatible with Teamviewer server version;

– web browser: Internet Explorer, Netscape, Mozilla, etc.

8.4. Use of a remotely operated laboratory via the Internet

8.4.1. Procedure instruction sheet

An access instruction sheet is provided to each web client after his registration in the database of local web servers. Table 8.2 presents a sample of an instruction sheet that requires frequent updating by the system administrator of this remotely operated laboratory, which has been installed on a site in lecture hall number 300 of the ENSET campus of Douala, as part of a PhD research project on the subject of industrial automation and computing [PAU 16].

No.	EXPERIMENTS	CONCEPTS TO BE TESTED

An MMMI as shown previously will be displayed on the screen of your Internet terminal as soon as your web query for access to our automation laboratory is validated by the host server.

Experiments and concepts to be tested		
No.	EXPERIMENTS	CONCEPTS TO BE TESTED
1	Open loop without disturbance	Input delay, damping, static error
2	Open loop with disturbance	Sensitivity
3	PID control without disturbance	Response time, overshoot, stability, accuracy
4	PID control with disturbance	Robustness
5	Variation of parameters K_{pd}, T_i and T_d	Complementarity of PID parameters K_p, T_i and T_d
6	Variation of T	Sampling and the Nyquist theorem
Procedure		
0	Three formats of experimental responses to specified settings on MMMI: a) graph; b) video image of the lighting device on the right and at the top of MMMI; c) video image of the lighted working surface on the right and at the bottom of MMMI.	
1	Click the "Run" arrow of the menu to start the system	
2	"PID" button in low position: "Open-loop" mode	
3	"PID" button in high position: "PID control" mode	
4	"Setting Lux" bar: variation of light setting	
5	"Disturbance control" button: sets the disturbing lamp on	

Table 8.2. *Instruction sheet for REOPAULAB remote operators*

8.4.2. Samples of test results obtained with REOPAULAB

Figure 8.6 shows the test results obtained via a PC connected to the Internet network of the ENSET campus of Douala. Figure 8.6(a) corresponds to the active open-loop control mode with a setting of 350 Lux in the presence of a light disturbance of the order of 125 Lux. Under these conditions, a steady state response of around 600 Lux can be noted, which means that a light disturbance has an additional lighting effect, which contributes to improved energy savings. On the contrary, Figure 8.6(b) shows that in the presence of a PID controller, the response to a light step with a setting of 450 Lux offers, in the presence of disturbance and after a brief transient, a null static error. These results illustrate the practical interest of computer-aided automated control of power lighting systems.

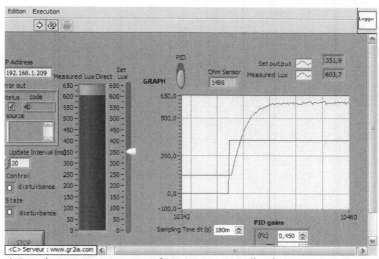

a) Open-loop response to a step of 350 Lux step 125 disturbance

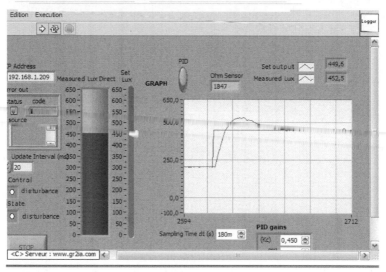

b) Step response with a PID controller in operation

Figure 8.6. *Examples of test results via a local Internet network. For a color version of this figure, see www.iste.co.uk/mbihi/regulation.zip*

Further important test results that were obtained locally are summarized in Figure 8.7, which shows the robustness of the PID control system when settings change (see Figure 8.7(a)) and when it is subjected to a permanent or brief disturbance (see Figure 8.7(b)).

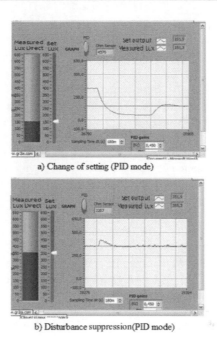

a) Change of setting (PID mode)

b) Disturbance suppression(PID mode)

Figure 8.7. *Further test results obtained using a local Internet network. For a color version of this figure, see www.iste.co.uk/mbihi/regulation.zip*

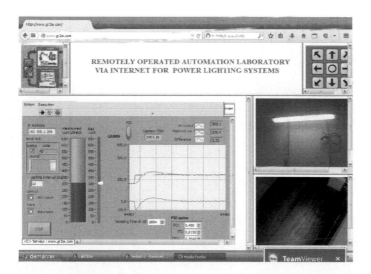

Figure 8.8. *REOPAULAB test results obtained from Lens in France. For a color version of this figure, see www.iste.co.uk/mbihi/regulation.zip*

On the contrary, Figure 8.8 presents a sample of obtained test results without online support in 2016, from Lens, by a remote operator during a post-doctoral program in France. As per our request, he had first downloaded and installed the TeamViewer client (default Labview server and Labview Runtime Engine) on its access terminal, which already featured the Mozilla browser. He had also received a copy of the instruction sheet presented in Table 8.2 as well as his user identification name (ID) and his password (PWD) by e-mail.

The experiments were conducted by this remote operator during his assigned time frame, without assistance or trainer presence, from his Internet terminal in Lens (France). He then sent the screenshots of several experimental results obtained in virtual reality from his terminal located in Lens by e-mail.

Thus, the presented results show that our REOPAULAB model, which has been described in this chapter, is effectively accessible from anywhere in the world by automation students, provided that they have access authorization and are connected to the Internet. This chapter has therefore revealed the secrets of the design and construction of a remotely operated automation laboratory via the Internet.

Finally, it is worth noting that the first REOPAULAB prototype, presented in this chapter, can be operated (online, on a wide scale due to 4G or 5G mobile communication technology) from anywhere in the world without trainer(s) or technician(s) assistance on the auto-pilot experimental site.

8.5. Exercises and solutions

Exercise 8.1.

The most frequently used real dynamic processes in remotely operated automation laboratories are servomechanisms. What are the main reasons that justify this fact?

Solution – Exercise 8.1.

The two main reasons that justify the use of servomechanisms in most remotely operated laboratories are:

– they are widespread and well-known dynamic systems;

– they are formed of mobile parts with perceptible controlled motion that generates an attractive visual effect for student operators.

Exercise 8.2.

What are the reasons for the creation of remotely operated automation laboratories based on a power lighting device?

Solution – Exercise 8.2.

The reasons for the creation of remotely operated automation laboratories based on a power lighting device are the following:

– power lighting represents a permanent social need in all sectors of human activity;

– important problems of increasing interest for automation:

- quality of lighting comfort according to NF EN 12464-1 standards;

- artificial lighting energy savings in the presence of uncertain or insufficient daylight sources.

– convenient deployment of disturbing lamps with controllable source;

– the level of perceptible lighting is an important visual factor for student operators.

Exercise 8.3.

A dynamic power lighting device exhibits a pure input delay of the order of $\tau_0 = 10$ ms. What interest might this delay phenomenon present in the context of a remotely operated automation laboratory?

Solution – Exercise 8.3.

In the context of a remotely operated automation laboratory that has a dynamic power lighting device, this significant delay of $\tau_0 = 10$ ms could absorb the average value and the variance of uncertain time of propagation of the setting through the Internet.

Otherwise, the Internet network would tend to have an upstream behavior on the web server side, similar to time-variant transmission media.

Exercise 8.4.

What are the hardware and software tools used in the implementation of the remotely operated automation laboratory described in this chapter?

Solution – Exercise 8.4.

Hardware and software tools used:

– hardware tools on the server side: fixed IP camera, rotating IP camera, lighting module equipped with two lamps with dimmable electronic ballast, disturbing lamp that can be controlled by a PC via electric relay, MDAQ (multifunction data acquisition module) and Ethernet;

– hardware tools on the remote operator side: PC for Internet access, TeamViewer client and Labview runtime engine;

– software tools on the local web server side: Labview application, MDAQ driver, Labview server, Labview web application and TeamViewer client/server;

– software tools on the local web server side: Labview runtime engine and TeamViewer client.

Exercise 8.5.

The use of several combined technologies is unavoidable when creating digital control systems for dynamic processes. Several typical examples of such technologies are the following:

– multimedia programming;

– object-oriented programming;

– Ethernet communication;

– virtual reality modeling;

– WiFi communication;

– Bluetooth communication;

– software driver of peripheral hardware.

From the above list, choose the technologies used for the creation of the Labview application that runs on the web server side. Then, give a reason for each choice of technology, specifying the corresponding target integration media.

Solution – Exercise 8.5.

Technological choices and underlying reasons:

– multimedia programming for the MMMI creation;

– Ethernet communication for the connection between local PC and MDAQ;

– WiFi communication for the connection between IP cameras, WiFi and PC;

– software driver for the peripheral hardware for MDAQ.

Exercise 8.6.

MMMI of the remotely operated automation laboratory presented in this chapter contains modifiable data fields (sampling period T, PID parameters, etc.).

a) What are the risks generated by arbitrary modifications of these data?

b) What strategies allow the elimination of these risks at the stage of development of the virtual instrumentation software module?

Solution – Exercise 8.6.

a) The risks generated by arbitrary modifications performed by remote operators are:

– the operator may input erroneous data;

– the operator may input data that are incompatible with the limit characteristics of the real equipment installed.

b) The strategy that allows the elimination of these risks involves planning preliminary data validation procedures before data processing.

Exercise 8.7.

What are the main concepts of basic automation that can be remotely tested in the virtual environment of the remotely operated laboratory presented in this chapter?

Solution – Exercise 8.7.

No.	Basic automation concepts that can remotely be tested
1	Dynamic process with pure input delay;
2	Shortcoming of an open-loop dynamic system: static error, sensitivity, etc.;
3	PID control of lighting comfort;
4	Complementarity of PID controller parameters;
5	Performance-related quantities: stability, rapidity, overshoot, accuracy, robustness, etc.;
6	Effect of setting change;
7	Lighting energy savings;
8	Effects of sampling period and the Nyquist theorem.

Table 8.3. *Solution to exercise 8.7*

Exercise 8.8.

Figure 8.9 presents the VMMI (virtual man–machine interface) of the remotely operated automation laboratory described in this chapter. Knowing that the time axis corresponds to the number of samples processed under a sampling period T = 180 ms, find the approximate characteristics of the observed step response of 250 Lux.

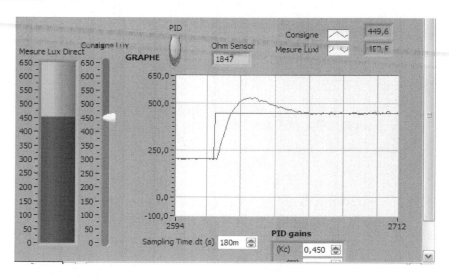

Figure 8.9. *MMMI of the remotely operated automation laboratory. For a color version of this figure, see www.iste.co.uk/mbihi/regulation.zip*

Solution – Exercise 8.8.

The approximate characteristics of the observed step response of 250 Lux in Figure 8.9 are:

– overshoot: 525 – 500 = 25 Lux;

– response time: (2712 – 2594) / 7 × 180 ms × 2 div ≈ 6 s;

– static error: 0.

Exercise 8.9.

Figure 8.10 presents a screenshot of VMMI of the remotely operated automation laboratory described in this chapter. The graph of the response in the PID control mode can be observed for a persistent light disturbance applied in a steady state.

a) Explain the shape of this response.

b) Prove that the disturbance effect is reflected by energy savings in the power lighting device.

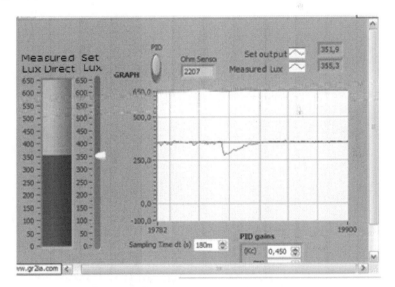

Figure 8.10. *Screenshot of MMMI of the remotely operated automation laboratory. For a color version of this figure, see www.iste.co.uk/mbihi/regulation.zip*

Solution – Exercise 8.9.

a) Response shape explained: before the disturbance there is a permanent control state with a null static error. The instant of disturbance application is followed by a brief transient state of automatic correction of the disturbance effect. Finally, the system goes back to the steady state, which is maintained due to instantaneous compensation of the persistent effect of the lighting disturbance.

b) Energy savings: let y_r, $y_s(t)$, w and $y(t)$ be the respective lighting quantities of setting, main source, disturbance and output. Then, according to the principle of superposition of linear processes, the following can be written:

$$y(t) = y_s + w$$

Or, knowing that after a brief transient period the static error in the presence of disturbance is again null, then:

$$e(t) = y(t) - y_r = 0 \text{ with } y_r = 350 \text{ Lux}$$

Thus:

$$y_s + w = y_r, \text{ or } y_s = y_r - w$$

In conclusion, the light level y_s generated by the lighting source is automatically reduced to the disturbing value w, which contributed to maintaining the same resulting lighting comfort y. This is the principle of artificial lighting energy saving in the presence of uncertain or insufficient daylight sources.

Appendices

Appendix 1

Table of z-transforms

T₀: Sampling period

Signal $x(t)$	X(s)	$X(z)$
$\delta_1(t) = \begin{cases} 1, & \text{if } t=0 \\ 0, & \text{if } t \neq 0 \end{cases}$	0	$X_z(z) = 1$
$u(t) = \begin{cases} 1, & \text{if } t \geq 0 \\ 0, & \text{if } t < 0 \end{cases}$	$u(s) = \dfrac{1}{s}$	$\dfrac{z}{z-1}$
$t.u(t)$	$\dfrac{1}{s^2}$	$\dfrac{T_0 \cdot z}{[z-1]^2}$
$\dfrac{t^2}{2}.u(t)$	$\dfrac{1}{s^3}$	$\dfrac{T_0^2 \cdot z \cdot [z+1]}{2.[z-1]^3}$
$e^{-a.t}.u(t)$	$\dfrac{1}{s+a}$	$\dfrac{z}{z - e^{-a.T_0}}$
$t.e^{-a.t}.u(t)$	$\dfrac{1}{(s+a)^2}$	$\dfrac{T_0 \cdot z.e^{-a.T_0}}{\left[z - e^{-a.T_0}\right]^2}$
$\dfrac{t^2}{2}.e^{-a.t}.u(t)$	$\dfrac{1}{(s+a)^3}$	$\dfrac{T_0^2 \cdot z.e^{-a.T_0}}{2.\left[z - e^{-a.T_0}\right]^2} + \dfrac{T_e^2 \cdot z.e^{-2.a.T_0}}{\left[z - e^{-a.T_0}\right]^3}$
$\left[1 - e^{-a.t}\right].u(t)$	$\dfrac{a}{s(s+a)}$	$\dfrac{\left(1 - e^{-a.T_0}\right).z}{(z-1).\left(z - e^{-a.T_0}\right)}$

Signal $x(t)$	$X(s)$	$X(z)$
$\left[t - \dfrac{1-e^{-at}}{a}\right].u(t)$	$\dfrac{a}{s^2\,(s+a)}$	$\dfrac{T_0.z}{(z-1)^2} - \dfrac{\left(1-e^{-a.T_0}\right).z}{a.(z-1).\left(z-e^{-a.T_0}\right)}$
$\dfrac{1}{2}\left[t^2 - \dfrac{2t}{a} + \dfrac{2}{a^2}.\left(1-e^{-at}\right)\right].u(t)$	$\dfrac{a}{s^3\,(s+a)}$	$\dfrac{T_e^2.z}{(z-1)^3} + \dfrac{(a.T_e-2).T_e.z}{2.a.(z-1)^2}$ $+\dfrac{z}{a^2.(z-1)} - \dfrac{z}{a^2.\left(z-e^{-a.T_e}\right)}$
$\sin\left(\omega_0 t\right).u(t)$	$\dfrac{\omega_0}{s^2+\omega_0^2}$	$\dfrac{z.\sin\left(\omega_0.T_0\right)}{z^2 - 2.z.\cos\left(\omega_0.T_0\right)+1}$
$\cos\left(\omega_0 t\right).u(t)$	$\dfrac{s}{s^2+\omega_0^2}$	$\dfrac{z.\left[z-\cos\left(\omega_0.T_0\right)\right]}{z^2 - 2.z.\cos\left(\omega_0.T_0\right)+1}$
$\left[1-\cos\left(\omega_0 t\right)\right].u(t)$	$\dfrac{\omega_0^2}{s\left(s^2+\omega_0^2\right)}$	$\dfrac{z}{z-1} - \dfrac{z.\left[z-\cos\left(\omega_0.T_0\right)\right]}{z^2 - 2.z.\cos\left(\omega_0.T_0\right)+1}$
$\left[1-(1+at).e^{-at}\right].u(t)$	$\dfrac{a^2}{s\,(s+a)^2}$	$\dfrac{(1-e^{-aT_0}-aT_0e^{-aT_0})}{(z-1)\,(z-e^{-aT})^2}\,z^2 +$ $\dfrac{(e^{-2aT_0}-e^{-aT_0}+aT_0e^{-aT_0})}{(z-1)\,(z-e^{-aT})^2}\,z$
$e^{-at}.\sin\left(\omega_0 t\right).u(t)$	$\dfrac{\omega_0}{(s+a)^2+\omega_0^2}$	$\dfrac{z.e^{-a.T_0}.\sin\left(\omega_0.T_0\right)}{z^2 - 2.z.e^{-a.T_0}.\cos\left(\omega_0.T_0\right)+e^{-2.a.T_0}}$
$e^{-at}.\cos\left(\omega_0 t\right).u(t)$	$\dfrac{s+a}{(s+a)^2+\omega_0^2}$	$\dfrac{z.\left[z-e^{-a.T_0}.\cos\left(\omega_0.T_0\right)\right]}{z^2 - 2.z.e^{-a.T_0}.\cos\left(\omega_0.T_0\right)+e^{-2.a.T_0}}$
$A\,e^{-\xi\omega_n t}\sin\left(\omega_n\sqrt{1-\xi^2}\,t\right)$ with $A=\dfrac{\omega_n}{\sqrt{1-\xi^2}}$	$\dfrac{\omega_n^2}{s^2+2\xi\omega_n s+\omega_n^2}$	$\dfrac{\omega_n\,e^{-\xi\omega_n T}\sin\left(\omega_n\sqrt{1-\xi^2}\,T\right)z}{z^2 - 2e^{-\xi\omega_n T}\cos\left(\omega_n\sqrt{1-\xi^2}\,T\right)z+e^{-2\xi\omega_n T}}$

Table A1.1. *Table of z-transforms (T: sampling period)*

Appendix 2

Matlab Elements Used in this Book

This table summarizing Matlab® elements previously appeared in [MBI 18].

Category	Elements	Description of elements
Specific symbols	%	Comment
	=	Assignment
	'	Transpose
	,	Argument separator/end of command
	;	No display of the result of command
	...	Line continuation
	[,], [;]	Brackets of vector/matrix elements
	:	Separator of indices of a sequential data
	( )	Parentheses of arguments of a function
Arithmetic operators (applicable to vectors/matrices according to context)	+ and .+	Addition
	- and .-	Subtraction
	* and .*	Multiplication
	/ and ./	Division
	^ and .^	Power
Relational operators	<	Less than
	<=	Less than or equal to
	>	Greater than
	>=	Greater than or equal to
	==	Equal to
	~=	Not equal to

Category	Elements	Description of elements
General primitives	clear	Data deletion in progress
	clg	Deletion of figure content in progress
	function	Function defined by the programmer
	load	Reading in the disk object *.mat
	num2str	Conversion from number to string
	save	Storage in the disk object *.mat
Graphic management of figure object in progress	axis	Ranges of axes of a figure layout
	deploy	Deployment of the Matlab application for Windows
	figure	Figure object
	get	Recovery of the property(properties) of GUI object
	grid	Grid drawing on the figure
	gtext	Text display at a point of a figure object
	guide	Activation of the Matlab GUI editor
	hold on/off	Management of figure content memorization
	image	(GUI) image object
	imshow	Image display in progress
	plot	Graph plotting with a default pattern "*"
	preview	Displays video data on GUI video window
	set	Writing of GUI object property
	stem	Graph plotting with a stem pattern
	subplot	Division of a figure into $n \times m$ cells
	text	Graphic display of x
	title	Titling of a figure
	videoinput	Creation of video object
	xlabel	Text display in the ordinate
	ylabel	Text display in the ordinate
Arithmetic calculation applicable to vectors/matrices according to context	cos	Cosine function
	diag	Creation of diagonal matrix
	exp	Exponential function
	floor	Rounding to nearest integer less than or equal to an element
	length	Dimension
	log	Logarithm of base e
	ones	Unit vector/matrix object
	rank	Rank of a matrix
	sin	Sine function
	sqrt	Square root

Category	Elements	Description of elements
Management of dynamic models	c2d	Discretization of continuous model
	ctrb	Returns the controllability matrix
	ctrbf	Returns the controllable form
	d2c	Reconstruction of continuous model
	eig	Calculation of eigenvalues and eigenvectors
	feedback	Object creation: feedback loop
	iddata	Data of identified model
	obsv	Calculation of observability matrix
	parallel	Object creation: parallel association
	obsvf	Returns the observable form
	p = tf('p')	Symbolic variable for the transfer function $G_c(p)$
	series	Object creation: series association
	ss	Object creation: state model
	s = tf('s')	Symbolic variable for $G_c(s)$
	tf	Object creation: transfer function
	tfdata	Data of the transfer function object
	tfest	Object creation: estimator of $G_c(s)$
	z = tf('z')	Symbolic variable for the transfer function $G(z)$
	place	Pole placement gain
Synthesis of controllers	acker	Pole placement Ackermann's gain
	dlqg	Parameters of discrete LQG controller
	dlqr	Parameters of discrete LQR controller
	lqr	Parameters of continuous LQR controller
	lqg	Parameters of continuous LQG controller
	Bode	Bode diagram
Model simulation (default plot of data graph)	dlsim	Discrete time response
	dstep	Discrete time step response
	lsim	Continuous time response
	step	Continuous time step response
Programming structures	for … end	Processing loop
	if … end	Simple/multiple conditional switch

Table A2.1. *Matlab elements used in this book*

Appendix 3

Discretization of Transfer Functions

A3.1. Discretization of transfer functions of dynamic processes

For a dynamic process modeled by a transfer function $G_c(s)$, the discretization of $G_c(s)$ is done using the step invariance method, which is defined by the following algorithm:

$$G(z) = \left(\frac{z-1}{z}\right) Z\left(\frac{G_c(s)}{s}\right)$$

where $Z(.)$ designates the z-transform of the argument $G_c(s)/s$.

Methods for the discretization of $D_c(s)$	D(z) obtained for the PID analog controller described by: $Dc(s) = Kp\left(1+\dfrac{1}{Ti\,s}Td\,s\right)$
First-order Euler transformation $s \rightarrow \dfrac{z\text{-}1}{T}$	$D(z) = K_p \dfrac{\dfrac{T_d}{T}z^2 + \left(1-2\dfrac{T_d}{T}\right)z + \dfrac{T}{T_i} + \dfrac{T_d}{T} - 1}{z-1}$
Second-order Euler transformation $s \rightarrow \dfrac{z\text{-}1}{T\,z}$	$D(z) = K_p \dfrac{\left(1+\dfrac{T}{T_i}+\dfrac{T_d}{T}\right)z^2 - \left(1+2\dfrac{T_d}{T}\right)z + \dfrac{T_d}{T}}{z^2 - z}$
Tustin transformation $s \rightarrow \left(\dfrac{2}{T}\right)\left(\dfrac{z-1}{z+1}\right)$	$D(z) = K_p \dfrac{\left(\dfrac{T}{2\,T_i}+2\dfrac{T_d}{T}+1\right)z^2 + \left(\dfrac{T}{T_i}-4\dfrac{T_d}{T}\right)z + \dfrac{T}{2\,T_i}+2\dfrac{T_d}{T}-1}{z^2 - 1}$

Table A3.1. *Discretization of transfer functions of the PID controllers*

A3.2. Discretization of transfer functions of analog controllers

There are several techniques for the discretization of transfer functions of analog controllers. Tables A3.1 and A3.2, which have been extracted from [MBI 18], summarize the results obtained by applying several discretization techniques to the respective cases of the PID and PIDF analog controllers.

Methods for the discretization of $D_c(s)$	$D(z)$ obtained for the PIDF controller described by: $$Dc(s) = Kp\left(1 + \frac{1}{Ti\,s} + \frac{Td\,s}{1 + Tf\,s}\right)$$
First-order Euler transformation $s \to \dfrac{z\text{-}1}{T}$	$$D(z) = \frac{K_p\left(a_0 z^2 + a_1 z + a_2\right)}{T_i(z-1)\,(T_f z + T - T_f)} \text{ avec}$$ $$\begin{cases} a_0 = T_i T_f + T_d T_i \\ a_1 = T_i(T - T_f) + (T - T_i)\,T_f - 2T_d T_i \\ a_2 = (T - T_i)\,(T - T_f) + T_d T_i \end{cases}$$
Second-order Euler transformation $s \to \dfrac{z\text{-}1}{T\,z}$	$$D(z) = \frac{K_p\left(a_0 z^2 + a_1 z + a_2\right)}{T_i(z-1)\left((T - T_f)z - T_f\right)} \text{ avec}$$ $$\begin{cases} a_0 = (T + T_i)\,(T + T_f) + T_d T_i \\ a_1 = T_f(T + T) + (T + T_f)\,T_i + 2T_d T_i \\ a_2 = T_i T_f + T_d T_i \end{cases}$$
Tustin transformation $s \to \left(\dfrac{2}{T}\right)\left(\dfrac{z-1}{z+1}\right)$	$$D(z) = \frac{K_p\left(a_0 z^2 + a_1 z + a_2\right)}{2\,T_i(z-1)\,((T + 2T_f)z + T - 2T_f)}$$ $$\text{with} \begin{cases} a_0 = (T + 2T_i)\,(T + 2T_f) + 4T_d T_i \\ a_1 = 2T^2 - 8T_i(T_f + T_d) \\ a_2 = (T - 2T_i)\,(T - 2T_f) + 4T_d T_i \end{cases}$$

Table A3.2. *Discretization of transfer functions of the PIDF controllers*

Bibliography

[AFN 11] AFNOR, Lumière et éclairage – Eclairage des milieux de travail: Partie I, lieux de travail intérieur, NF EN 12464-1, AFNOR Editions, June 2011.

[BAG 93] BAGCHI A., *Optimal Control of Stochastic Systems*, Prentice Hall, 1993.

[BEN 96] BENNETT S., "A brief history of automatic control", *IEEE Control Systems*, pp. 17–25, June 1996.

[BIS 09] BISSELL C., "A history of automatic control", in NOF S.Y. (ed.), *Springer Handbook of Automation*, Springer, Berlin, 2009.

[CHE 84] CHEN C.T., *Linear System Theory and Design*, Hold Rinehart and Winston Inc., New York, 1984.

[FOU 87] FOULARD C., GENTIL S., SANDRAZ J.P., *Commande et régulation par calculateur numérique: De la théorie aux applications*, Eyrolles, 1987.

[KAL 58] KALMAN R.E., KOEPCKE R.W., "Optimal synthesis of linear sampling control systems using generalized performance indexes", *Transactions on ASME*, vol. 80, pp. 1820–1826, 1958.

[KAL 60a] KALMAN R.E., "Contributions to the theory of optimal control", *Boletin de la Sociedad Matematica Mexicana*, vol. 5, pp. 102–119, 1960.

[KAL 60b] KALMAN R.E., "A new approach to linear filtering and predictions problems", *Transactions of the ASEM Journal of Basic Engineering*, vol. 82, pp. 35–45, 1960.

[KAL 61] KALMAN R.E., BUCY R.S., "New results in linear filtering and predictions", *Transactions of the ASME Journal of Basic Engineering*, vol. 83, pp. 83–108, 1961.

[LEW 95] LEWIS F.L., *Applied Optimal Control and Estimation*, Prentice Hall, 1995.

[LUX 04] LUX, "Cahier Technique", *Revue européenne de l'éclairage*, no. 228, pp. 45–50, June 2004.

[MBI 05] MBIHI J., *Informatique et automation – automatismes programmables contrôlés par ordinateur*, Editions Publibook, Saint-Denis, 2005.

[MBI 12] MBIHI J., MOTTO A., *Informatique Industrielle – Instrumentation virtuelle assistée par ordinateur: Principes et techniques, Cours et exercices corrigés*, Editions Ellipses, Paris, 2012.

[MBI 15a] MBIHI J., "A PC-based workbench for virtual instrumentation and automatic control using Matlab GUI/MEX-C++ application", *WSEAS Transactions on Advances in Engineering Education*, vol. 12, pp. 52–62, 2015.

[MBI 15b] MBIHI J., "A flexible multimedia workbench for digital control of input-delay servo systems", *Journal of Computer Science and Control Engineering*, vol. 8, no. 2, pp. 35–40, 2015.

[MBI 16] MBIHI J., "Graphical design and virtual simulation of deterministic and stochastic of optimal control systems", *European Journal of Automation*, Lavoisier, July 2016.

[MBI 17] MBIHI J., "Application Matlab/GUI déployée de conception et simulation graphique rapide de systèmes de commande optimale et stochastique", 5ᵉ *Colloque International du RAIFFET*, Douala, October 2017.

[MBI 18] MBIHI J., *Analog Automation and Digital Feedback Control Techniques*, ISTE Ltd, London and John Wiley & Sons, New York, 2018.

[PAU 14] PAUNÉ F., MBIHI J., KOM M. *et al.*, "A new architectural control scheme for power lighting systems", *Journal of Control Engineering and Technology*, vol. 4, no. 3, pp. 174–182, available at: www.ijcet.org, June 2014.

[PAU 16a] PAUNÉ F., Etude et prototypage d'un laboratoire d'automatique classique télé-opérable de systèmes dynamiques d'éclairage de lieux de travail, PhD thesis, ENSET, University of Douala, July 2016.

[PAU 16b] PAUNÉ F., MBIHI J., "A novel web based laboratory for remote control of power lighting processes", *WSEAS Transactions on Advances in Engineering Education*, vol. 13, pp. 7–19, 2016.

[PAU 17] PAUNÉ F., MBIHI J., "Nouvelle Topologie de Partage de Laboratoires Télé-Opérables via Internet", 5ᵉ *Colloque International du RAIFFET*, Douala, October 2017.

[RUB 12] RUBA M.K., HUMMANDI A.L., "Simulation of optimal speed control for a DC motor using linear quadratic regulator", *Journal of Engineering*, vol. 18, no. 3, pp. 340–349, 2012.

[SIO 96] SIOURIS G.M., *An Engineering Approach to Optimal Control and Estimation Theory*, John Wiley & Sons, 1996.

[ZIE 43] ZIEGLER J.G., NICHOLS N.B., "Optimum settings for automatic controllers", *ASME Transactions*, vol. 65, pp. 433–444, 1943.

Index

Other titles from

in

Systems and Industrial Engineering – Robotics

2018

BERRAH Lamia, CLIVILLÉ Vincent, FOULLOY Laurent
Industrial Objectives and Industrial Performance: Concepts and Fuzzy Handling

GONZALEZ-FELIU Jesus
Sustainable Urban Logistics: Planning and Evaluation

GROUS Ammar
Applied Mechanical Design

LEROY Alain
Production Availability and Reliability: Use in the Oil and Gas Industry

MARÉ Jean-Charles
Aerospace Actuators 3: European Commercial Aircraft and Tiltrotor Aircraft

MAXA Jean-Aimé, BEN MAHMOUD Mohamed Slim, LARRIEU Nicolas
Model-driven Development for Embedded Software: Application to Communications for Drone Swarm

MBIHI Jean
Analog Automation and Digital Feedback Control Techniques

SIMON Christophe, WEBER Philippe, SALLAK Mohamed
Data Uncertainty and Important Measures
(Systems Dependability Assessment Set – Volume 3)

2017

ANDRÉ Jean-Claude
From Additive Manufacturing to 3D/4D Printing 1: From Concepts to Achievements
From Additive Manufacturing to 3D/4D Printing 2: Current Techniques, Improvements and their Limitations
From Additive Manufacturing to 3D/4D Printing 3: Breakthrough Innovations: Programmable Material, 4D Printing and Bio-printing

ARCHIMÈDE Bernard, VALLESPIR Bruno
Enterprise Interoperability: INTEROP-PGSO Vision

CAMMAN Christelle, FIORE Claude, LIVOLSI Laurent, QUERRO Pascal
Supply Chain Management and Business Performance: The VASC Model

FEYEL Philippe
Robust Control, Optimization with Metaheuristics

MARÉ Jean-Charles
Aerospace Actuators 2: Signal-by-Wire and Power-by-Wire

POPESCU Dumitru, AMIRA Gharbi, STEFANOIU Dan, BORNE Pierre
Process Control Design for Industrial Applications

RÉVEILLAC Jean-Michel
Modeling and Simulation of Logistics Flows 1: Theory and Fundamentals
Modeling and Simulation of Logistics Flows 2: Dashboards, Traffic Planning and Management
Modeling and Simulation of Logistics Flows 3: Discrete and Continuous Flows in 2D/3D

2016

ANDRÉ Michel, SAMARAS Zissis
Energy and Environment
(Research for Innovative Transports Set - Volume 1)

AUBRY Jean-François, BRINZEI Nicolae, MAZOUNI Mohammed-Habib
Systems Dependability Assessment: Benefits of Petri Net Models (Systems Dependability Assessment Set - Volume 1)

BLANQUART Corinne, CLAUSEN Uwe, JACOB Bernard
Towards Innovative Freight and Logistics (Research for Innovative Transports Set - Volume 2)

COHEN Simon, YANNIS George
Traffic Management (Research for Innovative Transports Set - Volume 3)

MARÉ Jean-Charles
Aerospace Actuators 1: Needs, Reliability and Hydraulic Power Solutions

REZG Nidhal, HAJEJ Zied, BOSCHIAN-CAMPANER Valerio
Production and Maintenance Optimization Problems: Logistic Constraints and Leasing Warranty Services

TORRENTI Jean-Michel, LA TORRE Francesca
Materials and Infrastructures 1 (Research for Innovative Transports Set - Volume 5A)
Materials and Infrastructures 2 (Research for Innovative Transports Set - Volume 5B)

WEBER Philippe, SIMON Christophe
Benefits of Bayesian Network Models
(Systems Dependability Assessment Set – Volume 2)

YANNIS George, COHEN Simon
Traffic Safety (Research for Innovative Transports Set - Volume 4)

2015

AUBRY Jean-François, BRINZEI Nicolae
Systems Dependability Assessment: Modeling with Graphs and Finite State Automata

BOULANGER Jean-Louis
CENELEC 50128 and IEC 62279 Standards

BRIFFAUT Jean-Pierre
E-Enabled Operations Management

MISSIKOFF Michele, CANDUCCI Massimo, MAIDEN Neil
Enterprise Innovation

2014

CHETTO Maryline
Real-time Systems Scheduling
Volume 1 – Fundamentals
Volume 2 – Focuses

DAVIM J. Paulo
Machinability of Advanced Materials

ESTAMPE Dominique
Supply Chain Performance and Evaluation Models

FAVRE Bernard
Introduction to Sustainable Transports

GAUTHIER Michaël, ANDREFF Nicolas, DOMBRE Etienne
Intracorporeal Robotics: From Milliscale to Nanoscale

MICOUIN Patrice
Model Based Systems Engineering: Fundamentals and Methods

MILLOT Patrick
Designing Human–Machine Cooperation Systems

NI Zhenjiang, PACORET Céline, BENOSMAN Ryad, RÉGNIER Stéphane
Haptic Feedback Teleoperation of Optical Tweezers

OUSTALOUP Alain
Diversity and Non-integer Differentiation for System Dynamics

REZG Nidhal, DELLAGI Sofien, KHATAD Abdelhakim
Joint Optimization of Maintenance and Production Policies

STEFANOIU Dan, BORNE Pierre, POPESCU Dumitru, FILIP Florin Gh.,
EL KAMEL Abdelkader
*Optimization in Engineering Sciences: Metaheuristics, Stochastic Methods
and Decision Support*

2013

ALAZARD Daniel
Reverse Engineering in Control Design

ARIOUI Hichem, NEHAOUA Lamri
Driving Simulation

CHADLI Mohammed, COPPIER Hervé
Command-control for Real-time Systems

DAAFOUZ Jamal, TARBOURIECH Sophie, SIGALOTTI Mario
Hybrid Systems with Constraints

FEYEL Philippe
Loop-shaping Robust Control

FLAUS Jean-Marie
Risk Analysis: Socio-technical and Industrial Systems

FRIBOURG Laurent, SOULAT Romain
*Control of Switching Systems by Invariance Analysis: Application to Power
Electronics*

GROSSARD Mathieu, REGNIER Stéphane, CHAILLET Nicolas
Flexible Robotics: Applications to Multiscale Manipulations

GRUNN Emmanuel, PHAM Anh Tuan
Modeling of Complex Systems: Application to Aeronautical Dynamics

HABIB Maki K., DAVIM J. Paulo
Interdisciplinary Mechatronics: Engineering Science and Research Development

HAMMADI Slim, KSOURI Mekki
Multimodal Transport Systems

JARBOUI Bassem, SIARRY Patrick, TEGHEM Jacques
Metaheuristics for Production Scheduling

KIRILLOV Oleg N., PELINOVSKY Dmitry E.
Nonlinear Physical Systems

LE Vu Tuan Hieu, STOICA Cristina, ALAMO Teodoro,
CAMACHO Eduardo F., DUMUR Didier
Zonotopes: From Guaranteed State-estimation to Control

MACHADO Carolina, DAVIM J. Paulo
Management and Engineering Innovation

MORANA Joëlle
Sustainable Supply Chain Management

SANDOU Guillaume
Metaheuristic Optimization for the Design of Automatic Control Laws

STOICAN Florin, OLARU Sorin
Set-theoretic Fault Detection in Multisensor Systems

2012

AÏT-KADI Daoud, CHOUINARD Marc, MARCOTTE Suzanne, RIOPEL Diane
Sustainable Reverse Logistics Network: Engineering and Management

BORNE Pierre, POPESCU Dumitru, FILIP Florin G., STEFANOIU Dan
Optimization in Engineering Sciences: Exact Methods

CHADLI Mohammed, BORNE Pierre
Multiple Models Approach in Automation: Takagi-Sugeno Fuzzy Systems

DAVIM J. Paulo
Lasers in Manufacturing

DECLERCK Philippe
Discrete Event Systems in Dioid Algebra and Conventional Algebra

DOUMIATI Moustapha, CHARARA Ali, VICTORINO Alessandro,
LECHNER Daniel
*Vehicle Dynamics Estimation using Kalman Filtering: Experimental
Validation*

GUERRERO José A, LOZANO Rogelio
Flight Formation Control

HAMMADI Slim, KSOURI Mekki
Advanced Mobility and Transport Engineering

MAILLARD Pierre
Competitive Quality Strategies

MATTA Nada, VANDENBOOMGAERDE Yves, ARLAT Jean
Supervision and Safety of Complex Systems

POLER Raul *et al.*
Intelligent Non-hierarchical Manufacturing Networks

TROCCAZ Jocelyne
Medical Robotics

YALAOUI Alice, CHEHADE Hicham, YALAOUI Farouk, AMODEO Lionel
Optimization of Logistics

ZELM Martin *et al.*
Enterprise Interoperability –I-EASA12 Proceedings

2011

CANTOT Pascal, LUZEAUX Dominique
Simulation and Modeling of Systems of Systems

DAVIM J. Paulo
Mechatronics

DAVIM J. Paulo
Wood Machining

GROUS Ammar
Applied Metrology for Manufacturing Engineering

KOLSKI Christophe
Human–Computer Interactions in Transport

LUZEAUX Dominique, RUAULT Jean-René, WIPPLER Jean-Luc
Complex Systems and Systems of Systems Engineering

ZELM Martin, *et al.*
Enterprise Interoperability: IWEI2011 Proceedings

2010

BOTTA-GENOULAZ Valérie, CAMPAGNE Jean-Pierre, LLERENA Daniel,
PELLEGRIN Claude
Supply Chain Performance / Collaboration, Alignement and Coordination

BOURLÈS Henri, GODFREY K.C. Kwan
Linear Systems

BOURRIERES Jean-Paul
Proceedings of CEISIE '09

CHAILLET Nicolas, REGNIER Stéphane
Microrobotics for Micromanipulation

DAVIM J. Paulo
Sustainable Manufacturing

GIORDANO Max, MATHIEU Luc, VILLENEUVE François
Product Life-Cycle Management / Geometric Variations

LOZANO Rogelio
Unmanned Aerial Vehicles / Embedded Control

LUZEAUX Dominique, RUAULT Jean-René
Systems of Systems

VILLENEUVE François, MATHIEU Luc
Geometric Tolerancing of Products

2009

DIAZ Michel
Petri Nets / Fundamental Models, Verification and Applications

OZEL Tugrul, DAVIM J. Paulo
Intelligent Machining

PITRAT Jacques
Artificial Beings

2008

ARTIGUES Christian, DEMASSEY Sophie, NERON Emmanuel
Resources–Constrained Project Scheduling

BILLAUT Jean-Charles, MOUKRIM Aziz, SANLAVILLE Eric
Flexibility and Robustness in Scheduling

DOCHAIN Denis
Bioprocess Control

LOPEZ Pierre, ROUBELLAT François
Production Scheduling

THIERRY Caroline, THOMAS André, BEL Gérard
Supply Chain Simulation and Management

2007

DE LARMINAT Philippe
Analysis and Control of Linear Systems

DOMBRE Etienne, KHALIL Wisama
Robot Manipulators

LAMNABHI Françoise *et al.*
Taming Heterogeneity and Complexity of Embedded Control

LIMNIOS Nikolaos
Fault Trees

2006

FRENCH COLLEGE OF METROLOGY
Metrology in Industry

NAJIM Kaddour
Control of Continuous Linear Systems

Printed and bound by CPI Group (UK) Ltd, Croydon, CR0 4YY